THE FUTURE OF CHRIST

This book offers a mature assessment of themes preoccupying David Martin over some fifty years, complementing his book *On Secularization*. Deploying secularization as an omnibus word bringing many dimensions into play, Martin argues that the boundaries of the concept of secularization must not be redefined simply to cover aberrant cases, as when the focus was more on America as an exception rather than on Europe as an exception to the 'furiously religious' character of the rest of the world.

Particular themes of focus include the dialectic of Christianity and secularization, the relation of Christianity to multiple enlightenments and modes of modernity, the enigmas of East Germany and Eastern Europe, and the rise of the transnational religious voluntary association, including Pentecostalism, as that feeds into vast religious changes in the developing world. Doubts are cast on the idea that religion has ever been privatized and has lately reentered the public realm. The rest of the book deals with the relation of the Christian repertoire to the nexus of religion and politics, including democracy and violence and sharply criticises polemical assertions of a special relation of religion to violence, and explores the contributions of 'cognitive science' to the debate

Other titles by David Martin

Christian Language and its Mutations
Essays in Sociological Understanding

Christian Language in the Secular City

On Secularization
Towards a Revised General Theory

*To my wife Bernice
with love and gratitude for everything
over the past fifty years*

The Future of Christianity
Reflections on Violence and Democracy, Religion and Secularization

DAVID MARTIN

Adjunct Professor, Liverpool Hope University
Emeritus Professor of Sociology, London School of Economics

ASHGATE

Published by
Ashgate Publishing Limited
Wey Court East
Union Road
Farnham
Surrey, GU9 7PT
England

Ashgate Publishing Company
Suite 420
101 Cherry Street
Burlington
VT 05401-4405
USA

www.ashgate.com

British Library Cataloguing in Publication Data
Martin, David, 1929–
  The future of Christianity : reflections on violence and democracy, religion and secularization.
  1. Church and the world. 2. Secularism. 3. Secularization (Theology) 4. Christianity and politics. 5. Violence – Religious aspects – Christianity. 6. Christianity – Forecasting.
  I. Title
  261.2'1–dc22

Library of Congress Cataloging-in-Publication Data
Martin, David, 1929–
  The future of Christianity : reflections on violence and democracy, religion and secularization / David Martin.
    p. cm.
  Includes index.
  ISBN 978-1-4094-0658-7 (hardcover : alk. paper) – ISBN 978-1-4094-0669-3 (pbk. : alk. paper) – ISBN 978-1-4094-0659-4 (ebook) 1. Secularism. 2. Christianity and politics. 3. Christianity – 21st century. I. Title.
  BL2747.8.M34 2010
  261–dc22

                                                                            2010035263

ISBN 9781409406587 (hbk)
ISBN 9781409406693 (pbk)
ISBN 9781409406594 (ebk)

Printed and bound in Great Britain by the
MPG Books Group, UK

Contents

Acknowledgements and Sources

Chapter 1

This introductory chapter is, of course, newly composed, but it runs in parallel with a piece I would have included, had not the overlap with the introductory chapter been too great. It was published in *Dialog*, 46: 2 (2007): 139–52, as 'What I really Said about Secularisation'.

Chapter 2

Given in Dallas to a Catholic Episcopal Conference in January 2005 and published in *The Journal of Contemporary Religion*, 20: 2 (2005): 145–60. Republished, though in considerably revised form, by kind permission.

Chapter 3

This chapter extensively reworks a key note address to the American Academy of Religion meeting at Philadelphia on 20 November 2005.

Chapter 4

An unpublished paper originally given in Los Angeles at a conference organized by the University of Southern California for the centennial of the outbreak of Pentecostalism in Los Angeles in 2006. It has been totally recast. The recast version was given at the University of Graz on 4 May 2010, and at a conference in Antwerp in August 2010. It is partnered by two papers not included here, one given at University College, London in 2007, and published by Brill in 2010 in *The Call of the Homeland* edited by Anthony Smith, Athena Leoussi and Allon Gal, the other given at the Israel Academy of Sciences, Jerusalem, in December 2008, entitled 'Pentecostalism: a Christian Revivalism Sweeping the Developing World' and published in Eliezer Ben-Raphael and Yitzak Sternberg (eds), *World Religions and Multiculturalism: A Dialectic Relation* (Leiden: Brill, 2010).

Chapter 5

Given in Malta as a public lecture organized by Joe Inguanez for the Catholic Institute for Research into the Signs of the Times, 13 October 2009, and then in Manchester Cathedral as the Wickham Lecture for June 2010. Republished by kind permission.

Chapter 6

A critical response to the theme of an Insitut für Wissenschaften von Menschen conference at the French Institute in Vienna in June 2009 and published in German in the IWM Journal, *Transit*, 39 (2010): 58–76 as 'Religiöse Antoworten auf Formen des Säkularismus'. Republished by kind permission.

Chapter 7

Published in *The Scottish Journal of Theology*, 61: 1 (2008): 51–63. Republished by kind permission.

Chapter 8

Given at Košice, Slovakia, in September 2008 and published in Š. Marinčák (ed.), *Religion*: *Problem or Promise*? *The Role* of *Religion in the Integration of Europe* (Košice: Dobra Knina publishers, Series Orientalia et Occidentalia, 4, 2009: 129–44). Republished by kind permission.

Chapter 9

Given at the Max Planck Institute, Halle, July 2006 and much revised and greatly expanded for *Books and Culture*, 15: 5 and 6 (Sep.–Oct. 2009 and Nov.–Dec. 2009). Reprinted by kind permission.

Chapter 10

A chapter in Eileen Barker (ed.), *The Centrality of Religion in Social Life: Essays in Honour of James Beckford* (Aldershot: Ashgate, 2008: 161–74). Republished by kind permission.

Chapter 11

Given at the Archiepiscopal Palace, Prague in 2007, for a conference organized by the University of Virginia on Jefferson's Wall of Separation between Church and State, and published in 2009 in R. Patton and R. K. Ramanzani (eds), *Religion, State and Society: Jefferson's Wall of Separation in Comparative Perspective* (New York: Palgrave Macmillan, 2009: 137–54). Republished by kind permission.

Chapter 12

A version of a paper given in Istanbul in November 2008 for the Heinrich Böll Foundation.

Chapter 13

A version of a review written for the *Times Literary Supplement*.

PART 1
Secularization and
the Future of Christianity

Chapter 1

Christianity and the World, the Religious and the Secular

Introduction

This book follows a continuous train of my thinking over the last four years or so, about secularization and related themes – themes that have kept me intermittently preoccupied over the last forty years since 1964. They overlap of course, because each time I focus on a particular topic to a specific (and usually lay) audience I recapitulate my basic approach, but in every case I have found this recapitulation rapidly taking off in fresh directions, usually with varied examples. Initially I tried to cut out these disconcertingly insistent 'establishing shots', especially where they involved reference back to my own contributions. I found it very difficult, especially given severe problems with my eyesight, to disentangle restatements of old themes from fresh variations, novel directions and new examples, as well as internal cross-references within chapters. I have let most of them stay. I have also made intermittent attempts, for example in chapter 4, to simplify my writing and make it more spare, rather in the mode of Fauré's *Chanson d'Eve*, if such a comparison is not too absurd. I would like to help purify the dialect of my tribe.

The last two chapters on the social incarnations of Christianity, in particular as they relate to the secular realities of established polities and violence, as well as to democracy, are also closely linked. However, they are repetitive in a different way because they all depend on a conception of Christianity as a repertoire of themes selectively drawn upon according to the kinds of situation and the types of society in which they are embedded.

Any topic in this area of debate will imply several of the other topics, and the arguments will be mutually dependent. They also intertwine because certain themes are fundamental, like the contrast between universality and particularity, or between the voluntary transnational religious association and the territorial national or transnational Church, or between individual and community. In addition to these fundamental contrasts there is the complex difference and partial unity of the political and the religious, as well as the dialectic relations built into the binary distinctions of the religious and the secular.

These fundamental themes, these contrasts and these binaries, with their attendant paradoxes, recur throughout the text. In several chapters I stress again how the dialectic of the religious and the secular, or more precisely of faith and the world, has its roots in Christian categories. To understand this dialectic we need to follow though the 'transformational grammar' of these categories as they intersect at different periods with very different social worlds, and also with something we recognize as the 'real world', otherwise social science has no object, only a subject. I believe in subjects and objects, for example religious visions of worlds to come and the objective status of the dynamics of social and political action.

I underline the extent to which there are elements in the European situation supporting the notion of European 'exceptionalism', as originally proposed by Peter Berger and discussed in several crucial interventions by Grace Davie. Berger and Davie have argued that secular Europe is the exception to the 'universality' of religion rather than religious North America an exception to the universal process of secularization.[1] I also reiterate my doubts about some claims made for genetic explanations of religion. Setting aside the besetting problem of how and why the very concept of 'religion' has been constructed, I simply do not see how the variable presence and absence of religion can be explained by a constant. The relation between evolved strategies and the objective dynamics of in group and out group, irrespective of whether these dynamics include a religious component, is another matter, and one on which I would not want to hazard a judgement. What I do notice is the partial congruence between cost-benefit analysis, biological approaches, and realist accounts of political and personal strategies, and that suggests to me the variety of languages and analytic levels at our disposal in the quest both for explanation in the positivistic sense, and for understanding or *verstehen* in the hermeneutic sense. I am pretty clear that whatever the relations between evolved strategies and the objective dynamics of 'the social' may turn out to be, the posited 'explanations', whether or not correct at their own analytic level, add *nothing* whatever to our 'understandings'. Leaving aside their novel terminology they tell us nothing we did not already know.

I believe the analysis of religion, nationalism and politics can be undertaken in a unified framework. I am not saying that religion – meaning here post-axial religion – and politics are identical, but I am pointing to very similar processes and dynamics, in spite of these being inflected in absolutely crucial ways by the different repertoires of those religions. Particularly in Christianity and Buddhism, the horizons of height and depth and time stretch far beyond the immediacies of politics, and the love of the brethren and the peace of God differ from the fierce intimacies of political comradeship. A parish Eucharist as an act of worship is not a party meeting to discuss policy, tactics and leadership. But crusading Templars might exemplify a fraternity comparable to the kind of comradeship found in a political or religio-political cell, and every universalism generates an exclusive border of some kind. That is a point made in a different way in chapter 3. At any rate the commonalities governing religion and politics are great enough to treat them in a single frame. As examples of the common elements I might offer the

---

[1]　Davie, Grace, *Europe: The Exceptional Case: Parameters of Faith in the Modern World* (London: Darton, Longman and Todd, 2002); Berger, Peter, Davie, Grace, and Fokas, Effie, *Religious America, Secular Europe? A Theme and Variations* (Aldershot: Ashgate, 2008).

processes and practices of sect formation and fragmentation, of ritual induction and fraternity, of heresy and excommunication, as well as the uses of motivating myths with their accompanying kinds of rhetoric and imagery, the modes of authority, legitimation, commemoration and doctrinal formulation, the role of charisma and founding fatherhood and motherhood, and the intermittently violent relation between love and hate, us and them. It cannot be said too often that these are fundamental to sociality *as such*.

Some Comments Concerning Secularization

Secularization is the most important single subject, and my criticism of secularization theory has focused on those versions that treat secularization as a universal and unilateral trend. Perhaps that kind of formulation is today more often taken-for-granted in popular treatments than in the serious literature. In a personal conversation, Steve Bruce, a major and effective advocate of the 'standard' version of secularization, wondered nevertheless whether it might be dependent on the global advance of liberal individualistic democracy about which he entertains serious doubts.[2]

Secularization is not a myth,[3] even though it has profound mythic and ideological sources and resonances. My initial treatments began by specifying the mythic and prescriptive ideological elements but they continued with an empirical theory of the key patterns of secularity and religiosity. An empirical treatment has to delimit what is to be covered by secularization, and in my *A General Theory of Secularisation* I confined it to declines in more or less Christian belief and practice.[4] Though I tried extending the frame to Turkey, partly because Turkey is a country infiltrated by European concepts, even there the patterns and processes, and the conceptual demarcations, were sufficiently disparate to dissuade me. I concluded there was a certain Christian specificity about secularization, even though one might reasonably talk of secularization (say) in Central Asia under the Soviets or in China under Mao.

Some of the problems of secularization theory arise because secularization is bound in with dangerous 'nouns of process', like modernization, rationalization and bureaucratization, and matters are made more complicated because secularization brings many dimensions into play, not all of them closely related or even mutually compatible. That was what I argued in 1965 and 1969, mainly in response to sociological assumptions but also in response to theological uses, for example

---

[2]   Steve Bruce, personal communication.

[3]   Glasner, Peter, *The Sociology of Secularisation: A Critique of a Concept* (London: Routledge, 1977); Joas, Hans, 'State, Society and Religion: their Relationship from the Perspective of the World Religions: An Introduction', in Hans Joas, and Klaus Wiegandt, (eds), *Secularization and the World Religions* (Liverpool: Liverpool University Press, 2009).

[4]   Martin, David, *A General Theory of Secularisation* (Oxford: Blackwell, 1978).

in the widely read work of Harvey Cox, rooted in a very different intellectual genealogy.[5] Cox espoused secularization in a manner that reminded me of Comte, and he has since blamed sociologists for misleading him in his *Fire from Heaven*, a book in which he discusses what his blurb (with a rare insouciance) called the 'largely unexamined' phenomenon of Pentecostalism. In my experience, as a sociologist writing in the sixties, I recollect the difficulty I had countering the enthusiasms he engendered, in company with numerous death of God theologians and people writing about 'secular Christianity', or (somewhat later) bidding farewell to God in extended exequies.[6] Cox disavows any connection with the death of God theologians on the ground that he had a different 'God' in mind, but he was certainly part of the anti-institutional fervour of the time which gave an extra impulse to self-destructive tendencies in the Christian Church itself. In discussing secularization one should not entirely neglect what fashions in the Church contribute.

Within my own academic tribe I have been unhappy with the redefinition of secularization to cover aberrant cases, especially when the focus has been on America as an exception to the theory of secularization rather than on Europe as an exception to global religiosity. The twentieth-century American case has been dismissed as 'internally secularized' according to criteria that would plausibly categorize eighteenth-century Britain and France or Renaissance Italy as internally secularized. Those criteria make perfectly good sense, and the history of Christianity revolves ninety degrees when you deploy them, but they cannot be applied selectively to bolster an argument in trouble. They need to be applied over the whole course of Christian history, and when that is done we uncover religious thrusts, such as monasticism, pietism and Evangelicalism, and secular recoils. Christianity drives salients into 'society', if I may use the reified concept of society for historical times where it was of dubious relevance. These salients deploy those sectors of its repertoire of themes responding to and appropriate for the type of society and the specific historical situation. At the same time internal secularization is endemic throughout Christian history, as the visions and revisions of faith compromise with 'the world'.

I have also been unhappy with the way my own academic tribe has treated that other noun of process, privatization. Indeed I doubt very much whether privatization is the right word for what has happened. It is certainly true that Christians, maybe Catholics in particular, can no longer expect laws to reflect ecclesiastical norms, that the impact of the religious factor on voting has declined, for example, in Holland, a Christian Democratic hegemony has collapsed, and in the case of the USA, the religious right has influenced the election of presidents

---

[5]   Cox, Harvey, *Fire from Heaven: The Rise of Pentecostal Spirituality and the Reshaping of Religion in the 21st Century* (Reading, MA: Addison-Wesley, 1994: xvi); Cox, Harvey, *The Secular City: Secularization and Urbanization in Theological Perspective* (New York: Macmillan, 1965).

[6]   Smith, Ronald Gregor, *Secular Christianity* (London: Collins, 1966).

without significantly achieving its aims with respect to the law. On the other hand, when Steve Bruce, for example, says that commentary has to put its case in terms of what is likely to have general appeal rather than in terms of 'God says', that is a general truth about all pressure group politics, supposing one wants to gain ones point as well as to make it.[7] More crucially, the role of religious bodies in the public sphere has been and largely remains ubiquitous. Moreover, if one looks at major reports and commentaries, for example, those of the Catholic bishops on peace and the economy in the USA, or on the criteria of the just war and faith in the city in Britain, they are not based on reading off prescriptions from the Bible or on invocations of what 'God says' in a conservative Protestant manner, but on philosophical norms which draw on long term Christian traditions and sources. These sources are to some extent shared with people of good will, in part because certain understandings of personhood, of creation, or the good society, have been built into the foundations of western civilization. There is, after all, simply to take the British case, a Christian critique of utilitarianism going back to Ruskin and indeed to Burke, that constitutes a continuous seam in British political culture and influences all political parties. Christian commentary simply exploits this wider resonance even though the foundations may be partly invisible.

From the start my argument has been that the theory of secularization, (as summarized in empirical correlations between religious belief and practice and urbanization, industrialization, degrees of prosperity, class and gender amongst others) is profoundly inflected by particular histories, which in the modern period are national histories qualified in a minor or major way by regional variations, particularly between centres and peripheries, and by micro-nationalisms often in a territorial or professional niche. Considerations of space prevented me including two extended chapters on the religious social geography and architectural emplacements of centre and periphery.

I have also argued there are many versions of modernity apart from our Western European version, and all of them are compatible with religion in some form or other. Those two propositions about the importance of variable histories, and about the variable modes of modernity compatible with religion, have been fundamental to my position from the mid-sixties till now. The empirical correlates and historical inflections were first brought together in my argument, given at LSE in 1968 and published in the *European Journal of Sociology* in 1969[8] outlining

---

[7] Bruce, Steve, 'Secularisation in the UK and the USA', in Callum Brown, and Michael Snape, (eds), *Secularisation in the Christian World: Essays in Honour of Hugh McLeod* (Aldershot: Ashgate, 2010: 204–18).

[8] Martin, David, 'Towards a General Theory of Secularisation', *European Journal of Sociology* (Dec. 1969): 192–201. The theory was in a sense created by accident: Ernest Gellner was chairing a seminar and when the paper reader failed to turn up he asked me to make something up on the spur of the moment. That encouraged me to risk what I might otherwise have felt inhibited about saying. Gellner then arranged for a cleaned up version to be published.

the main features of *A General Theory of Secularisation*. About the same time I argued in the *British Journal of Sociology* that the global future was not necessarily prefigured either by the secularism of France or the secularity of Scandinavia. The world is not travelling in the wake of Europe and José Casanova has shown in many seminal contributions how secularization theory emerged in Europe by way of a simultaneously descriptive and prescriptive response to European conditions, which then became built into the European 'knowledge regime', including the contemporary media through which it is promoted.[9] A magisterial overview of the earlier phases of these debates by a prominent participant has been provided by Karel Dobbelaere.[10]

The Future of Christianity: Master Narratives, Catholic and Protestant; Transnational Pentecostalism

Chapters 2–4 on the future of Christianity are concerned with master narratives about the direction of past and future developments, and reach back to arguments in my *On Secularization*.[11] Chapter 2 concentrates on the contrast between Catholic and Protestant patterns of secularization. Chapter 3, which occasionally veers in a theological direction, examines master narratives in general as well as associated categories like authenticity and corruption as they are embedded in social science and historical writing. Chapter 4 examines the master narrative of Pentecostalism as a viable path to an alternative modernity based on the crucial shift from the territorial Church to a transnational voluntary association. Pentecostalism is a fusion of black and white revivalist motifs, which expands most easily in the inspired continents in the world unless repelled by a powerful territorial religion with spiritist elements, but it also expands in the form of charismatic Christianity in middle-class business and professional sectors all over the world from Indonesia to Brazil and Nigeria.

  Master narratives have not gone away, and both the religious and the secular forms of master narrative, including the secularization story, share fundamental characteristics. These constantly appear in religion, nationalist ideology and politics as suggested in the final chapter. Particularly in chapter 3, I point to the endemic attempts of each master narrative to pull its rivals into is own ambit and I indicate how attempts to explain and neutralize frustrations experienced en route to eventual triumph, are somehow built into the story. Among radical expressions

---

[9] Casanova, José, *Public Religions in the Modern World* (Chicago: University of Chicago Press, 1994).

[10] Dobbelaere, Karel, 'Some Trends in European Sociology: The Secularization Debate', *Sociological Analysis*, 2 (1987): 107–37; 'Secularization: a Multidimensional Concept', *Current Sociology*, 29: 2 (1981).

[11] Martin, David, *On Secularization: Towards a Revised General Theory* (Aldershot: Ashgate, 2005).

of the master narratives of an unfolding *telos* (in time) there are anarchic and totalitarian versions that fragment into political, religious and religio-political sects. I also underscore how some great figure, a Cromwell, a Napoleon, a Lenin or a Mao, converts the seeming triumph of a universal revolution, English, French, Russian or Chinese, into something resembling its reversal, in particular as it is *partly* incorporated in an imperial system, just as the original Christian Revolution was incorporated in the Roman Empire. I think I first picked up this trope from an adolescent reading of Spengler's *The Decline of the West*.[12]

The master narrative of secularization is haunted by several spectres. There is a useful but dangerous historical construct frequently referred to as *the* Enlightenment Project. Then there are approaches to religion subliminally absorbed from Marxism and associated theories to do with imperialism; and there are also concepts based on Durkheim, like anomie and the effervescence of the *conscience collective* that are too easily imposed on very varied religious phenomena. Exorcising the spectres haunting our intellectual subconscious is no easy task. Our procedures, our vocabulary, and even more our mental apparatus for organizing our material, seem so natural that we excommunicate alternatives.

Chapter 4 is the third chapter on master narratives and it emphasizes the variety of routes to a viable modernity, including the route through the Cultural Revolution represented by Pentecostalism. In many places where Marxism has failed Pentecostalism has taken off, for example in Ethiopia and China. Pentecostalism is a major route to modernity rather than a reaction to it, in company with Marxism, several forms of liberalism, Catholicism, Buddhism and Islam.

At the core of chapter 4 is a contrast between political revolutions with a territorial base or religions with territorial base, and a transnational cultural revolution like Pentecostalism mainly working below the level of the state, though occasionally picking up the pull of the territorial and re-entering the political. A key element in this chapter is the failure of politics and of the state and the role of voluntary religious association in mediating between the individual and the state. In a University College paper published in *The Call of the Homeland*, edited by Gal, Leoussi and Smith, which serves as a partner to chapter 4, I explicitly take off from a contrast between Judaism and its Christian offshoot, framed by *heimat* and *diaspora*, and I have further developed these themes in 'Pentecostalism: a Christian Revival sweeping the Developing World' in a volume edited by Eliezer Ben-Raphael and Yitzak Sternberg.[13]

However, while voluntarism and multiculturalism are waves of the future they do not represent all the future there is, especially given the homogenizing logic of nationalism and ethno-religious nationalism. The study of nationalism is the natural complement of the study of religion, as I argue in the final chapter. Nationalism

---

[12]   Spengler, Oswald, *The Decline of the West* (London: Allen and Unwin, 1932).

[13]   Ben-Raphael, Eliezer, and Sternberg, Yitzak, (eds), *World Religions and Multiculturalism: A Dialectic Relation* (Leiden: Brill, 2010: 93–118); Gal, Allon, Leoussi, Athena, and Smith, Anthony, (eds), *The Call of the Homeland* (Leiden: Brill, 2010: 345–62).

is strong in the developing world, for example India, Eastern Europe and Russia, and it resists the development of transnational voluntary associations. Indeed it sometimes looks as though the old heartlands of Christianity are becoming more multicultural while much of the rest of the world extrudes minorities and inhibits religious pluralism. China may become hospitable to an increasing degree of religious pluralism which includes Christianity, given that Christianity does not threaten the social order, even though it now probably outnumbers the membership of the Communist Party.

Religious Responses to Modes of Secularism?

The chapter on 'Religious Responses to Modes of Secularism' (chapter 6 in the sequence) picks up my earlier comment on the problem of exorcising the spectres haunting our disciplinary subconscious. It deploys the title of a conference in Vienna to ask why we think in terms of religious 'responses' (for which read 're-actions' rather than actions) to secularism, and why over recent years we have increasingly fused and confused the *ideology* of secularism with the social *processes* of secularization.[14] In the course of this chapter I return to my persistent concern with the major difference between the way intellectual and media elites view the world and what is actually happening. This brings us back again to the (Western) European 'knowledge regime'. I have always aimed, in company with Berger, Casanova, Joas, Taylor and others, to spread suspicion about the 'masters of suspicion'. It is a difficult balancing act, because I want to defer to what is happening empirically on the ground rather than parroting what public intellectuals say, without reverting to the restrictive protocols of Scientism or Positivism.

Numbers and metrics are kinds of control over what we assert, but they do not provide their own interpretation or hermeneutic. If we find that the proportion of people answering to 'no religion' increases we have to ask about changing meanings attached to religion just as we interrogate what people mean when they tick the box marked Christian. Language is not stable and social concepts are embedded in fluid usages, as the increasing 'use' of secularism in the media, and now among academics, indicates. Secularization, secularity and secularism are – or have been – different things, and it is characteristic of contemporary linguistic changes that important discriminations are elided, like the vital distinction for our analytic purposes in the study of religion between disinterested and uninterested.

In this same chapter I also ask how a precarious thesis about the key role of the privatization of religion in secularization, has been hijacked by influential intellectuals to bolster a rational restriction on religious contributions in the public sphere. It is really odd that in Germany of all places, where the contributions of religion to the public sphere have been and largely remain omnipresent, there

---

[14]   Margaret Archer and Edward Tyriakian are two sociologists who have tried to expose the hidden foundations of the way sociologists see the world and elucidate it.

should be an assumption about the privatization of religion let alone a debate about the appropriate conditions under which religion may make a public contribution.[15] Public intellectuals delimit such contributions in terms of what they define as rational, while others defend such contributions as rational.[16] Both sets of arguments are otiose. Religious contributions to public debate are not subject to rational restrictions promulgated by academics in seminars, in part because public debate is a sphere of clashing interests. Politics is more about master narratives, power and the motivating myths that sustain power, than reason and logic.

Secularization in Reverse?

The answer to this question in chapter 5 is negative, with the exception of regions where Marxism has dramatically retreated, for example in the Orthodox and Chinese worlds. That apart, the vitality of religion is either associated with ethno-religion, as in India, or manifests itself in continents where secularization had so far failed to make serious headway. Books like *God is Back* by John Micklethwait and Adrian Wooldridge are thoroughly misleading.[17] Such well-publicized ideas about the return of religion and the so-called 'Revenge of God' depend on the assumption that it was once privatized, which is false, even in Western Europe. Maybe contemporary Israel is a partial exception on account of a need felt among some younger Israelis to reinvestigate the deeper religious roots of Israel, even though 50 per cent of Israelis are secular, 30 per cent 'traditional', and 20 per cent Orthodox.

Throughout my analysis I emphasize both the expansion of voluntary transnational forms of religion (for example Pentecostalism) and the resistance offered by forms of religion (for example Buddhism and Orthodoxy) rooted in automatic belonging to a solitary group and usually based on a territory or recollecting a sacred homeland. This is a fundamental theme linked to my two decades and more of work on Pentecostalism. I also use this chapter to include an assessment of arguments about the reversal of secularization understood as disenchantment, for example in the work of William Gibson and Christopher Partridge.[18]

---

[15]   I am grateful here to Professor Klaus Tanner of Heidelberg University for letting me see his unpublished paper offered at Stanford University on issues in genetics and religious views in Germany.

[16]   Trigg, Roger, *Must Faith be Privatised?* (New York: Oxford University Press, 2007).

[17]   Micklethwait, John, and Wooldridge, Adrian, *God is Back* (New York: Penguin, 2009).

[18]   Partridge, Christopher, *The Re-Enchantment of the West* (London: T. & T. Clark 2005: vol. 1); Gibson, James William, *A Re-enchanted World: The Quest for a New Kinship with Nature* (New York: Henry Holt, 2009). For a brilliant if idiosyncratic statement of disenchantment there is Gauchet, Marcel, *The Disenchantment of the World: A Political History of Religion* (Princeton: Princeton University Press, 1997).

The history of enchantment and disenchantment, like the semi-related history of the sacred, is importantly different from the history of secularization, because sometimes Christianity and Judaism are in cahoots with the sacred and/or the enchanted, while at other times they have themselves actively promoted both the concept and the reality of the secular, or the disenchanted, or the profane. Post-axial religion, especially Judaism, Christianity and Buddhism, with their reservations about 'the world', especially sacred kingship and sacred nature, made it in principle mundane long before modern science.[19] It began to banish human apprehensions of the animation of spirits from the processes of the natural world, even as it half-absorbed them, so that up to quite recently God was still thought of as bringing about natural disasters like the Lisbon earthquake and the Virgin praised for graciously averting them. People still ask why something or other happened to them, as though tsunamis and even terrorist actions like Beslan, were really 'acts of God' for which He might be held responsible. No matter how often ahistorical and purist definitions of science and religion are deployed by polemicists and apologists, in their concrete practice both religion and science have simultaneously challenged and incorporated superstition. That is true of Pentecostalism at the present time as the largest and latest Christian salient driven into contemporary society, changing and absorbing it in all its varied manifestations. Pentecostalism flourishes in particular in environments which remain inspirited, but it also demonizes the older inspirited world. Whether it is, as David Voas would maintain, a transitional phenomenon en route to a more recognizably 'Western' secular modernity, or an alternative way of being modern is as yet unclear.[20]

There is a link here with contemporary discussions, for example the work of Linda Woodhead, Paul Heelas, and Christopher Partridge, pointing to the rise of spirituality and the expansion of 'the holistic milieu' at the expense of organized religion.[21] Some important discriminations have to be made here, and varied *kinds* of enchantment and disenchantment canvassed. Here we partly leave behind empirical indices and cautiously venture into the history of ideas and of sentiment. Again the instability of meanings over time and cultural space, and the shifting frontiers of the religious and the secular, recognized as binary distinctions rooted in a Christian world-view, have to be taken into account as they relate to shifts in empirical indicators. Some contemporary modes of 'religion', like neo-paganism, and post-romantic nature worship, lack the binary distinction altogether, and it is problematic in Islam. The boundary between the religious and the secular also varies within Christianity, not only as between Catholic, Orthodox and Protestant, but also between the USA, England, France and Germany, let alone sub-Saharan

---

[19]   Berger, Peter L., *The Social Reality of Religion* (London: Faber, 1969).

[20]   Voas, David, 'The Continuing Secular Transition' in Detlef Pollack and Daniel Olson, (eds), *The Role of Religion in Modern Societies* (New York/London: Routledge, 2008: 25–48).

[21]   A useful source for these debates is Flanagan, Kieran, and Jupp, Peter, (eds), *A Sociology of Spirituality* (Aldershot: Ashgate, 2007).

Africa. Religion itself is a historically conditioned category, and philosophically it is 'essentially contested'.

Secularization and the Advance of Science?

Chapter 7 picks up my earlier point about religion and science simultaneously incorporating and challenging superstition. The idea that secularization is mainly driven by science is fed by a particular account of the historical clash between religion and science, with a focus on the Darwinian revolution, though one might also stress the huge impact made by the advent of a 'realist' political science with Machiavelli. In relation to Darwin, the notion of a simple clash between religion and science has been undermined by scholars like John Brooke and Ronald Numbers, but it is deeply embedded in the world of the media and in the presuppositions of the global intelligentsia.[22] Sociologists for their part have not endorsed any simple relation between science and secularization. Sociology has focussed instead on the indirect rather than the direct impact of scientific and of technological change. Sociology has also emphasized social processes like the shift to individualism in some cultures, the process of functional differentiation whereby different spheres of activity, including science, acquire autonomy, and the process of rationalization understood as the technically efficient adjustment of means to ends. I make clear I have the same kind of reservations about the impact of rationalization as I have with respect to disenchantment, since religion seems to flourish in highly rationalized environments, like the business class in the US, South Africa, Chile, Singapore or Korea. Highly generalized explanations like rationalization need to be handled with care and not invoked automatically. Automatic recourse to generalized explanations, whether based on Weberian rationalization or Durkheimian anomie, is to be avoided.

Case Studies of Secularization: East Germany and Eastern Europe

The linked Chapters, 8 and 9 on East Germany and Eastern Europe take different instances of secularization in the special European context. I try to bring out their distinctive characteristics by comparative analysis of how they are historically inflected, following my original arguments in the *General Theory*, particularly about the role of nationalism, or how, in current parlance, they are 'path dependent'.[23]

---

[22]   Brooke, John, 'Science and Secularization', in Linda Woodhead, (ed.), *Reinventing Christianity: Nineteenth Century Contexts* (Aldershot: Ashgate, 2001); Numbers, Ronald, and Lindberg, David, (eds), *God and Nature: Historical Essays on the Encounter between Religion and Science* (Los Angeles and Berkeley: University of California Press, 1986).

[23]   Norris, Pippa, and Inglehart, Ronald, *Sacred and Secular: Religion and Politics Worldwide* (Cambridge: Cambridge University Press, 2004).

In a further chapter, excluded on grounds of space, I also discussed Denmark as a prime case of what I originally identified in the *General Theory* as the Scandinavian pattern of high identification combined with diffuse belief and low practice, and an almost uniform mutation from state Lutheranism to state welfare promoted by social democratic politics. I raised once again the question as to whether Denmark, like the rest of Scandinavia, is just a singular niche or a presage of the global future, and concluded, as before, it is the former. I also used Denmark to illustrate again the relevance of geographical space to historical time, and included a comparison with the historic-geographical configuration of Britain as a country exemplifying an affiliated pattern of secularization. In my *General Theory* I identified an Anglo-Scandinavian pattern of secularization.

In analysing East Germany, the former DDR, I am dealing with the most secular country in the western world, in that respect rivalling the Czech Republic, especially Bohemia. Obviously it presents a key case for comparative investigation. It seems clear that East Germany has *not* emerged as the pre-eminent example of secularization on account of being more modern, more prosperous or more rationalized than West Germany or the USA, as major secularization theses might suggest. East Germany is not an instance of superior prosperity sapping religion or of a particularly advanced form of rationalized modernity, at least when compared with West Germany. My own argument is that the former DDR is secularized, (and nowadays without even the ideology of communism to provide the decrepit ghost of a functional alternative to religion), on account of a long-term history, and a bargain struck by the communist victors releasing its demoralized people from Nazi guilt if they accepted the complete secularist package. I also use the example of East Germany to criticize the notion of 'post secularity' as a construction of the intelligentsia, no doubt useful for obtaining grants, but lacking secure root in the empirical and historical data.

In my analysis of Eastern Europe as a whole I use a comparative survey of most of the countries that experienced an ideological programme of enforced secularization to ask why the outcomes in the DDR, the (current) Czech Republic and Estonia were so different from those in Poland, Slovakia, Croatia and Romania. At the same time the indices nearly all point in a downward direction, whether from a high point or a low point, especially when you look at the variations by generational cohort.[24]

I stress, of course, the important historic and continuing role of nationalism, with the vitality and influence of religion partly dependent on whether a particular nationalism is aligned with or athwart religion. For example, Lithuania is less firmly Catholic than Poland, given the greater historical role of secular motifs in its nationalist movements against both Catholic Poland and Orthodox Russia. I also contrast the Orthodox resistance to secularization as a religion deeply embedded in culture and in tangible objects of devotion and pilgrimage, with the vulnerability

---

[24]   Zulehner, Paul, and Tomka, Miklos, *Religionen und Kirchen in Ost (Mittel) Europa* (Wien: Pastorales Forum, 2008).

to secularization of Protestantism. Under the specific conditions of state religion in Northern Europe rather than those of the USA, key elements in Protestantism, such as inwardness and subjectivity, can mutate into a secular modernity, especially as self-sacrifice gives way to self-expression and 'self-actualization'.

It is, parenthetically, interesting that this Protestant potential can be found in the 'religious' USA as well as in 'secular' Western Europe. Historically, according to Benjamin Friedman, the shift in Calvinism to optimism about human motivation away from depravity may have facilitated the advent and reception of Adam Smith's economics.[25] Here a Christian motif mutates and arguably then becomes entered in the account sheet of secularization. By way of a contemporary example one might cite the tendency of the penitential and confessional character of Evangelicalism to turn, under the influence of psychoanalysis, into the confessional style of politicians whose sexual misdemeanours have been publicly exposed. However, in the USA this shift can go on inside religious bodies, alongside an increasing religious interest in the arts, whereas in Europe it more often migrates outside. In any case there are several European countries, such as France and Italy, where sexual misdemeanours on the part of politicians do not matter much, and there are important clues here to the range of religious and cultural differences between the USA and Europe discussed in chapter 7 of my *On Secularization*.[26]

Social Incarnations of Christianity: Democracy and Violence

The final chapters take up issues that bear both on the ways Christianity has inserted or incarnated itself in society and on secularization as a category intimately connected with the Christian approach to 'the world', above all as discussed in two classic essays by Max Weber.[27] Sections of these chapters deal with Christianity and violence and they treat Christianity as an 'axial religion' with strong reservations about the world and the worldly, including violence and sex, *and* strong eschatological claims over it in terms of overcoming the world.[28] Once Christianity is adopted as the faith of the Roman Empire, and even before that as a faith that has come to include senators, it renegotiates both the reservations and the claims.

---

[25]   Benjamin Friedman, in personal conversation; cf. Friedman, Benjamin, *The Moral Consequences of Economic Growth* (New York: Vintage, 2005).

[26]   Martin, *On Secularization*; Martin, David, *Christian Language and its Mutations* (Aldershot: Ashgate: 2002).

[27]   Weber, Max, 'Religous Rejections of the World' and 'The Social Psychology of the World Religions', in Hans Gerth, and C. Wright Mills, (eds), *From Max Weber* (London: Routledge, 1957: 267–301; 323–61).

[28]   Cavanaugh, William, *The Myth of Religious Violence* (Oxford: Oxford University Press, 2009).

Christian reservations about 'the world' or the *saeculum*, established in its formative stages by its status as a voluntary transnational movement, generate a symbolic logic, or a table of symbolic affinities. This discloses itself in a branching repertoire profoundly inflected by its social location and by the type of society in which it is incarnated, whether imperial, feudal, mercantile, 'enlightened autocratic', capitalist' or whatever.[29] Gary Runciman expresses this in the language of 'memes', but the point is identical: 'the memes constitutive of the Christian idea of brotherly love run up against the practices constitutive of the institution of serfdom'. John Teehan, as a cognitive psychologist, would reinforce that by arguing that the positive traits selected for by way of sustaining solidarity against the 'Other' ran up against the negative traits selected for to sustain intra-group solidarity.[30] Whatever language you deploy, the result in the specific conditions of the Middle Ages was a combination of courtesy, subordination and mayhem. Those who rail in an ahistorical, decontextualized manner against what Christian knights did in Jerusalem or in everyday feudal practice are using 'Christian' criteria when they might from a social scientific or cognitive psychological point of view spare their breath to cool their porridge.

The symbolic logic of Christianity, and its bifurcation into both radical and socially legitimizing icons with established access to the state semi-monopoly of the means of violence, was the theme of my book *The Breaking of the Image*.[31] Violence has to be discussed in relation to the type of society in which it occurs, and with reference to all the expressions of developed social solidarity (and therefore of conflict) in relation to the 'Other', located in secular nationalism and secular ideology as well as in religion. Otherwise comment degenerates into mere pointing at instances and a naive moral accountancy totting up St. Francis against Torquemada, or Torquemada and the Wars of Religion against Stalin, Pol Pot and Mao. This wretched pabulum feeds the public controversies promoted by Dawkins, Hitchens and Harris.

I am not here arguing that there are *no* variations within or between religions with respect to a propensity to violence, because they have different attitudes to power based on their initial type of social carrier, though they inevitably converge, once installed in power, by partially conforming to the dynamic of political action even as they attempt partially to shape it. Clearly, a faith, like Christianity, nurtured by outsiders with no access to power, will differ from a faith, like Islam, associated with a territorial entity. It cannot be said too often that the crucial initial symbolic repertoire of a textually stabilized religion is always drawn upon selectively according to the type of social location in which it becomes embedded. For exemplary comparisons between Islam and Christianity where they are of

---

[29]   Runciman, W. Gary, *The Theory of Cultural and Social Selection* (Cambridge: Cambridge University Press, 2009: 97).

[30]   Teehan, John, *In the Name of God: The Evolutionary Origins of Religious Ethics and Violence* (Oxford: Oxford University Press, 2010).

[31]   Martin, David, *The Breaking of the Image* (Oxford: Blackwell, 1980).

roughly equal strength but somewhat skewed in terms of social and territorial location, there are John Peel's as yet unpublished Birkbeck lectures on conversion to the two world religions among the Yoruba.[32]

Sometimes one has the impression that religion is being deployed as a synonym for fanaticism in a way that would include Stalin in the category 'religious' and exclude Ghandi and William Penn. From a social scientific viewpoint, trading rival atrocities against each other for rhetorical advantage is so much moral masturbation insofar as it goes beyond noting the patterns of violence associated in different modalities with secular and religious utopianism alike, or secular and religious empires alike. The key analytic category is *not* to be located in particular modes of social activity, whether these take the form of a religion or of a secular ideologies, including nationalism among secular ideologies. Moreover, from a social scientific viewpoint, it is irresponsible and dangerous to select a uniquely culpable source of violence and oppression (and untruth), and then to conclude all too easily that this source needs to be eliminated as far as possible, even by the kind violence of which the twentieth century provides a myriad of examples.

The analytic problem lies rather in the modalities and dynamics of power, in the nature of 'the political' (for example, as discussed in David Runciman's *Political Hypocrisy* and John Gray's *Black Mass*), and in the social science of international relations, of which sociologists take too little account.[33] Power is at its most naked in inter-state relations and the subject of international relations is as much neglected in sociological understandings of power, as the subject of geography is neglected in sociological understandings of the distribution (or ecology) of different types of religion. In his classic analysis, *Peace and War*, Raymond Aron makes rather little reference to religion and certainly does not select religion as an especially potent source of social violence.[34] It requires (say) no more than a reading of Schiller's *Wallenstein* to have at least some idea of the issues of power as well as faith at play even in the so-called Wars of Religion. The central role of great power politics in the immensely destructive Palatinate wars in the late seventeenth century, *not* designated part of the wars of religion, is particularly obvious. One concludes that the Westphalian Settlement of 1648, touted as an attempt on the part of the 'secular' state to bring the special destructiveness of religion to heel, is a mythical construct. Of course, it is equally possible to view a recent twentieth-century war, like the 1914–18 conflict, entered into initially by way of a power struggle for European hegemony, as having an ideological component, for example a struggle between German idealism and

---

[32]   Peel, John, Birkbeck lectures delivered at Trinity College, Cambridge in the autumn of 2009.

[33]   Runciman, David, *Political Hypocrisy* (Princeton: Princeton University Press, 2006); Gray, John, *Black Mass: Apocalyptic Religion and the Death of Utopia* (Harmondsworth: Allen Lane, 2007).

[34]   Aron, Raymond, *Peace and War: A Theory of International Relations* (London: Weidenfeld, 1962).

French scepticism. If we leave out of account wars that are primarily dynastic, both men *and* ideas are mobilized for war. The Wars of the Enlightenment (to coin a term) put universal ideas at the service of French imperialism and the mobilization of a nation in the form of the Grande Armée, spreading devastation from Salamanca to Speyer and Speyer to Moscow, and stimulating several other nationalisms in the process, above all in Germany.

Considerations of an equally complicated kind apply to the questions of religion and democracy discussed in some of these chapters. It all depends on the type of religion understood in the context of different types of society. There is no inherent connection between Christianity and democracy, but there are elements in its repertoire which can be given a democratic inflection under particular and favourable circumstances, as these are discussed in several sections on Protestantism and democracy. Of course, religious motifs which might favour democracy, other things being equal, encounter situations where 'things' are conspicuously unequal and stacked in a contrary direction. There are always unintended consequences following the pursuit of objectives one considers admirable and it is not always easy to gauge the unacceptable 'collateral damage'. Nor do we enquire just where in the 'really existing' contemporary world, from the USA to India or Chile, our confident criteria for passing adverse judgements on others are securely achieved, or what one needs to take into account in order to compare like with like before rushing to condemn. The problem is not too little moralization in alliance with a pervasive relativism, but too many stones thrown by moralizers who think they live in impregnable castles when they inhabit glasshouses. Imposing democracy and peace by force has its difficulties, as William Cavanaugh has argued in *The Myth of Religious Violence.*[35]

Circumstances alter cases, so that Buddhist monks in Burma may be aligned with democracy and in Sri Lanka against, or the Catholic Church in Latin America maybe at one time more aligned with conservative autocracy and at another more aligned with liberation while retaining hegemonic ambitions and traditional linkages with elites. Obviously what applies to religious motifs favouring democracy applies in equal measure to political motifs favouring democracy. There will always be countervailing influences that work in an opposed direction or combinations of causes and effects that result in initially democratic impulses generating unintended and undemocratic consequences. That is most conspicuously the case where democratic systems give power to undemocratic parties. There is nothing under the sun that is not capable of being corrupted, including the pursuit of incorruption, and if anyone supposes corruption not a social scientific category they had better read the literature more attentively.

Enlightenment, whether secular or religious, has its shadow side through a process of ineluctable entanglement. John Gray has even criticized the shadow side of the secular enlightenment as carrying forward Christian delusions by more

---

[35]   Cavanaugh, William, *The Myth of Religious Violence.*

mundane means, but that may be a paradox too far.[36] I have constantly tried to bring out the paradoxes and opportunity costs attending all prospects of amelioration: one cannot simultaneously create educated elites capable of competing internationally, and ensure that all shall win and all shall have prizes. Paradox and irony are at the heart of the social scientific endeavour and this is one area where a realistic theological or humanist understanding of the ironies and paradoxes of political action can play an important ancillary role'.[37]

The chapter on 'The Religious and the Political' has two main themes. The first is the challenge of Christianity to the Durkheimian social sacred. In several important ways primitive Christianity is a secularizing movement, for example by removing the aura of the sacred from an elect people defined by ritual prescription in a promised land with a holy city and a holy temple, as well as by rejecting fate and fortune and the *sacramentum* of loyalty to the god-emperor. These shifts cannot be contained within a simplistic articulation of the religious-secular distinction, partly because what is sacred for Judaism in terms of ritual purity is profaned and secularized by Christianity in its quest for an inward and intangible purity of heart and its partial shift from rules to sentiments, and even to the sentimentality that now infuses public debate. The crucial shift occurs when Christianity itself succumbs to a partial secularization in terms of its original thrust by providing sacred insurance cover for the empire, which is something quite abhorrent to the secularizing impulse in the Hebrew Scriptures in respect of sacred kingship. In examples of this kind the meanings of the sacred and secular change places, because, as I have said earlier, the histories of the sacred and of the Christian are not identical, as they can easily appear to be in the work of Roger Scruton. In one way Louis the Fourteenth was a Catholic Christian, but the aura of the sacred attracted into the sphere of an aggrandizing French monarchy, can be accounted as a secularization closely parallel with the secularization achieved by Constantine when he adopted Christianity as the sacralizing agent of the Roman empire.

The *partial* absorption of Christianity in order to provide the sacred legitimation of empire in the Constantinian era is countered by voluntary protest movements partly operating outside the social space of political necessity, such as monasticism, the Friars, the Radical Reformation, Pietism and Evangelicalism. Christianity makes successive but differently and historically inflected incursions into the world. These religious protest movements in turn *partially* succumb to worldliness. The Cluniac Order helped finance the Crusades and Pietism was adapted to the needs of Prussian imperial administration. The Quakers became respected bankers, like Barclays, as well as opponents of slavery, creators of model townships and prison

---

[36]   Gray, John, *Straw Dogs: Thoughts on Humans and Other Animals* (Cambridge: Granta, 2002).

[37]   Here, of course, I am much indebted to Reinhold Niebuhr. For a recent reassessment of Niebuhr there is Harries, Richard, and Platten, Stephen, (eds), *Reinhold Niebuhr and Contemporary Politics: God and Power* (Oxford: Oxford University Press, 2010).

reformers, and Evangelicals contributed to the economic ethos of industrializing Britain as well as stimulating the ethos of voluntary association and works of social amelioration and improvement.[38]

If this sounds complicated, it is. The question is not so much whether we are experiencing a unilinear movement to the secular but whether the successive and different incursions of Christianity into 'the world', including contemporary Pentecostalism, have finally used up its symbolic repertoire. The secular also has a constant and a variable history. As a secular or worldly political practice its manifestations are remarkably uniform and singularly ruthless over millennia, but its nature and dynamic is only demythologized, and then not entirely, with Ibn Khaldun and Machiavelli. In a parallel manner the character and dynamic of the natural world was only theoretically exposed to view with Darwin and others engaged in the study of evolution. One might even add here the exposure of the dynamics of the human affections by Freud, except that in the Freudian case one mythology partly displaces another, and the whole exercise is of debatable value by the stricter scientific canons. In another paper not included here, I discuss this obdurate persistence of the secular and its tardy exposure in theoretical form through Machiavelli and Darwin.[39] Needless to say, these exposures morally scandalized much religious thinking, though the scandal provoked by Machiavelli lasted much longer than the scandal provoked by Darwin. 'Mankind cannot bear very much reality'.

These successive exposures feed into the theme of Christianity's encounter with the social sacred and a persistently raw political secularity. As I have just suggested, this raw reality achieves social scientific articulation quite late in western history by way of a tradition that runs from Machiavelli to Hobbes and Sorel. There are, of course, many acute as well as theologically normative accounts of the tense relation of the City of God to the secular City of Man from Augustine onward. The point is that Machiavelli comes out brutally with the way things are in 'the world', the *saeculum*, as Augustine of Hippo or Gregory the Great do not.

The kind of analysis I propose shifts the boundaries of what we conventionally mean by the world, the secular, secularization and the transcendent, to achieve a fresh perspective, notably on the religious as it relates to the political. This shifting of conceptual boundaries helps us to see secularization in varied perspectives and not just as a univocal and unilinear process. In the course of this analysis I challenge various assumptions about the privatization of religion and have some reservations about the negative relation between rationalization and religion. I question some formulations of the clash of religion and science, and I point to

---

[38]   Hilton, Boyd, *The Age of Atonement: Influence of Evangelicalism on Social Thought, 1795–1865* (Oxford: Oxford University Press, 1986).

[39]   Martin, David, a chapter based on a paper given at Erfurt in July 2008 at a conference in honour of Robert Bellah entitled 'Axial Religion and the Problem of Violence', to be published in Robert Bellah, and Hans Joas, (eds), *The Axial Age and its Consequences* (Cambridge, MA: Harvard University Press, 2010/11).

the shifting and shifty boundaries of the religious and the secular as they relate to shifting empirical indices. I am worried about the blurring of the distinction between Judaeo-Christianity and the sacred or enchanted, about the indifference in the cruder forms of debate to the modes whereby Christian motifs are incarnated in, and inflected by, different *types* of society, most notably when the issue turns on the specific role of religion in relation to violence. And I underline constantly the partial but crucial shift within Christianity back to its original form as a transnational voluntary association.

The appended chapter 13 in the form of a Review expresses my overall approach to the issue of violence and religion. In the context of the present book it gives a sympathetic account of William Cavanaugh's argument to the effect that we literally do not know what we are talking about if we ignore the circumstances in which the idea of a specifically religious violence was produced. This is not the same as the broader argument about how we maintain stable and accepted criteria about what is to count as religion over cultural time and space. Rather, Cavanaugh emphasizes how the idea of a specifically religious violence was constructed and deployed by the secular nation state in the early modern period as part of its rhetorical armoury over against other and rival forms of social solidarity, whether imperial or ecclesiastical.

The idea of the 'innocence' of the secular generated, and was reinforced by, a retrospective account of the thirty years war as a 'war of religion' brought to an end by the secular nation state in 1648. This supposition is extraordinarily widespread, and one can find it in writers who should know better, like Ronald Gregor Smith in his *Secular Christianity*, perhaps because it offers conventional fuel to the secularization thesis.[40] In fact major motives for these wars included the resistance of local elites to incorporation in larger entities and an attempt on the part of these entities to extract revenues. The idea of the innocence of the secular has been revived by the nation states of the West as part of their characterization of the 'Other', notably the Muslim 'Other', since the inauguration of the war on terror. Here it seems to me it is important to take into account the dynamics of real-politik, not merely as a concept invented in the same early modern period, but permanently operative as the principles governing the relationships between political actors, whether sovereign cities, sovereign states or rival empires.

These dynamics might be summarized as follows. In any given contest between two states plus one other, alliances for defence or attack, the two being closely related, will ignore religious or ideological affinities in favour of securing the optimum chance of survival. Thus the Catholic French will ally themselves with the Ottoman Muslims against the Catholic Hapsburgs. Survival is the key to violence, not particular modes of religious or ideological expression. This could well mean that sociological and socio-biological accounts of violence coincide, but if that were so then an analysis such as has been provided by John Teehan of the biological sources of a specifically religious violence is otiose. Moreover,

---

[40]   Smith, Ronald Gregor, *Secular Christianity*.

were religious violence written in biologically then moral indignation about it such as is regularly expressed is equally otiose. Ought implies can. Inability to do otherwise removes the concept of agency from our vocabulary and at the same time endangers the concept of culture. The concept of agency and with it concepts of culture and of the dignity of human beings, as responsible creatures 'looking before and after', is shared by Christianity and any serious kind of humanism.

However, and here I draw on my own much earlier analysis of religious and other kinds of pacifism, it is absolutely clear that religious pacifism arises *culturally* and that it arises very *late* in the social evolution of religion, as part of the crucial shift identified as the 'Axial Age' and involving several different kinds of reserve towards the givens of our world, including the datum of violence. I am not even sure it makes coherent sense to discuss religious forms based on inspired Nature as though they were on all fours with forms based on visions of transformation, personal, social and natural. In any case, it would be salutary to recollect that as a result of the shift in the Axial Age, and specifically in relation to Christianity and Buddhism, a major plaint against religion has *not* been on account of its violence but on account of its passivity and politically irresponsible pacifism. In the case of Christianity, both religious passivity and violence, *and* its secular analogues, arise in the context of a transcendent hope in the coming of a kingdom of peace and righteousness.

I should say it again: we are here no longer largely dealing with an animated and inspired religious world, but one in which transcendent anticipations and apprehensions generate visions of a new world order. In the religious version of the coming of that order, agency is attributed to God, and pacifism is much more usually recommended in the interim than violence, whereas in the secular and secularized versions agency may be understood as active human violence for justice of the familiar kind found in secular revolutionary movements. It is in this context that Eisenstadt's analysis linking the Christian radical tradition to radical secular revolution makes sense.[41] By contrast, established Christianity realizes its radical potential for a peaceful kingdom in the safe sidings of monasticism and in special provision for those whom Max Weber refers to as religious virtuosi. Established Christianity concentrates on the occasions of justified warfare by way of traditions of reflection about the appropriate conditions for the use of violence. Rather oddly those who discuss what they take to be a specifically religious mode of violence rarely talk of reluctant but justified violence. It is almost as though they worked with an idea of the inherently unjustified nature of violence derived from traditions of Christian pacifism.

In all that has gone before I have stressed the protean character of religion, and in addition emphasized the central importance of the shift to transcendent visions arising in the Axial Age, and the world historical consequences for politics and religion alike of that shift. But the problem of what we understand by 'religion'

---

[41]   Eisenstadt, Schmuel N., *Fundamentalism, Sectarianism and Revolution* (Cambridge: Cambridge University Press, 1999).

and by the adjective 'religious' is much more subtle than most discussions of the appropriate criteria for defining religiosity allow, especially now that we find many people taking Protestant interiority to the point where they disclaim any interest in institutional religion in favour of personal spirituality. I can only illustrate what I mean by examples from the classical arts over the four or five centuries taken to be a crucial arena of 'secularization': Machaut to Shostakovich, the Siennese masters to Andy Warhol. After all, the arts, along with popular culture, are often cited as a sphere in which the religious impulse has been relocated. Supposing that in the area of (serious) music one takes the liturgical music of Palestrina and Bach as providing a benchmark for religion, then how are we to place (say) Handel's *La Resurrezione*, Mozart's *Coronation Mass*, the last Quartets of Beethoven, the Berlioz *Te Deum* and Mahler's song 'Ich bin der Welt abhanden gekommen'? Or supposing that in painting one takes Grünewald and Botticelli as unequivocally religious, how are we to place the religious woodcuts of Dürer, Raphael's *Stanze*, or such radically different artists as Poussin and Blake, and in the modern period Barnett Newman and Kandinsky? If religion is understood as a mode of being in the world then it is very clear the religious mode resists capture in definitions.

And the Future of Christianity?

It is notorious that even the best observers failed to anticipate the crucial events of the past half century which with regard to religion included the cultural upheaval of the sixties, the Iranian Revolution and the fall of the Berlin Wall. It follows that my ambition in this book is limited to providing a thematic index, tracing contractions and expansions, and indicating how and when the repertoire of Christianity is appropriated according to social context. I approach this enterprise from some of the many angles available for the observation of trends according to varied time scales. There is the long time scale including many centuries in which Christianity precariously covered just a part of Europe and was subject to a millennium of Muslim invasions and folk wanderings. Then there is the time scale which runs from the variable dawns of modernity, when Christianity was mostly confined to the global North, to the present when its centre of gravity has shifted to the global South. In that perspective we may actually be observing one of the great expansions of Christian history, with all that could entail for the emergence of hybrid religious forms, as well as for the distribution of religious power and religious demographics.[42] This then is the background of this modest exercise in the discussion of religion and secularization, democracy and violence.

---

[42]   Joas, Hans, 'The Future of Christianity', to appear in a forthcoming issue of *The Hedgehog Review*.

Chapter 2

Secularization and the Future of Catholicism and Protestantism

Problems of Master Narratives

If sociologists could not predict the fall of Communism or the rise of Pentecostalism or the cultural revolution of the 1960s, then my chapter title smacks of hubris. But the future is not the only problem. Even when sociologists deal with the past they are selective, because only approved routes to modernity, like ascetic Protestantism, are allowed to count. That is why Pentecostalism, in spite of its clear modernizing potential, could be so long ignored. It was discounted because it was presented as politically the wrong kind of modernity or treated as an alarming case of reactive fundamentalism or dismissed as simply a phase before genuine modernity set in. As for movements like the Catholic Reformation, the ultramontane revival or the role of Catholic thought and power in the emergence of Europe post 1945 and in the resurgence of Eastern Europe post 1989 up to events in 2004 in Ukraine, there has been scant interest. These major events do not belong to the standard story or master narrative of how we arrived where we are. Secularization is a major component in that master narrative and is a master narrative in its own right.

This climate of skewed but 'Enlightened' anticipations about the future and of skewed history reflects the influence of European secularist ideologies on sociology and secularization theory, and both José Casanova and Grace Davie have pointed to the way the specifically European experience of modernity has entered into the warp and woof of secularization theory in the hands of some of its European exponents.[1] Our observations as Europeans can be slanted by an exceptional historical experience, and one which includes Enlightened anticipations, themselves quasi-Providential, of a move from obscurantist superstition to the glorious liberty of reason or political revolution or existential autonomy.[2]

Even if we are neither sociologists nor partisans of the Enlightenment, we need to be wary of barely conscious assumptions about the future fate of the Christian faith and the way these are related to scholarly or popular ideas about the origins,

---

[1]   Casanova, José, *Public Religions in the Modern World*; Davie, Grace, *Religion in Modern Europe: A Memory Mutates* (Oxford: Oxford University Press 2000).

[2]   Clark, Jonathan, 'Providence, Predestination and Progress: or, did the Enlightenment fail?' *Albion*, 35: 4 (2003): 559–89; Martin, David, 'Towards Eliminating the Concept of Secularisation', in Julius Gould, (ed.), *The Penguin Survey of the Social Sciences* (Harmondsworth: Penguin, 1965).

role, and social basis of religion. Theories of religion and theories of secularization are closely related, which means you can infer an author's concept of what constitutes religion from what he believes causes secularization, such as greater wealth and security. At the same time, that does not preclude theories of religion, for example, as hard-wired or neurological, which simultaneously regard religion as illusory and imply a denial of secularization. An illusion can have a future. Conversely nothing prevents a Christian holding a strong view of secularization.[3]

Ideological contamination does not in itself show a theory is mistaken. Having criticized it, I then tried to produce *A General Theory of Secularisation*, sketched in embryo in 1969.[4] I tried to restrict the power of unwanted ideological resonances by focusing on Church-related religiosity and its penumbra. Moreover I concentrated on a particular branch of secularization theory indebted to Talcott Parsons and based on social differentiation rather than rationalization and privatization. Social differentiation refers to the clearly identifiable process whereby social spheres, such as the state, administration, welfare, education, and the arts, are no longer under ecclesiastical oversight or governed by the deliverances and modalities of theology.

Clearly such an approach generates questions relevant to master narratives of past and future. Does differentiation marginalize religion in its own specialized ghetto or does it create a space in which faith can discover its own specific character, freed from the constraints of establishment and seductive opportunities for political influence? Standard secularization theory, according to the model set up by Bryan Wilson, rests not only on differentiation but on other grand nouns of process like rationalization, bureaucratization, and privatization. I was uncertain about these terms just as I was wary of just-so historical stories based on Then and Now, such as once upon a time there was Community and now there is Association. There is *something* in this, and it greatly influenced Bryan Wilson, but it is not a straightforward story, any more than the Durkheimian transition from Mechanical to Organic Solidarity, or Ernest Gellner's rift between modernity and all previous periods is straightforward.[5] One needs to subject nouns of process and binary distinctions of Then and Now to careful scrutiny.[6] That kind of scrutiny led me on to the issue of the assumed religiosity of the past and to a slightly different question about how recent and superficial the Christianization of Europe sometimes was.[7] Such questions puzzle historians, let alone sociologists, as the

---

[3]   Fenn, Richard K., *The Secularization of Sin* (Louisville, Kentucky: John Knox Press, 1991).

[4]   Martin, David, *A General Theory of Secularisation*.

[5]   Gellner, Ernest, *Thought and Change* (London: Weidenfeld, 1964).

[6]   Martin, David, *The Religious and the Secular* (London: Routledge, 1968); Wilson, Bryan, *Religion in Sociological Perspective* (Oxford: Oxford University Press, 1982).

[7]   Stark, Rodney, *One True God* (Princeton: Princeton University Press, 2001).

difference in emphasis between Keith Thomas and Peter Laslett shows.[8] One is brought up short when a major historian like Friedrich Heer can say it takes up to a couple of millennia for a religion really to sink into a cultural system.[9] Above all, one needs to think on an adequately long time scale about the viability of alternative master narratives, such as the long-term advance of monotheism or master narratives based on alternations rather than on continuous movement forwards to an assured destination.

As well as the role of ideology in constructing our master narratives I have emphasized how particular histories, for example, the very different histories of Poland and France, give rise to very different styles of secularization. History matters and it is contingent. We can list numerous general tendencies inherent in secularization, but they are greatly affected by different histories, and different histories can even reverse seemingly general tendencies, as in the case of contemporary Islam. The distinctive history of Russia generates a distinctive pattern of secularization and religious revival. Moreover, one cannot reduce the Russian religious revival following the collapse of Communism to the survival of elements from the past which the regime failed to snuff out or just a 'reaction' to the partial abolition of an 'enlightened' tyranny. Religion acts as well as reacts, as I argue in a later chapter.

There are many other major examples of a particular history associated with a particular kind of secularization. Most obviously the history of liberal and republican France differs from the history of Protestant and post-Protestant Britain and Scandinavia. There are great gulfs fixed between the histories of religion and secularization in Catholic Southern and Catholic Central Europe and what happened in Northern Protestant Europe. Protestant Europe also differs markedly from the Protestant USA. In the early stages of modernity, Pietism and Evangelicalism in Northern Europe built up massive denominational sub-cultures which then declined, if at different rates, although some lasted up to the mid-twentieth century, whereas in the US, these sub-cultures accompanied modernity throughout and expanded with it.[10] The same Pietist and Evangelical impulse, particularly in the contemporary form of Pentecostalism, then became indigenized in Latin America. There, it created a hybrid and pluralistic Catholic-Evangelical pattern very different from either Western Europe or North America. Eventually it became the most expansive form of Christianity in the world and entirely comparable to Islamic revivalism. At the very least, Islamic revival and the kind of Christian revival represented by Pentecostalism, need to be integrated into secularization theory. One cannot

---

[8] Laslett, Peter, *The World We Have Lost: England before the Industrial Age* (London: Methuen, 1965); Thomas, Keith, *Man in the Natural World: Changing Attitudes in England, 1500–1800* (London: Allen Lane, 1983).

[9] Heer, Friedrich, *The Medieval World 1100–1350* (London: Weidenfeld and Nicolson, 1961).

[10] Blaschke, Otto, (ed.), *Konfessionen in Konflikt: Deutschland zwischen 1800 und 1970: ein Zweites Konfessionelles Zeitalter* (Göttingen: Göttingen University Press, 2002).

automatically save the theory by dismissing such revivals as the kind of religious intensification that ushers in secularity, a way station en route to secular destiny. It could be that these revivals are phenomena of the interim before real secularity sets in, and that the fate of Pentecostal churches all over the two-thirds world is presaged by the forlorn chapels of North Wales or North-East Scotland. The sheer cunning of future history is not easily penetrable.

My emphasis on how much outcomes differ, especially when factor D alters the whole direction taken by the combined effects of factors A, B and C, led me to bring together all the material on Pentecostalism in three books.[11] In the latest, entitled *Pentecostalism: The World Their Parish*, I compared the vitality of Catholicism in the developing world with the vitality of Pentecostalism, looking at their differing appeals and also where they converge and exhibit or borrow common characteristics. This chapter simply extends that comparison. Both expressions of Christianity are tangible faiths, exhibiting the spirit through theatre and the senses, in spite of neo-Puritan and iconoclastic strains in the wake of Vatican II. The concern for the Holy Spirit and for a narrative faith we find in Catholic theological thinking is potently echoed in Pentecostal practice. When one observes these covert convergences one is even tempted to construct a master narrative based on Troeltsch's sequence of Church, sect (or denomination), and mysticism, and/or the Joachimite scheme of the Age of the Father, followed by the Ages of the Son and the Holy Spirit. I suspect an empirically grounded combination of Troeltsch and Joachim could be rather impressive, and what Steve Bruce has to say in *Religion in the Modern World: From Cathedrals to Cults* might well be assimilated to it.[12] The Age of the Spirit could be located under numerous forms: Spiritualism, primal spiritism as revived by contemporary pagans, the Latin American spiritism partly derived from Kardecist spiritualism in Spain, mystical gnosis or illuminationism, 'spirituality' as contrasted with religiosity, mainstream charismatic movements, and Pentecostalism.

There is yet another master narrative available, extrapolating from the two books on the social implications of one God by Rodney Stark, and it would be based on the global advance of monotheism over the last three millennia.[13] José Casanova as a Catholic scholar could easily construct a Catholic master narrative, and there are hints of one in Michael Novak.[14] I have explored what an

---

[11]   Martin, David, *Tongues of Fire: The Explosion of Protestantism in Latin America* (Oxford: Blackwell, 1990); *Pentecostalism – The World Their Parish* (Oxford: Blackwell, 2002); *Forbidden Revolutions: Pentecostalism in Latin America, Catholicism in Eastern Europe* (London: SPCK, 1996).

[12]   Bruce, Steve, *Religion in the Modern World: From Cathedrals to Cults* (Oxford: Oxford University Press, 1996).

[13]   Stark, Rodney, *One True God* (Princeton: Princeton University Press 2001); and 'Efforts to Christianize Europe 400–2000', *Journal of Contemporary Religion*, 16 (2001): 86–105.

[14]   Novak, Michael, *Spirit of Democratic Capitalism* (New York: Simon and Schuster, 1982).

Evangelical and Pentecostal master narrative might look like.[15] Indeed, Evangelical demographers have themselves devised schemes based on successive waves of Christian expansion and recession. If the Catholic and Evangelical or Pentecostal narratives were combined, Pentecostalism could be treated as Eastern Orthodox *stasis* transformed into *dunamis* and one might then explore the various dialectics, for example, between a religion of territory or sacred geography with portable faiths based on movement and transit; or between the local, the national, and the transnational; or between inward spirituality and objective sacrament; or between the free-floating and individual and the communal and stabilized. These would not be just-so stories based on Then and Now but intersecting and dialectic alternatives. In terms of these dialectics Catholicism and Pentecostalism are both transnational. However, Catholicism moves backwards and forwards between the God of sacred space as realized in parishes, dioceses and holy lands, and contemporary 'deterritorialization'. By contrast Pentecostalism is a 'movement' expressing social and geographical mobility and recapturing the voluntary character and the portable God of early Christianity, but also drawn back by the perennial pull of a people in a territory and by the power of sacred geography. This I discuss in chapter 4.

So far as my preferred master narrative of social differentiation goes I have also tried to explore another kind of dialectic based on the different kinds of sacred and secular space that have emerged over the eight or so centuries that have passed from the time when there was a simple differentiation of cathedral and city government following the extensive administrative role the Western Church played, initially in the persons of Ambrose and Gregory, when the Roman Empire collapsed. Today this simple differentiation has fragmented into multiple fragmentations by the extension of the sacred to art galleries, gallerias, stadia, universities, war memorials and supreme courts. In this way the shifting dialectic of sacred and secular space is patient of a translation in spatial and architectural terms.

I am simply illustrating just how numerous viable narratives and approaches are. One could find a place both for the master narrative of liberal Christianity and the secular advance of what Peter Berger has called 'faculty club culture' and one might even take into account the collapse of all master narratives that strikes the French as so appealing and obvious. At this very moment there may be some successor to Ibn Khaldun (the great Muslim sociologist who devised a theory of the alternation of Catholic and Puritan, rural and urban elements in Islam), who is busying himself with constructing the story of a future Islamic triumph after a two-century interlude of western secular and Christian domination. I recently met a scholar who has put together a version of Confucianism as a plausible compromise between all warring narratives, which was officially tried out for a while in Singapore.[16] It is an ideologically impoverished group that cannot devise a master narrative of its special place in the scheme of things.

---

[15]   Martin, David, *On Secularization*.

[16]   Yao, Xinzhong, 'Who is Confucian Today?' *Journal of Contemporary Religion*, 16 (2001): 313–38.

Of course the New Testament has its own master narrative, though it is partly concealed in the hidden purposes of God. The New Testament both embodies a sectarian approach based on the text 'When the Son of Man comes shall he find faith on the earth?' and a churchly or Catholic approach based on the 'great commission' to spread the faith to all nations at the conclusion of Matthew's gospel. Analogous tendencies exist in contemporary secular thinking, for example, Francis Fukuyama's liberal 'end to history' without apocalypse, and apocalyptic denunciations of advancing irrationality, fundamentalism, and predatory capitalism.[17] The morphologies of religious thinking reappear transposed in secular thinking, as do religious metaphors for epochs, like Light and Age.

I am trying to lift discussion out of a taken-for-granted rut and exploring what might be involved in a model of what Eisenstadt has called 'multiple modernities'.[18] I am re-iterating my suspicion articulated over the last four decades that the future of the world may not be prefigured by post-Protestant Holland or post-Catholic France.[19] In the same way it may not be prefigured, although it is certainly influenced by, the American model of Protestant pluralism, which today overtakes the French model of secularism once so influential in, for example, Turkey and Brazil.

I am also suggesting that the social distribution of different takes on secularization must tell us something about the social location and culture of sociology. American sociologists are impressed by the resilience of religion, by its successful democratization, and its autonomous power, while European sociologists assume otherwise. Likewise, American sociologists are often drawn to a market model of religion and the advantages for faith of competition, whereas European sociologists are prone to stress the limits of setting up a true market and the limited impact of such pluralism as exists.[20]

Sociologists on both sides of the Atlantic are inclined to select particular themes as key explanatory devices, for example, the current stress on the highly persuasive theme of subjectivization and the corrosion of authority and long-term institutional loyalties, to the neglect of the countervailing appeal of the communitarian impulse and charismatic leadership: kolkhoz and kibbutz. Inwardness is already embedded in the Christian repertoire as well as the earthing of 'the kingdom', the birthing of the divine in the human and the polarities of the religious and the secular, the

---

[17]   Fukuyama, Francis, *The End of History and the Last Man* (New York: Free Press, 1992).

[18]   Eisenstadt, Schmuel N., 'Multiple Modernities', *Daedalus*, 128: 1 (2000): 1–30.

[19]   Van Rooden, Peter, 'Long-Term Religious Developments in the Netherlands 1750–2000', in Hugh McLeod, and Werner Usdorf, (eds), *The Decline of Christendom in Western Europe 1750–2000* (Cambridge: Cambridge University Press, 2003: 113–29).

[20]   Stark, Rodney, and Finke, Roger, *Acts of Faith: Explaining the Human Side of Religion* (Berkeley CA: University of California Press, 2000); Bruce, Steve, *Choice and Religion: A Critique of Rational Choice Theory* (Oxford: Oxford University Press, 1999); and *God is Dead: Secularisation in the West* (Oxford: Blackwell, 2002).

Church, and the world.[21] If we examine this bringing 'down to earth' and this manifestation of the divine in the secular we recognize a dialectic of religious and secular, divine and human, and if that seems rather theological we at least need to realize how such polarities frame and inform our whole discourse and help create the distinctive experience of Christian civilization. All this is implicit in a Durkheimian understanding of how fundamental categories underpin our grasp of the world. Given that Christianity is the prime context of secularization, major contemporary keys to profounder currents in secularization may lie in the slackening of the tension between nature and history and between the cyclic rotations of the natural and the forward historical thrust of transcendence. One of the important shifts often attending the arrival of Christianity is found in the increased potential for a forward thrust capable of disrupting cyclical rotations, and the result is an inbuilt structure of teleological and quasi-Providential anticipations, especially in secular politics.

Catholicism and Modernity

I now want to explore the impact of uniquely rapid change, first on Catholicism with its historical pattern of conflict with secular radicalism, and second on the pattern of successive mutations of Protestantism, focusing on Pentecostalism and including the kind of inwardness found in today's free-floating spirituality.

As we examine what has happened to the old conflict characterizing Catholic, especially Latin Catholic culture, we can now see how it came to a climax in the Third French Republic and the Spanish and Mexican civil wars, before entering a plateau with Christian democracy post 1945. It then experienced virtual death with the collapse of communism. What began in 1789 died in 1989. At the same time, this conflict had various outcomes, country by country, which remain influential even now. We have to compare these outcomes to see where the Catholic Church is well-placed and where it is vulnerable. We also need to compare the different effects of reform carried out by the two sides, in the communist case, collapse, and in the Catholic case, a slackening of cohesion. Cohesion always suffers with the collapse of an enemy, as we can see from what happened to European Christian Democracy after 1989.

At its height, conflict creates solidarity on both sides and the Polish movement called 'Solidarity' was well named, until its aims were achieved and freedom secured. Historically we observe the vigour of ultramontane sub-cultures threatened by Protestant elites in Germany or England or by radical elites in Latin Christendom. The division of Europe after the Second World War resulted in a clash between a

---

21   Taylor, Charles, *Sources of the Self: the Making of Modern Identity* (Cambridge MA: Harvard University Press, 1989*)*; Debray, Régis, *God: an Itinerary* (London: Verso, 2004); Seligman, Adam, *Modernity's Wager: Authority, the Self and Transcendence* (Princeton: Princeton University Press, 2000).

Catholic Christian Democracy, sponsored by Adenauer, Monnet, Schuman, and De Gasperi, and communist Central and Eastern Europe, and for a while, the result was a high level of identification with the Church in Western Europe as well as a vigorous ethno-religious resistance in Eastern Europe. This resistance was most successful in Poland, Slovakia and Croatia and least successful in the GDR (the home of Luther) and what was then the western half of Czechoslovakia especially Bohemia (the sphere of Hus). Much depends, of course, on whether religion has or has not been positively associated with national survival.

By the 1960s, various changes had smudged the lines of confrontation, including the arrival of John XXIII, the pursuit of an up-dated Catholicism at the Second Vatican Council, and a certain Catholic disillusionment with the secular capitalist dynamic animating Christian Democratic parties. There was increased support for the Catholic left, and in Latin America there were progressive initiatives on the part of the bishops and the advent of liberation theology.[22] On the other side, Stalin died, Euro-communism emerged until eventually Gorbachev attempted to revive communism with the full-scale reforms associated with *glasnost* and *perestroika*.

It is inevitable that reform initiated by modernizing elites in political or religious institutions based on unity and authority has uncontrollable consequences. For example, the reforms of Tsar Alexander II, beginning with the emancipation of the serfs in 1861, led to his assassination some two decades later. Following the same Russian tradition, Gorbachev's attempt to save communism by reforming it led to its dissolution, although not to his. What remained were rumps composed of *apparatchiks* reinventing themselves as national kleptocracies, as in Romania and Serbia, or as renamed opportunist parties aiming to pick up the discontents of change, as in East Germany.

By contrast, the Catholic world did not break up. This was because Catholicism was not part of a system of absolute power and also because Catholicism became associated with movements for freedom and/or national identity and autonomy. From having defended up to quite recently the special rights of the Church in collusion with the state, the politics of Catholicism moved to the defence of the rights of the person, including the free exercise of religion.[23] The latest phase of this (February, 2010) is represented by Pope Benedict's critique of the British Equality Law for infringing both natural law and John Locke on the rights of religious bodies, perhaps oblivious to Locke's explicit exclusion of 'papists'.

The shift within Catholicism was momentous and it went hand in hand with movements world-wide to disentangle the Church from the direct legitimation of power and take up a stance of critical solidarity. A certain loss of cohesion and authority was inevitable, following what looked like changes of mind on the part of the *magisterium*. Moreover, the Church did not everywhere abandon conservative

---

[22]   Keogh, Dermot, (ed.), *Church and Politics in Latin America* (London: Macmillan, 1990).

[23]   Woodhead, Linda, *Introduction to Christianity* (Cambridge: Cambridge University Press, 2004).

alliances with state power and the social hierarchy, especially with respect to elite education. The clash between progressive and conservative elements was significantly reflected in the clash between the international orders or priests from elsewhere and local hierarchies and priesthoods.[24]

Some examples may help. In Chile, where tensions between the Church and the Pinochet regime grew apace within two years of the coup of 1974, lines of communication were maintained and compromises eventually sought. Once democracy was restored, members of the economic elite, previously worried by the clash over human rights between the Church and an economically successful regime, re-engaged with an ethos of paternal Catholic responsibility, whether or not they actively practised their religion.[25] They also showed considerable interest in movements like Opus Dei and the Legionaries of Christ, and in particular appreciated their schools and their combination of modernity and rigour. The Catholic hegemony remained in place, in spite of an Evangelical presence of over 15 per cent, although democratic politicians were increasingly wary of attempts to convert ecclesiastical norms into state law.[26]

In Brazil, the Church opened up a discreet dialogue with the military regime to ameliorate the most severe outbreaks of conflict over human rights.[27] With the return of democracy and the achievement of some stability under Cardoso, more conciliatory attitudes were adopted towards Catholicism and Pentecostalism by Lula and what has been for some time the governing Workers Party. The traditional divides became less significant and the Evangelical Presidential candidate, with 18 per cent of the vote, actually threw his weight behind the election of Lula. The overarching role of the Catholic Church remained, in spite of the massive rise in Evangelicalism and Pentecostalism and the increasingly independent influence of a syncretic Spiritism.

In Uruguay, however, the war of Church and state, and of whites and reds, had ended in a secularist victory, so that Christian symbols and the liturgical calendar were both expunged from public space. The secularism of Uruguay is due to the

---

[24] Vasquez, Manuel, *The Brazilian Popular Church and the Crisis of Modernity* (Cambridge: Cambridge University Press, 1998).

[25] Thumala, Maria Angelica, *Riqueza y Piedad El Catolicismo de la elite economica chilena* (Santiago, 2007).

[26] Fleet, Michael, and Smith, Brian, *The Catholic Church and Democracy in Chile and Peru* (Notre Dame IN: University of Notre Dame, 1997).

[27] Serbin, Kenneth, *Secret Dialogues* (Pittsburgh, PA: Metanexus Institute, 2000); Bruneau, Thomas, *The Political Transformation of the Brazilian Catholic Church* (Cambridge: Cambridge University Press, 1974); Hewitt, William, *Christian Base Communities and Social Change in Brazil* (Lincoln NE: University of Nebraska Press, 1991); Bruneau, Thomas, and Hewitt, William, 'Catholicism and Political Action in Brazil: Limitations and Prospects', in Edward Cleary, and Hannah Stewart-Gambino, (eds), *Conflict and Competition: The Latin American Church in a Changing Environment* (London: Lynne Rienner, 1992: chapter 3).

high proportion of European migrants who arrived at a time of vigorous anti-clericalism in Europe.[28] Nearby Argentina also had a high proportion of European migrants, yet it retained a conservative Catholic Church through various political vicissitudes and since the nineties has experienced the late arrival of a strong wave of non-denominational neo-Pentecostalism.[29] The Philippines offer yet another resolution of the traditional tension. Revolutions associated with dissident Catholic elites overthrew corrupt regimes, with ecclesiastical and popular support, and largely succeeded in dealing with communist insurgency.

At any rate, we may say that with varying outcomes, of which France and Uruguay offer examples of Catholic vulnerability, the Church came through. Liberation theology and the base communities both raised popular consciousness and made a serious contribution, along with important sectors of the episcopate, to human rights and resistance to dictatorship. They also pre-empted the Marxist threat until it receded and, apart from Nicaragua under the Sandinistas, the 'popular church' stayed under Episcopal control.[30] In a similar way, charismatic Catholicism, for example in Brazil, or New Evangelization and the Neo-Catechumenate, may to some extent have pre-empted Pentecostalism. Competition is good for monopolies, because it motivates them to find out need and meet it. At the same time, part of the appeal of Pentecostalism lies in enabling people, especially the aspiring poor, to walk away from all the hierarchies, social, ecclesiastical, and intellectual, whether or not they exercise 'an option for the poor'. They can walk out into a haven, where others like themselves enjoy equality before God. They can create their own space for faith, where they have an opportunity to lead and to give voice and tongue in their own words. In their churches, they enjoy mutual support among the brethren and can mediate the Gospel on their own account rather than have it mediated to them. No Church retaining access to power and the social hierarchy can fully pre-empt that without internal contradiction. It cannot avoid religious dissidence, and political opposition will always be able to mobilize new and subordinate social groups (or indeed elites in waiting) outside the sacred canopy of the traditional Church. That is a painful lesson the Church has learned over the past two centuries. The most the Church can expect is to exercise broad cultural influence as a pressure group, while distancing itself from any dangerous identification with power elites in the state. It has to arrive at workable compromises in the field of politics, while retaining a critical or prophetic role.

---

[28]   Sobrano, Eduardo, 'Influencia social de la Iglesia Catolica en el Uruguay', *Aportes*, 10 (1968): 106–35.

[29]   Miguez, Daniel, *Spiritual Bonfire in Argentina* (Amsterdam: CEDLA, 1998).

[30]   Williams, Philip, 'The Limits of Religious Influence: The Progressive Church in Nicaragua', in Edward Cleary, and Hannah Stewart-Gambino, (eds), *Conflict and Competition* (London: Lynne Rienner, 1992: 147–66): Gill, Anthony, *Rendering Unto Caesar: The Catholic Church and the State in Latin America* (Chicago: University of Chicago Press, 1998).

We now need to itemize varied historical situations and their likely outcomes for the Church. Where Catholicism has been opposed to the mobilization of the nation and specifically set itself against liberal nationalism, the compromise may be very disadvantageous and lead to the spiral of decline that has occurred in France. Of course it is always possible to criticize the exploitative character of liberal elites and so turn the tables on the liberal critique of Catholicism, but this has often taken the form of an *integrista* attack on individualism, liberalism and capitalism alike. In countries where periods of ambivalence, collusion, and compromise alternate with periods of vicious conflict, as they have done in Mexico, the partial recovery of privileges may be delayed many decades.[31] Where the Church has been associated with national struggle, even reluctantly as in Ireland, the positive identification will persist for some time, with the attendant danger the Church may become complacent and even exploitative in its enjoyment of unchallenged power. In Poland today, the vitality of vocations helps the wider Catholic Church in the crisis of the priesthood elsewhere.

There are other situations where Catholics constitute a minority, either because they are mixed with a Protestant majority as in the US and the UK, or mostly concentrated in a territorial base, as in Canada, Germany, Holland, and Switzerland. To begin with, the Catholic Church organizes itself as a separate culture with a ghetto mentality, but with social and geographical mobility; Catholics increasingly reflect wider national trends, including the growth of secular and Protestant individualism.[32] They may on occasion prefer to find secular means of political expression distanced or completely separated from the institutional Church. There will be breaches in the fortress mentality and its ring of defensive institutions which will widen when Catholics are disoriented by rapid change within the Church itself. In the US, Britain, and Australia, this resulted in lower levels of practice, while in Holland, the denominational ghettos were so tightly organized that once breaches occurred, the fall-out was catastrophic. It was also catastrophic in Quebec, where a Catholic nationalism turned into a more explicit cultural and economic nationalism. It is an easy transition.[33]

Nowhere can the Church assume that loyal identification is permanent or that it can be translated into obedience to Catholic norms or support for their embodiment in secular law. That is all part of the distancing of the Church from the state, of Catholic morality from the law, and of ecclesiastical elites from social elites, and it illustrates what is meant by secularization in the limited sense of social differentiation. Italians voted for divorce in 1976, while in Ireland, insensitive

---

[31]   Louaeza-Lajous, Solidad, 'Continuity and Change in the Mexican Catholic Church', in Keogh, Dermot, (ed.), *Church and Politics in Latin America* (London: Macmillan, 1990: 272–98).

[32]   Campiche, Roland, (ed.), *Croire en Suisse(s)* (Geneva: Slatkine, 1992).

[33]   Baum, Gregory, 'Catholicism and Secularisation in Québec', in David Lyons, and Margaret Van Die, (eds), *Rethinking Church, State and Modernity* (Toronto: University of Toronto Press, 2000: 149–65).

assumptions about automatic respect crumbled at the touch of moral scandal. A Church that too much looks after its priestly personnel at the expense of the laity and does not understand the ways of modern public relations is at the mercy of the secular media.[34]

Thus clerical immunity has departed for good, even in the most favourable circumstances. Increasingly, Catholics assume it is up to them to choose what they conscientiously regard as right according to their life experience and the evidence is clear enough in the declining birth rates of Brazil or Mexico or Italy. To be a Catholic in modern society does not carry assent to the *magisterium* or to a certain kind of logic based on natural law or inferences from dogma. Moreover, some internal changes within the Church, such as the removal of familiar marks of Catholic identity or the downgrading of individual confession and folk practices, can throw authority into question. The Catholic Church has always known how to deal with sin and errant humanity and it has successfully canalized movements of the spirit without disrupting its unity, but it has not found a way to meet overt and principled criticism without inviting comparisons between what it recommends politically to the secular world and how it orders its own internal affairs.

All the varied outcomes just outlined reflect the negotiation of the Church with modernity in the form of radical and liberal politics, nationalism, democracy, and human rights and with something more subtle, which I will call 'mutations of the Protestant and existential principle'. These mutations came to a head in the spirit of the 1960s and were an extension to nearly everybody of the self-cultivation, even the bohemianism, earlier enjoyed by elites, for example, in the 1890s and 1920s.[35] In those earlier decades, self-cultivation, particularly in the arts, might include personal mysticism and a renewed appreciation of the organic and communitarian and it often led to Catholic (or Anglo-Catholic) conversion.[36]

However, in the North Atlantic world of the 1960s and 1970s, the search for a personal pathway combined a legitimation of aggressive greed with an existential rejection of markers, limits, and boundaries, in particular all markers of authority, social cohesion and control, and all limits of respect. Individuals were disinclined to sink long-term psychic capital in the maintenance of institutions and viewed forms and manners, rituals and vestments, as mere external constraints.[37]

This relativistic subjectivity not only undermined religious institutions, but was also hostile to the proclaimed objectivity of science and the restrictive protocols of philosophical positivism. A space for religion was still there, except that it was as

---

[34]   Dillon, Michele, 'Catholicism, Culture and Politics in the Republic of Ireland', in Ted Jelen, and Clive Wilcox, (eds), *The One, the Few and the Many: Religion and Politics in Comparative Perspective* (Cambridge: Cambridge University Press, 2002: 47–70).

[35]   Davies, Christie, *The Strange Death of Moral Britain* (London: Transaction, 2004).

[36]   Cate, Shannon, 'Transcendentalists and Catholic converts in Emerson's America', in Linda Woodhead, (ed.), *Rethinking Christianity* (Aldershot: Ashgate, 2001).

[37]   Martin, Bernice, *A Sociology of Contemporary Social Change* (Oxford: Blackwell, 1981).

often occupied by immanence as by transcendence, and fostered an eco-mysticism devoid of long-term ethical community though not devoid of a capacity for interim mobilizations. Idealistic criticism of political and religious institutions proved more seductive than self-criticism. In other words, prophecy trumped sin, just as aesthetics trumped ethics, and rights trumped duties.

In earlier times, these impulses might have been canalized in tempered and realistic form by a Christian humanism or personalism, but that is not so easy where educational practices based on self-expression worked in alliance with consumerism, youth culture, and the pressures of the media. The consequence for religion was a 'spirituality' retranslated as working out your own salvation without fear and trembling. Clearly that allows us to move from Catholic to Protestant modes of secularization.

Protestantism and Modernity

Protestant trajectories vary as much as Catholic ones, but in general, one can say that as the inwardness and moral discipline of the Reformation breaks out of the protective fabric of the Church, Protestant faith grows passive and focused on ethical behaviour, which is paradoxical given the original stress on faith alone. Where Catholicism generates an antagonistic secular ideology, Protestantism mutates into a piecemeal pragmatism and utilitarianism.

Yet passivity and apathy only characterize the Protestant state churches of Northern Europe, and not always even there. In the US, vital religion goes together with pluralism and the separation of Church and state. Canada, with its quasi-establishments region by region and its less vital pluralism, lies between the American and European trajectory, and over the decades up to the nineteen-nineties it saw a shift from a very active Christianity to a passivity somewhat more in the European style. In the US, the extent and vitality of Evangelicalism is at its greatest and decreases progressively as you move to Canada, Britain, and Northern Europe.[38] Moreover, American nationalism conceives of America itself as a Light of the World, whereas Canada and Britain confine their national claims to being righteous peoples. In the American and British cases, one suspects *some* link between religious confidence and imperial confidence, with American confidence still undimmed, and British confidence undermined.

In the developing world, Protestantism has a very different character, especially in sub-Saharan Africa, where life remains inspirited and competition and pluralism are universal. The mainstream churches in Africa, Catholic and Protestant, often act as Non-Governmental Organizations in 'critical solidarity'

---

[38] Noll, Mark A., *American Evangelical Christianity: An Introduction* (Oxford: Blackwell, 2001); Stackhouse, John, *Canadian Evangelicalism in the Twentieth Century* (Toronto: Toronto University Press, 1993).

with the state.[39] The mainstream Protestant churches in Africa are morally and theologically conservative and that leads to tensions with the liberal Protestantism of the North Atlantic. That is not a problem for the rapidly expanding Pentecostals or the popular charismatic megachurches, which are fissiparous and in any case tend to represent new and younger groups outside the centres of power. However, once Pentecostals and charismatics grow in numbers and appeal to middle-class or university people, they lose their traditional reluctance about political activity and aspire (with some corporate and personal aggrandizement) to be influential in the state, for example, in Zambia and in Ghana where there is a veritable 'Christianity fever'.[40] They can also create powerful transnational communities through their massive influence in the popular media. In sub-Saharan Africa as a whole, the conditions that bring about decline in Europe do not obtain. As in the US, Christianity flourishes in an atmosphere of competitive pluralism and faith is identified with greater education and with modernity. One in five Christians today is African, part of the move southward of Christianity analysed by Philip Jenkins, even though Rome is not yet moving to central Africa, or Canterbury to Nigeria or Uganda, or Geneva to Malawi.[41] Demographically the 'centre' of Anglicanism might lie somewhere around Burkina Faso.

The US as the contemporary super-power is arguably the only genuinely Protestant country in the developed world, given that to survive the Protestant impulse in Northern Europe assimilated itself to established power as well as to the nation, its culture, and its language. By extending principles incubated, but only partly realized, in Britain, the US broke the historic mould by separating Church and state, accepting pluralism and combining the Enlightenment with Christianity.[42] Today, this combination is under strain on account of 'culture wars' between those who stress the undoubted religious elements built into the revolutionary settlement and those in the metropolitan media and academia who seek a secular Enlightenment pure and simple.[43]

American Christianity adjusts competitively to changes in the market of souls, and promotes religion as an indubitable social good and a form of social capital capable of yielding psychological, bodily, and communal benefits. Although individualism has made inroads into the regularity of religious practice, it mostly stays within the churches in the form of a Christian search for personal fulfillment. Whereas in Europe, spirituality often moves outside the churches, in America, it

---

[39]   Gifford, Paul, *African Christianity: its Public Role* (London: Hurst, 1998).

[40]   Gifford, Paul, 'Chiluba's Christian Nation: Christianity as a Factor in Zambian Politics 1991–1996', *Journal of Contemporary Religion*, 13 (1998): 363–82.

[41]   Jenkins, Philip, *The Next Christendom: The Coming of Global Christianity* (Oxford: Oxford University Press, 2002).

[42]   Clark, Jonathan, 'Providence, Predestination and Progress: or did the Enlightenment Fail?' *Albion*, 35 (2004): 559–89.

[43]   Clark, Jonathan, 'Liberty and Religion: the End of American Exceptionalism', *Orbis*, 49: 1 (2005): 21–46.

mostly stays inside them. That is also true of the spirituality sought in the arts, even among American Evangelicals.[44] Perhaps the North American evidence suggests that the intermittent warfare in Europe and Latin America between religion and the creative arts, like the political warfare, is in its final stages. That too is momentous, in spite of the prejudices still lodged in the cultural and media elites.[45] Modern media recruit disproportionately from people who represent the 'expressive revolution'. That kind of person and that type of media have an elective affinity.

Just as the relation of Catholicism to the arts has been more positive than that of Protestantism (or at least of Evangelical Protestantism), so the relation of Protestantism to nationalism has been more positive than that of Catholicism. Partly that follows from a tension between the nation state and the international claims of the Catholic Church, however much these claims were restricted by the *patronato* in Iberia and Latin America. It also follows from the forced collusion of the Catholic Church with the enlightened autocracy of the Spanish and Austrian empires and the conflict between the Catholic Church and aspirations to national independence in Latin America and central Europe. Perhaps today, an international Church stands to gain by declines in nationalistic fervour.

The price of Protestant assimilation to the nation, and of its educated clergy to the national elites, was *Kulturprotestantismus*. In North America and Britain, many of those in the enlightened elite, including many clergy, looked forward with Thomas Jefferson and Joseph Priestley to the universal triumph of a rational faith. Instead, the masses in Britain and the new American Republic were enthused by Methodism and in Germany by Pietism. All three countries were affected by Romanticism, with its revival of the mystical, including an invocation of medieval Catholicism. Some Transcendentalists even converted to Catholicism.

However, that is too tangled a tale for present purposes. Looking forward to the global present and future we need select only that Anglo-American version of Pietism and Methodism that became metamorphosed into Pentecostalism at the beginning of the twentieth century. Pentecostalism combined black and white revivalism in a potent mixture capable of crossing cultural barriers always resistant to the more verbal, ethical, and cerebral expressions of mainstream Protestantism. Pentecostalism also had the advantage of being based on semi-autonomous explosions of spiritual energy in places as widely separated as Korea, India, Wales, Norway, Chile, and South Africa.[46]

Perhaps there is some parallel between such movements of the spirit, with their expansive missionary aspirations, and the ultramontanism of the Catholic world, with its own readiness for expansion and mission. Yet these missionary energies

---

[44]   Wuthnow, Robert, *All in Sync*: *How Music and Art are Revitalizing American Religion* (Berkeley, CA: University of California Press, 2003).

[45]   O'Toole, Roger, 'Seeing and Believing: Reframing Christian Imagery in Secular Society', in J. Harris, (ed.), *Image Makers and Image Breakers* (New York: Legas, 2003).

[46]   Anderson, Allan, *An Introduction to Pentecostalism* (Cambridge: Cambridge University Press, 2004).

differed from those associated with the first wave of European colonialism, either because, as in the British case, mission had been largely eschewed for reasons of commerce and state, or because, as in the Spanish and Russian cases, political, religious, and economic expansion went straightforwardly hand in hand. Political expansion and religious expansion could now be in conflict, so that we have another example of social differentiation. Indeed, Protestant missions could, in the long run, feed African nationalism. All over Africa, missions created educated elites able to take over the governance of new nations, so contributing to the unexpected efflorescence of Christianity in the post-colonial period.[47] Of course, this mainstream Christianity also faced Africanist ideologies and independent African churches, as well as, in due course, the spread of Pentecostalism.[48]

From the viewpoints of national intelligentsias, including Catholic ones, and from the viewpoints of liberal Protestants and Catholics in the North Atlantic as well as their more conservative co-religionists in Africa, the growth of Pentecostalism and associated charismatic megachurches is problematic. It can be dismissed as sectarian or inspired by an American prosperity gospel or as a brand of fundamentalism indifferent to the authentic culture of Africa. Yet these dismissals set aside much contrary evidence about genuine indigenization, and Pentecostalism is a Christian movement fully comparable to Islamic revivalism, but entirely without a militant and violent wing. The fundamentalist label is misleading, partly because Pentecostalism focuses as much on spiritual gifts as on the text, but also because fundamentalism in the developing world arises with the formation of the nation state. The Christian parallels reach back to the *Reconquista*. That was when the militant unity of religion and the Spanish state led to the persecution and ethno-religious cleansing of minorities. Such ethno-religious cleansing has been characteristic of nationalism in the Balkans, the Caucasus, the Islamic Middle East, and North Africa and is present today wherever militant religiosity and nation-building fuse together. The fissiparous pluralism of Pentecostalism has little in common with this, even in places like Brazil, Nigeria and Ghana where some Pentecostals harbour serious political ambitions.[49]

Pentecostalism finds its characteristic location among the aspiring poor, particularly women, seeking moral integration, security, modernity, and respect, above all in Latin America and Africa. It also flourishes in ethnic groupings in Latin America and Asia that have been historically overshadowed by the weight and power of larger civilizations, as the Maya have been by Spanish hegemony and

---

[47] Ferguson, Niall, *Empire: How Britain Made the Modern World* (Harmondsworth: Penguin, 2003); Ranger, Terence, 'Evangelical Christianity and Democracy in Africa', *Transformation*, 19: 4 (2002): 265–7.

[48] Maxwell, David, *African Gifts of the Spirit* (Oxford: James Curry, 2007); Meyer, Birgit, *Translating the Devil: Religion and Modernity among the Ewe in Ghana* (Edinburgh: Edinburgh University Press, 1999).

[49] Freston, Paul, *Evangelicals and Politics in Asia, Africa and Latin America* (Cambridge: Cambridge University Press, 1998).

the Koreans by China and Japan. Pentecostal and charismatic Christianity make considerable headway among new transnational middle classes the world over, from Brazil to Nigeria and Singapore to Seoul.[50] Above all, perhaps, Evangelical and Pentecostal Christianity advance rapidly in China, where Protestantism has overtaken Catholicism, and both are influential in the Chinese diaspora in Malaysia and Indonesia. There seems to be an affinity between the Protestant and the Chinese spirit, which could prove very significant for the future of Christianity.

The Inward and the Bounded

I have suggested a number of patterns and trajectories from the immediate and longer-term past that affect the immediate and even the longer-term future. I have underlined the exceptional situation in parts of Western Europe, due in part to historical factors, including religious monopoly and/or establishment, not present on the global scene, except in Latin America.[51] However, it is also true that the war over religion and its political influence in Europe is largely over, in spite of continuing prejudice. Some observers, among them Andrew Greeley and Yves Lambert, even regard the European decline as bottoming-out.[52] Greeley in particular points to the virtual disappearance of the negative relation between level of education and religious belief, a shift also discernible in the USA. In any case, a declining European population in the future may make European developments less significant for global Christianity.

In Latin America, where some of the conditions in Europe also obtained, the enlightened elites rarely succeeded in erasing the inspired world of the majority. As in Europe, the combination of change, both in the Church and on the political left, has eased the conflict over religion as such, and with the rise of Pentecostalism the continent is now religiously pluralistic, even though the Church mostly retains a major cultural influence and some traditional privileges. The developments common to Europe and most other parts of global Christianity are those I put under the heading of social differentiation: the loosening of ties between Church and state, between ecclesiastical and social elites, between the Church and specific religious parties, and between ecclesiastical moral norms and secular law. To that I would add the ways in which the welfare and educational professionals, whose purposes link them to the Church, make pre-emptive strikes in favour of secular criteria of performance, even when under ecclesiastical aegis.

---

[50]   Corten, André, and Marshall-Fratani, Ruth, (eds), *Between Babel* and *Pentecost: Transnational Pentecostalism in Africa and Latin America* (London: Hurst, 2001).

[51]   McLeod, Hugh, and Usdorf, Werner, (eds), *The Decline of Christendom in Western Europe 1750–2000* (Cambridge: Cambridge University Press, 2003).

[52]   Greeley, Andrew, *Religion in Europe at the End of the Second Millennium* (London: Transaction, 2003); Lambert, Yves, 'A Turning Point in Religious Evolution in Europe', *Journal of Contemporary Religion*, 19 (2004): 29–46.

Another way of putting all that is to say that the *integrista* project has failed, although the Church can retain a role as chaplain to the nation, provided it does not openly attempt to exercise political power in its own favour. All that is as true of mainstream Protestant churches in Europe as it is of the Catholic Church. For all churches, loyal identification does not entail agreement with ecclesiastical pronouncements, and lay Christians make their decisions in terms of what makes moral sense in the life-world. Christians (and Catholics in particular of course) mostly respect the charisma of the Pope and his office, but if they agree with the critique of narcissism and consumer hedonism at the expense of justice, it is because the critique awakes an answering response and accords with conscience.

This supremacy of conscience, which in one way the Catholic Church recognizes, is linked to other changes in spirituality with variable consequences in Europe, North America, Latin America, Africa, and elsewhere. It is mainly in Europe that spirituality tends to be free-floating. In France, for example, where only one in ten attends mass regularly and vocations are in crisis, young people often believe in reincarnation and confuse it with resurrection. In many European countries, as Régis Debray has put it, the Twilight of the Gods turns out to be Morning for the Magicians. Of course, in Latin Christendom, there has always been a syncretistic underlay of semi-magical paganism and the ancient gods of fortune, but this now emerges as a mélange of attitudes outside the sacred canopy of the Church.[53]

Such a mélange is hardly the anticipated triumph of reason, but just as important is a mutation of Protestant inwardness, embracing spirituality as a personal path, and so far mostly confined to the North Atlantic.[54] This may well be ethical in character, even passionately so, for example, regarding environmental issues and the status of women. Yet there is also a culture of complaint about reality. The claims of unlimited freedom breed endless litigation over incompatible rights and assaults on respect, authority and the boundaries of the person and the sacred, while utopian illusions breed a sense of alienation displacing moral guilt.

The spiritual impulse turns inward through an exploration of eastern mysticism or outward in cults of 'positive thinking', some of them Christian. This represents the culmination of William James's view that religion is about personal experience, while its collective, institutional, sacramental, and intellectual expression is treated as derivative.[55] It also corresponds to Troeltsch's anticipation of a time when mysticism would supersede the polarity of Church and sect. Interestingly the search for a personal path and the mystical may also express itself in the liminal experience of pilgrimage to sacred sites, Christian and pagan, which grows in popularity year by year. In Europe, the pilgrimage to Santiago is virtually as

---

[53]   Debray, Régis, *God: An Itinerary* (London: Verso, 2004).

[54]   Woodhead, Linda, *An Introduction to Christianity*; MacLaren, Duncan, *Mission Implausible* (Milton Keynes: Paternoster Press, 2004).

[55]   Taylor, Charles, *Varieties of Religion Today: William James Revisited* (Cambridge MA: Harvard University Press, 2002).

popular as it was in the Middle Ages and for equally mixed, if somewhat different, motives.[56]

The charismatic movement within both the Catholic and Protestant Churches can be thought of as a middle-class version of Pentecostalism and, like Pentecostalism, it embraces modern technology and the concern for a personal spirituality within the ethical constraints required by group loyalty and mutual support. In the US and elsewhere, an older Evangelicalism has in part shifted towards megachurches frequented by young professionals and their families, anxious to secure an environment resistant to contemporary moral relativism.[57] The same impulse creates a demand for Christian education and education in schools with a Christian ethos, even among otherwise secular people, in Europe, North America, Australasia, and for that matter Latin America. The charismatic movement picks up modern spirituality while maintaining boundaries and personal discipline, and it represents a significant convergence of Protestant and Catholic, of mainstream and Pentecostal.[58]

Postscript

I earlier suggested that the future of Christianity is influenced by the question as to how far we have abandoned the tensions of transcendence and immanence, history and nature, either in favour of a paganism embedded in nature or a positivistic naturalism based on the manipulation of nature.[59] Neither pagan naturalism nor scientific naturalism leave space for the distinctive institution of the Church, eliciting a voluntary commitment to an ethical community pointed towards the transcendent. Such a distinctive institution embodies a distinctive understanding of the human as a creature transcending nature as well as part of it. That creature is not just a body in pursuit of happiness, but is seen as exercising choice within a drama of innocence and experience, moral aspiration and guilty regret, and redeemed by the gift of grace made manifest in the self-offering of Christ. The future of Christianity depends not on what scientific advance may show, but on whether the Christian drama continues to make sense.

---

[56]   Albert-Llorca, Marlène, 'Renouveau de la religion locale en Espagne', in Grace Davie, and Daniele Hervieu-Léger, (eds), *Identités Religieuses en Europe* (Paris: Decouverte, 1996: 235–52).

[57]   Miller, Donald, *Reinventing American Protestantism* (Berkeley, CA: University of California Press, 1997).

[58]   Percy, Martyn, *Power and the Church* (London: Cassell, 1998).

[59]   York, Michael, 'New Commodification and Appropriation of Spirituality', *Journal of Contemporary Religion*, 16 (2001): 361–72; Woodhead, Linda, 'Post-Christian Spiritualities', *Religion*, 23: 2 (1993): 167–82.

Chapter 3
Master Narratives and the Future of Christianity

In this chapter I look at the particular master narratives of sociology and anthropology, before turning to the broader master narratives in which they are embedded, as these bear on the future of Christianity. At the heart of the discussion are the two binary themes of individualism and the collective, universalism and the particular, and both binaries run into major paradoxes. The theme of individualism, (or individuality), and the collective, (or the communal), encounters paradoxes plaguing all our visions of political promise. To the extent that power is devolved downward to individual or community it reproduces and reinforces the existing pattern of difference and privilege, whereas to the extent it is concentrated upward in the market or the state it creates over mighty and potentially corrupt 'masters of the universe'. Paradigmatically all power to the people ends up with all power to Kim Jong Il, while the invocation of the freedom of the market ends up with all power to Bernard Madoff. To quote the Scripture 'their end is destruction'.

As for my second binary, the universal and the particular, I shall mainly focus on a major example of the principal paradox it encounters. I shall discuss how the universalism of Liberty and Enlightenment has perforce been carried by the particular nationalisms of the USA and France. I shall also take account of the more modest universalism and more modest Enlightenment carried by the particular nationalism of Britain, lying somewhere in between its American brother and its French second cousin. To include the German variant would simply take us too deep into intellectual history and too far afield, though many analyses, for example Marx, would treat the German case as of central importance.

This is an analysis of anticipations, limits and paradoxes, which is why it is implicitly theological. All our master narratives, considered as visions of 'the life of the world to come', are constrained and obstructed by the inherent structure of available options, the dynamics of power and the political, the contingency of culture and the wildness of history. They have to devise defensive strategies to explain away these obstructions and constraints, including the perverse persistence of rival tales. Christianity for example has to explain the persistence of Judaism and the emergence of Islam, and vice versa, and the protagonists of American and French universalism have to explain the failure of history to end with the triumph of their nations as privileged bearers of their rather different Enlightenments.

Our Social Scientific Narratives

The kind of sociology and anthropology that appeals to the public speaks directly to our experience and presents us with a story line. It offers a narrative, and narrative is our principal mode of understanding. But there is more to it than that, because the seemingly scientific enterprises of sociology and anthropology also draw on the deep structure of hope and loss, both individual and communal, at the heart of the religious project. They tap into an implicit and pre-theoretical understanding of 'the authentic', and evoke an intimation of a world we have lost or that remains half ruined and unfinished. So much social scientific writing implies a fall or regression from previous grace, and hopefully anticipates a better world to come. I am thinking of works like Riesman's *The Lonely Crowd* and Putnam's notion of *Bowling Alone*.[1]

We lament and we anticipate, we contrast authentic and fulfilled living with waste and frustration, and we intuit just when and how it was things started to fall away and fall apart. In the more usual laments things fell apart when the lone wolf of individualism entered the fold of community, and yet these same laments celebrate the 'turn to the self' and emergence of individual autonomy from oppressive communal constraints. The world of politics follows suit. Unless politicians are self-deluding they find they have to concelebrate both selfhood and community as though these alternatives exacted no opportunity costs. They are then pushed into a persistent invocation of 'tough choices' in general to obscure what such choices must mean in particular cases.

The ideal of self-realization strains against the bonds of community, and finds its anti-hero in the figure of the marginal outsider, invested with the glamour of the raggle-taggle gypsies or even the pagan unfettered by inhibitions and sin. This is a figure of guaranteed authenticity just because he stands outside, or even because he is maimed.[2] We are lay moralists haunted by Paradise Lost and Regained, as though Christianity still provided the unquestioned horizon of our experience. The trope of crisis harks back to the stark alternatives of Christian eschatology, while the pursuit of personal authenticity feeds on Christian inwardness and heart-work. Our response to victimage is in a strict and historic sense sentimental but it looks back to a religious reverence for the 'victim divine', while our yearning for community is reinforced by a subconscious recollection of Christian fraternity. We know what we are, but as Charles Taylor points out, we no longer know what we have been.

---

[1]   Riesman, David, *The Lonely Crowd: A Study of the Changing American Character* (New Haven: Yale University Press, 1950); Putnam, Robert, *Bowling Alone: The Collapse and Revival of American Community* (New York: Simon and Schuster, 2000).

[2]   This is very much the theme of the play *Jerusalem* by Jez Butterworth (2010) where the anti-hero is a drug addict on the margin of a West Country wood in a manner analogous to Shakespeare's 'rude mechanicals'. It also takes a more directly Christian form in the operas of Benjamin Britten.

The anthropologist Fenella Cannell has argued, and very persuasively, that the sometimes antagonistic relation between the social sciences and Christianity hides a deeper mutuality, and indeed it would not be difficult to cross-reference the sociological word-book against the theological word-book.[3] Crises beget judgement, and our social commentary identifies systematic sources of evil, like corporate capitalism, pervasive patriarchy, authoritarian collective tyranny or exploitative individualism. The times may be a-changing but whatever else changes the times will always be 'out of joint'. As William Blake warned us, the intrusive worm 'does our secret life destroy'. Original sin achieves high definition and acquires 'a local habitation and a name'. Indeed, 'sociology is the documentation of original sin by those who believe in original virtue'.[4]

I am suggesting that the language of social commentary remains saturated in the vocabulary of an occluded master narrative, no matter how strenuously we try to dehydrate it and engage in a linguistic purge of resonances to validate our claim to scientific objectivity. It is not only in theology that descriptive sentences operate as covert performatives, and although this is explicit in critical sociologies promoting an 'emancipatory project' it is far more widely pervasive than that. Even positivistic theses are presented in the persuasive tones of the legal brief.

In common with Scripture and European mythology we deal in ages and stages, and our sense of moving through stages and crises generates categories of 'lateness' or posteriority, for example our vocabulary of the 'post-modern' and its insubstantial companion ghost the 'post-secular'. Arthur Vidich was right some decades ago when he wrote of our worldly rejections of religion and their direction, by way of parodying Weber's famous religious rejections of the world and their direction.[5] That is by no means to imply that religion and politics are identical, or that politics continues religion by other means in a historical narrative sequence, only that they can be treated in a common framework for certain purposes, as argued in chapter 14. The suggestion one finds in John Gray and Norman Cohn, that passionate politics is only shame faced and covert religion, implies that religion is just over-generalized and/or mystical politics, which in the view of the Marxist author, Alberto Toscano, amounts to a reductionist blasphemy against religious faith.[6] As I said in the initial chapter, a parish Eucharist is not a party meeting to discuss strategy or elect the right faction to leadership.

In cultural anthropology the nostalgia for the uncorrupted ways of past times is quite striking. Supposedly objective scholars openly admire holistic forms of life before the fragmentations of modernity, and before linear conceptions of time disrupted the slow rotations of more natural ways of life. As Derrida pointed

---

[3] Cannell, Fenella, (ed.), *The Anthropology of Christianity* (Raleigh-Durham, NC: Duke University Press, 2006).

[4] Martin, David, *Christian Language and Its Mutations*.

[5] Vidich, Arthur, *American Sociology: Worldly Rejections of Religion and their Directions* (London: Yale University Press, 1982).

[6] Toscano, Alberto, *Fanaticism: On the Uses of an Idea* (London: Verso, 2010).

out, moral positions are smuggled in as worldly knowledge. The distinguished Africanist, Terence Ranger, comments on the tone that used to be adopted by anthropologists about missionaries on account of the tone the missionaries adopted when pressing health, education, and worst of all progress and civilization, on indigenous peoples.[7] How else could 'civilization' have become such a dirty word that one hardly dare pronounce its name? Even today those who analyse religious change in the developing world without adequate expressions of disapproval find themselves mightily disapproved of. The multicultural diversity celebrated as right and proper for Europeans is roundly condemned as cultural intrusion among indigenous peoples, as though it were the snake in a hitherto harmonious garden.

Authenticity confronts corruption, though neither authenticity nor corruption belong in the lexicon of objective science. That does not prevent these loaded words from pervading the academy and the media. The real world comes into existence once you cross the Rio Grande del Norte from the corrupt comforts of the USA into the authentic earthiness of Mexico, a country which acts as a collective unconscious for lost souls on the wrong side of the border. For Britons there is a Celtic fringe to compensate for the human damage wrought by the industrial revolution and Puritanism. In his *Shamans, Sorcerers and Saints* Brian Hayden, a self-identified scientific archaeologist, celebrates an authentic and aboriginal paganism now re-emerging after many centuries of oppression inaugurated by Moses and monotheism.[8] This may be nonsense as science but it is part of the contemporary narrative of Paradise Lost and of re-sacralization. Aboriginal perfection returns, improved with modern abundance rather than primitive scarcity, and time runs back to fetch the Age of Gold.

Narratives in General

What are the general characteristics of master narratives, especially when they are blocked by rival tales, by the cunning and perversity of history and by the structure of real alternatives in our fallen world? Most narratives proclaim a triumph of peace and justice coextensive with their own triumph. They are inclusive and therefore exclude those attached to rival narratives. That is what makes the one God jealous and creates a border excluding those who reject inclusion or happen to live strictly 'idiotic' lives of hapless ignorance. Rival stories have to be corralled and cornered to prevent the energy of a stray truth disrupting the new dispensation of the redeemed, or Socialist Reality, or the last best hopes of liberal democracy, or the peaceful House of Islam. If history does not cooperate, or turns ambiguous and whimsical, without positively proving itself beyond redemption, then true

---

[7]   Ranger, Terence, 'Some Second Thoughts', in Peggy Brock, (ed.), *Indigenous Peoples and Religious Change* (Leiden: Brill, 2005: 15–32).

[8]   Hayden, Brian, *Shamans, Sorcerers and Saints* (Washington: Smithsonian Books, 2005).

believers may need to take things into their own hands by destroying books or persons. They must inscribe their triumph on the bodies of their adversaries, like the Grand Inquisitor in Schiller's *Don Carlos*, and bury them beyond identification or resurrection, in case broken bodies themselves rise up as witnesses.

The trinity of universal truth, liberty and equality, like any other kind of universalism, is potentially aggressive, because it is the ultimate true story. Hence the way we service the trope of a fine enthusiasm degenerating into an unlovely fanaticism. To know the Truth is often the ultimate justification for the Lie: one dare not be without the truth and yet its possession is always dangerous. As for liberty it usually begins at home, like charity, before it is reluctantly extended to others, as in the British case, or too enthusiastically imposed on them, as in the American case. Liberty puts the rest of the world under tutelage as slow learners not yet entirely prepared for the full glare of the light. Slow learners, most of them concentrated in the Middle East, viewed as the contemporary equivalent and recrudescence of the Middle Ages, are all too prone to misuse liberty for illiberal ends and attack their tutors. As for equality, it is a necessary hope, rooted in the universal and shared image of the divine, however defaced, but its costs are as high as the universalistic monotheism from which it mostly takes its modern origin. This is the real appeal of kolkhoz and kibbutz, but once manifested in a demand for the unremitting participation of equals whatever their other proper interests, and by way of the immediate existential availability required by the enthusiasts of '68, it is a nightmare.

The options available all have disadvantages. Culturally sensitive liberals think the over-vigorous export of liberty and liberalism disrespectful to the 'Other' as well as much more trouble and expense than it is worth. On the other hand, those subject to, or fleeing, sadistic and illiberal regimes, particularly tribes oppressed by another tribe in control of the state, are prone to take an encouraging view of liberal imperialism, and their complaints are assumed to be true simply because they are victims. The Albanians knew how to play this card with the Americans, and so did the *Mujahideen*, aka the Taliban, when the Russians oppressed them with schooling for women and other insults to sacred custom and traditional culture.

Unfortunately it cannot be assumed that victims will be friends of liberty once in power, and indeed there are plenty of examples of noble victims, like Mugabe, deploying their status as sometime victims to destroy the liberties of fellow countrymen with insouciant impunity late into their dotage. The indigenous inhabitants of inappropriately named Liberia found that out under the heel of ex-slaves, and the Russians have not enjoyed the rule of liberated Estonians. In Western Christian culture this is not merely a sad reflection of the propensity of the oppressed to turn into oppressors once liberated, but has a theological root in the exaltation of the divine Victim to highest heaven.

Other cultures, free of the moral inconveniences of Christianity, like the Turks, do not feel penitent the moment they are faced with victims of their oppression, but merely note the erstwhile victims are now free to commit mayhem on their own account and should if possible be sharply restrained. The cult of apology to those who no longer suffer by those who have not themselves committed the wrong is restricted to the sometime borders of Christendom. The pejorative deployment of imperialism and colonialism, in itself usually justified, is similarly restricted. The descendants of the Moghuls have very little to say about it, and the trickle of Han Chinese going on a pilgrimage of apology to Lhasa remains unreported. A Kemalist general told me the Turks had only retired from Vienna because it looked too beautiful to suffer rape and mayhem.

I return to the power of truth as embedded in master narratives: 'You shall know the truth and the truth shall set you free'; '*magna est veritas et prevalebit*'. All our western sacred sources confirm this view, but it can be appropriated too simplistically. In his pamphlet *Areopagitica* in favour of liberty of the press John Milton declared truth was never defeated in open encounter with error. Such confidence is surprising, given the track record of the modern media, but we too believe something similar when we prematurely claim Mission Accomplished or chant 'We shall overcome one day', when the time of troubles ends and the wildness of history is tamed. So far as the USA is concerned, the victory of liberty and of the USA and the greater glory of God run in tandem, whereas for the Russians up to 1989 the reverse was true. Kruschev told Nixon 'We shall bury you first', whereas Reagan assured Gorbachev of 'the end of the evil empire'. Once the latter turned out to be true Francis Fukuyama could imagine 'the End of History' forgetting that Islam harboured in its basic repertoire other ideas about that.

Any impasse apparently frustrating the received narrative has to be symbolically overcome by being designated as a House of War in the case of Islam or as *in partibus infidelium* in Catholicism, or as malignants and refusniks. According to Augustine's political interpretation of Christ's parable of the reluctant, unlikely and astonished invitees to the wedding feast of the Lamb, all such should be 'compelled to come in'. Effectively Augustine reversed the meaning of the dominical saying about bringing in the outsiders at the expense of the established insiders.

This is the classic reinterpretation undertaken by established religion, which always knows how to turn the gospel upside down to serve the seeming necessities of its real-politik. In exactly the same manner the Grand Inquisitor invited King Philip to kill his own rebellious son, Don Carlos, for the sake of the body politic, in devout emulation of the divine Father who spared not his own Son for the sake of humanity. Christ's parable of the talents turns out to be perfectly adaptable to capitalist society once you convert being rich unto God into being rich in the sight of men, and therefore the more able to dispense charity. As Mrs. Thatcher told the elders of the Church of Scotland, Good Samaritans who have accumulated no money by hard work are not much use to a man wounded by robbers en route to Jericho and in need of palliative care in a hostelry.

Should blockages in the way of the approved course of history persist, then bedevilment and satanic intrusion may be invoked. This is where ingenious retelling of master narratives comes into is own. Perhaps the believers are being chastised for lack of faithfulness to the true or pristine faith. They must be rooted out, or if rulers they must be cast down, else God or the predestined movement of history cannot inaugurate the otherwise assured and glorious future. The English, French, Russian, Chinese, and now the Islamist, revolutions, all knew how to root out the corrupt and the slack-minded who slow down the march of destiny, or stain and dishonour the blood of the martyrs and the perfection of the elect.

Here, however, there is an alternative available and one based on the religious repertoire of world rejection. One may depart into the wilderness or solitary place to create a new and uncorrupted human cell in a utopian community and abandon the *luxuria* and the snares that have led astray even the elect. This alternative also has its dangers, because the most rigorous *askesis* has a habit, especially in the case of monasticism, of enabling the meek to inherit the earth. The figure of the Christian Friar and the Buddhist Monk is generally portrayed as fatter than his ostensible profession might warrant.

In the case of Islam, however, more adjusted from the beginning to the quasi-necessities of power, violence and social regulation than Christianity, triumph in this world is not readily construed as disaster, certainly not as requiring retirement to the wilderness and the solitary place. As already suggested, one does not expect Muslim scholars as a matter of course to interpret the achievements of Islamic dynasties as exemplary spiritual disasters any more than one expects Turks to apologize for Ottoman imperialism. The attitude of Islam to peoples and outsiders who get in the way of God's sovereignty is robust, rather like Joshua's approach to the indigenous peoples of the Promised Land, an attitude more recently adopted by some Israelis. It is a dogma of secular nationalism that some peoples are intended by history to occupy the sacred dirt of particular allotments on earth, particularly when bounded naturally by the sea, like Ireland and the USA, or by mountains, like Switzerland.

Here we arrive at something resembling the fundamental grammar of master narratives, informing secular and religious ideologies alike. In the latest secularist manifestation the maxim *Ecrasez l'infame* has been roughly translated as an imperative need to prevent pious parents 'abusing' children by foisting deleterious fables on them. Provided one cuts off the past as a 'time of ignorance' the bright future will look after itself. The question is, to commandeer Bernard Lewis's question about Islam after centuries of science, civilization and triumph, 'What Went Wrong?' Who or what is to blame for the cunning and perversity of history?[9] History is too cunning for mortals easily to chart its course. Perhaps we all need to make sense of what is happening and fit things in to a story, a master narrative. But could the story be no more than 'one damn thing after another'? What kind of *telos* are we talking about? Did the expulsion of the Russians from Afghanistan really help bring down the Berlin Wall, or was it rather the invisible divisions mustered by the Pope that brought down what Vaclav Havel designated 'the Kingdom of the Lie'? Is there spiritual as well as empirical causation? Vaclav Havel certainly thought so. What he said clearly implies the Kingdom of the Lie cannot stand for ever.

---

[9]   Lewis, Bernard, *What Went Wrong? The Clash between Islam and Modernity in the Middle East* (Oxford: Oxford University Press, 2002).

For secular and Christian westerners the re-emergence of Islam itself poses problems. How could a religion rightly fallen on bad times at the imperative behest of Progress or Providence be resurgent in a truly modern time in a properly modern way? The left has an answer, though one it offers with increasing unease since it functions as an excuse for mayhem and murder, including the murder of Muslims adopting a less violent response. For the Left Muslim resurgence is an understandable response to western imperialism and cultural aggression, conveniently ignoring the fact that non-Islamic populations with greater grievances than wealthy and educated dissidents in Saudi Arabia or elsewhere, respond quite differently. For other observers Islamic revival is not a perverse form of modernity but a re-action *against* modernity, a move which for them preserves the master narrative of progress towards a common modernity. The idea of a re-action, as I shall argue in chapter 6, implies there can be no real and autonomous action to locate and build up an alternative version of modernity. This approach can also be deployed against 'conservative' movements within Christianity. Is Russian Orthodoxy capable of devising a contemporary form compatible with modernist discourse?[10] What we see around us in the contemporary world are mere simulacra of the modern.

This is how fundamentalism comes to be such a remarkably useful term of abuse and excommunication, as well as useful for grant applications, because it enables one to catch so many disparate fish in the same basket to feed a liberal moral panic. Fanaticism as a key motif in western intellectual constructions of the Cold War, serves a similar purpose, for example in Norman Cohn's psycho-analytic and de-contextualized conflation of Christian eschatology and modern totalitarianism. I discussed the uses and abuses of the construction of fundamentalism in *Forbidden Revolutions* – and there is an excellent Marxist analysis of the polemical uses of 'fanaticism' in Alberto Toscano *Fanaticism: On the Uses of an Idea*.[11]

T. E. Hulme caught very well the role of periodization in annihilating the past in favour of some New Age or major mutation of the old. He wrote that 'The best-known work on the Renaissance ... describes the emergence of a new attitude towards life ... as it might describe the gradual discovery of the concept of gravitation – that is, as the gradual emergence of something which once established would remain always, the period before it being characterized as a privation of the new thing'.[12] What emerges is a conception of the self based on the Shakespearean aphorism put in the mouth of the old fool Polonius: 'This above all: to thine own self be true'.

---

[10]   Stoeckl, Kristina, *Community after Totalitarianism: The Russian Orthodox Intellectual Tradition and the Philosophical Discourse of Modernity* (Frankfurt: Lang, 2008).

[11]   Martin, David, *Forbidden Revolutions* (London: SPCK, 1996); Toscano, Alberto, *Fanaticism*.

[12]   Hulme, T. E., *A Notebook*, published in seven instalments in *The New Age* between Dec. 1915 and Feb. 1916.

Of course, almost everybody, except militant and self-consciously unsentimental atheists, respects the 'Other' provided everybody understands where it is out of place and provided it is not allowed to intrude on our own advanced time zone. Cairo, Damascus and Abu Dhabi are none of them our genuine contemporaries. As for Afghanistan it is pre-feudal and two or three ages or stages behind. That might help justify invasion as an attempt to jerk it forward or else justify disdain for the violent and corrupt Afghan 'Other' and a sensible recognition of practical impossibilities. Saudi Arabia is wealthy and technically sophisticated but remains 'medieval' even though using such a term of any version of the 'Other' is politically incorrect. In any case 'medieval' sits rather oddly with 'fundamentalist', in part because the term 'medieval' suggests guilds, Dante and Chartres, and in part because Protestants and secularists alike have used it to impugn the perverse persistence of Catholicism into modern times.

Chartres both figures in the genealogy of western culture, and is also used controversially in a clash of civilizations within western culture itself by way of contrast with the Parthenon. The Parthenon represents the genealogy of secular classicism and perfection of form over against the asymmetrical medieval mystery of Chartres. Master narratives are constantly justified by the reference to a genealogy, and the citation of Chartres and the Parthenon as rivals for pre-eminence can look like a rather modern mode of contestation dependent on the idea that narratives may be judged in terms of their artefacts, both aesthetically and in relation to size and potent reference back to previous revered achievements. Albert Speer had precisely this in mind when he planned to inaugurate the millennial Nazi Reich with monuments that not only outdid all local predecessors like Schinkel but completely dwarfed St. Peter's in Rome. You prove the superiority of your master narrative by knocking down the buildings that represent rival stories, or by building higher, quicker and better. At a Buddhist theme park near Shanghai they explain that the vast new temple represents a Chinese Renaissance, partly because it took five years to put up whereas the West took many decades to build St. Peter's.

Should one knock down the Palace of the People's Republic and then rebuild the Berlin Schloss? It all depends on whose nostalgia is at stake and what continuities are being asserted. Stories are embedded in stone and also in great human monuments, hence the heat engendered by the argument about whether Shakespeare was a Catholic or even about whether Bertrand Russell was a more impressive human being than Albert Schweitzer. Size and beauty both matter in the clash of civilizations, and a master narrative feels obliged to assert its real presence in the modern world by building bigger and better. 'Impression management' is one of the most ancient of arts and all the tropes of rhetoric are marshalled to bolster each carefully managed impression. London was extolled as the world's biggest city in the nineteenth century, and now the same symbolism is revived for Shanghai and Tokyo. Small is not all that beautiful when it comes to the contestation of civilizations.

Master narratives often split into two or more versions. The form the splits take tells you a great deal about the fundamental character of the narrative, so that Islamic splits are quite differently based from Christian ones. Physical genealogy and lineage do not matter much in Christianity. The split that most interests me here arises between the heroic advance guard and those who inherit the revolutionary kingdom. The sailors of Kronstadt saved the revolution in its hour of need only to be crushed once the hour of need had passed. That has been the usual fate of true believers at the hands of the established representatives of true belief from Savonarola and the Spiritual Franciscans to Robespierre. In France in the 1830s Lamennais tried to reconcile liberalism with loyalty to the international Papacy only to be put down by the Pope. There is always a Cromwell, a Napoleon, a Lenin or a Pope, to deal with the true believers and the revolutionary heroes, or better still, to redirect their energies into some combination of religious or political faith with an imperial project. The legacy of Cromwell is North America and the legacy of Napoleon is Western Europe.[13]

Excursus: Individualism and Individualization

So much for the general character of master narratives, the structures that constrain the options in practice available, and the attempts made to circumvent whatever and whoever lies in the way of an anticipated fruition. I turn now to the first of my two intersecting master narratives, individualism and individualization and to the blockages lying athwart the path to fruition.

There is a seeming contradiction here. When I discussed our social scientific narratives, especially in anthropology, I remarked that individualism is treated like the wolf in the fold or the snake in the garden. But in relation to the *institutional* sphere in modern society, whether religious or political, we cherish a quite contrary account of individualism, or rather of *individuation* considered as a nicer and more positive way of referring to individualism. This stress on the autonomous individual rather than the rapacious individual patently contributes to a generalized scepticism about institutions as such rather than religious institutions in particular. This scepticism derives from and feeds the idea that, when faced with institutional demands, authenticity inheres in the sincere individual, though it can also be realized in intense if short-lived communal experimentation outside the conventional institutional framework.

Of course, individuation has a venerable genealogy in the Hebrew Scriptures and Christianity, as well as in the Renaissance, but I focus here on its Protestant realization and the post-Protestant sequel. Whitman is one obvious source in his *Song of Myself* as well as Thoreau and Emerson. In his book on the centenary of the publication of *The Varieties of Religious Experience*, Charles Taylor sees William

---

[13]   Clark, Jonathan, *The Language of Liberty, 1660–1832: Political Discourse and Social Dynamics in the Anglo-American World* (Cambridge: Cambridge University Press, 1994).

James as an archetypical pioneer of the modern self for whom personal experience is primary, and sacramental realization at best secondary.[14] The institutional form, the ordered rite and the letter of the law incarcerate the spirit, just as logic and mere fact inhibit freedom of opinion. 'Do I contradict myself? Very well then I contradict myself'.[15]

That has clear implications for post-Catholicism as well as for a Protestantism deprived of Scriptural anchorage. Of course, the echo of Scripture with respect to the ultimate supremacy of spirit over law, and love over letter, is unmistakable, but in the Scripture such sentiments are firmly checked by the nurture of stable habits of the heart, meditation on divine statutes, care for neighbour, responsibility towards God and solidarity with the brethren. In the contemporary version the emphasis is firmly on authentic selfhood and being true to it. John Wesley was well aware of the possible corrosions of individualism and of religion as 'the Flight of the alone to the Alone' when he declared 'No religion that is not social'. Jonathan Sachs has (on television) described religion as 'the redemption of solitude'.

From John Kennedy's speech about not merely asking what your country can do for you, till now, politicians in the western world have had to appeal for a return to neighbourliness and neighbourhood, and to the basics of citizenship. They even call religion in aid, whether or not themselves religious, just at the point where religious institutions are weakened by the tendencies they are called upon to counteract. The key blockage in the path of the triumph of the individual is a head-banging incapacity to comprehend the inherent dilemmas and dynamics of collective and political life, or the proper role of authority, self-control and ritual procedure in sustaining any humane civilization.[16] I have already mentioned the difficulty of using the word civilization, with its connotations of civility, though that is unsurprising when commentators on the BBC can attribute 'musical greatness' and 'genius' to Michael Jackson and call Damien Hirst and Tracey Emin 'Great British Artists'. For the individual intent solely on discovering the true self the more important truth about the nature of political reason is harsh indeed, and politicians, when not themselves deluded, have to spend much linguistic ingenuity in pretending reality is governed by generalized slogans and sentiment rather than a strict form of economic and political accountancy. Tony Blair, facing the Chilcot Enquiry of 2010, could not explain the nature of political calculation and the full range of his reasons for going to war beyond saying he believed it was right on the calculus of risk following the Twin Towers, and yet he was *still* asked to apologize *personally* for the deaths of British soldiers. Where sentiment reigns undeterred by the actually available choices at a particular time, for a decision-maker with ultimate responsibility to ask what the opportunity cost of leaving Saddam Hussein

---

14   Taylor, Charles, *Varieties of Religion Today.*

15   Whitman, Walt, *Song of Myself*, Part 51.

16   Seligman, Adam, Weller, Robert, Puett, Michael, and Simon, Benedict, *Ritual and its Consequences: An Essay on the Limits of Sincerity* (Oxford: Oxford University Press, 2008).

and his sons in power counts as moral obliquity. Whether the decision to go to war was *mistaken* and ill-judged, even hubristic, is a separate question.

The disjunction between selfhood and political reason in part accounts for the increasing role over the past two centuries of the innocent eye in political commentary. Innocence need not imply any straightforward lack of political sophistication, as is very evident from John Bright's noble and knowledgeable critique of the Crimean War. The root of innocence lies rather in the privilege extended to the existential – almost the metaphysical – 'Why?' of war and of death in war rather than the analytic 'Why?'. However necessary and wholesome the role of the innocent eye may be in liberal society, it can become captious and trapped in the inveterate dissidence of dissent. Too often it repudiates Weber's 'ethic of responsibility', whereby understanding the nature of political reason depends on recognizing the limited range of choices, with the accompanying balance of more or less likely alternative ills, which is available to major political players.

Bertrand Russell inherited this role in the twentieth century from his Whig ancestry and from a tradition of writing going back to Hazlitt, Paine and beyond. The stream of moral consciousness in which Russell swam exemplified the transition from Christian Nonconformity to the dissidence of the philosopher-scientist up to Noam Chomsky, or of the artist-writer up to Harold Pinter. In 1936 Bertrand Russell admonished the western allies to emulate the disarmed helplessness of Denmark in response to the Nazi threat; some years later he was advocating using the threat of the atomic bomb before associating himself with the campaign for nuclear disarmament.[17] The problem of the innocent eye is the maintenance of consistency over time, calling for intervention when it does not happen and decrying it when it does. The politician is by definition always wrong, in particular because different circumstances demand a formal inconsistency, and even some hypocrisy, but even the innocent eye does not find consistency over time easy, as the examples of Russell and Chomsky indicate. Hazlitt was obsessively consistent, and by his mixture of nobility and excoriating righteousness succeeded in wounding or alienating almost all his friends and allies.

Universalism

Monotheistic universalism now has a global constituency of about half of humankind: one in three Christian, one in five Muslim. Enlightened universalism has a less well-defined constituency, because some of our varied enlightenments have historically and significantly overlapped Christianity, and because the Marxist variant now has its sphere in places like North Korea and the global Faculty Club.

---

[17]   Russell, Bertrand, *Which Way to Peace?* (London: Michael Joseph, 1936); Parkin, Frank, *Middle Class Radicalism* (Manchester: Manchester University Press, 1968).

If the first and great paradox of universalism, religious or secular, is exclusive inclusivity, excommunicating alternative universalisms, the second great paradox is its incarnation in particular nations and its fusion with the spirit of empire. Ikhnaton apart, it began in Israel and Persia. In the modern period it has become incarnate in civic nationalisms, like France and the United States, or organic nationalisms of ethno-religion and/or blood and/or language, such as burgeoned in late fifteenth-century Spain, or nineteenth-century Germany and Russia under the stimulus of Napoleonic aggression.

There are two ways of putting what I have in mind. One is to say that in the context of monotheistic religion we are talking about universalism and empire, in Cairo, Damascus, Granada, Samarkand, Isfahan, Baghdad and Delhi in relation to Mecca, and in Paris, the Escorial, London, Moscow and Washington in relation to Rome, Athens, Byzantium and Jerusalem. The other way is to say that we are talking about the Church, humanity and ummanity. If that sounds all too world-historical, then some of my examples will sound dangerously up-to-date, especially when it comes to the semi-Christian, semi-Enlightened universalism of the United States.

Universalism has to begin somewhere in a particular place, and the Hebrew Scriptures present features appearing regularly ever since. The Jews harboured a tension-ridden combination of a chosen nation which acquired a capital in Jerusalem with the idea that this spot on earth might become a universal point of convergence for all peoples made in the image of the universal God. The protection and survival of that inclusive vision meant that whatever benign provision might be made for 'strangers within the gate', 'the walls thereof' needed to be patrolled day and night. Thus a particular people had to be set aside by the rite of circumcision, and we have a model for an organic nationalism which could mutate into a universal faith round about AD 50 in an atmosphere of tension between Jews in diaspora, Jewish proselytes, Christian Jews and Gentile Christians. This was facilitated by the multicultural *oekumene* of the Roman Empire, as Acts, chapter 2 suggests. But there was a severe tearing of the womb as circumcision became converted, after much dispute, into baptism. The tear was permanent and became gangrenous, especially once a universal Christianity had fused with an imperial *Romanitas*. This *Romanitas* represented a particular location and one that first shifted to the Holy Roman Empire and eventually relocated itself in Hispanidad, a world-conquering faith rooted in a universal monarchy and based on a language and an ethnos. Hence the emergence of what a French imperialism later designated Latin America. Thereafter Latin America was to be inherently Catholic by historical, divine and papal dispensation. It is not widely known that the Pope not only gave Brazil to Portugal but was so ill-advised as to give Ireland to Catholic England. Universality works itself out in inviolable local patrimonies.

Since the expulsion of Jews and Muslims from Spain after 1492, universalism has shown its inclusive-exclusive face in alliance with local organic nationalism. The socio-logic works itself out from North Africa to the Middle East and Israel/Palestine, from the Balkans to the Caucasus and Central Asia, and from Sudan to Burma and even India. Tides of ethno-religious or ethno-ideological cleansing have swept the ancient territories of Christianity and Islamia, especially mixed and/or border lands, like Armenia and the sometime mixed areas of Turkish and Greek occupancy. The civil war in Sri Lanka that originally spawned 'suicide bombing' provides another obvious instance. In the sphere of enlightened and universalist Marxism there have been expulsions, deportations, intrusions and forced inclusions from the Baltics and the Balkans to Central Asia, China, Tibet, Vietnam and North Korea. We selectively blame religion or this or that secular master narrative whereas the terrible socio-logic of these happenings is written in from the outset. The universal acquires particular locations in sacred centres and holy cities, in the Christian case in Aksum or Aachen, Constantinople or Kiev.[18]

Here I pause to note a special feature of universal empire, both as idea, and as power projected around the world in the two great civic nationalisms of revolutionary France post-1789 and revolutionary America post-1776. Both were enlightened, both rapidly expansionist and both monotheistic, except that France became rapidly anti-Catholic and America rested on a firm Anglo-Protestant base. Each in different ways jettisoned the specificities of its religious patrimony by emphasizing the Supreme Being of Voltaire or the generalized Deity of Jefferson, Priestley and Paine. The Fatherhood of God gained at the expense of the divine and human Son, so reversing the emphasis within the Christian master narrative. Christian Churches are not dedicated to the Father, but they are frequently dedicated to the Son or his mother.

We have here a major break, initiated by France and America, but based rather differently. In the French case a principle of citizenship was established in close alliance with French nationalism, and citizens were expected to subordinate all other loyalties to the nation as part of the definition of citizenship. In the American case citizenship was also primary, and the rights associated with it, but the existence of a strong and stable Anglo-Protestant core enabled more and more Christian denominations and ethnic groups to be included, though with frequent nativist objections. In the USA a constantly expanding religious multiculturalism was able to flourish, though some of its limiting preconditions in the maintenance of certain core values can easily be ignored. One finds a British equivalent of the break initiated in America and France in the invocation of the Fatherhood of God and the Brotherhood of Man which used to be part of the idealistic rhetoric of the nascent Labour Party.

The universal master narrative of *laïque* France, once so influential world-wide from Brazil to Turkey and Russia, has probably hit the buffers though without quite knowing it. So I therefore concentrate here on the American successor to both the French and the British empires. The imperial republic encounters the classic quandary of all universalisms, whether religious or secular. Should it go for it in a big way and risk overstretch, or not? The relevance of this question to the future of Christianity lies precisely in the export, or rather the replication, of

---

[18]   Stringer, Martin, *A Sociological History of the Christian Worship* (Cambridge; Cambridge University Press, 2005).

the American pattern of religious voluntarism and multiculturalism to the world at large, though the remarkable aptitude of the Chinese for Christianity, much of it pluralistic in the American Protestant manner, may also be relevant as another superpower arrives on the horizon.

In geo-politics there is no alternative to the kind of policy the British in India called 'The Great Game'. What Lord Salisbury called 'splendid isolation' is never viable for long, given what another British prime minister, Harold Macmillan, called 'Events, dear boy, events'. You either go forward or retreat, since to stand still is to retreat. Go forward and you stimulate alliances between those you may humiliate, but if you stand still you retreat into irrelevance for any good you might do. You turn up the chance of any better ordering of the world and retire on the defence of your own interests and useful alliances, preferably with the like-minded if you are lucky.

This is where realism and idealism turn ambiguous and even change places under the pressure of unavoidable events and dilemmas. Realism can be construed as not interfering in appalling situations you do not understand, lest you are (rightly) accused of having mixed motives, such as wanting oil as well as democracy, lest things go wrong, as in the short term they generally do, and lest you stimulate hostile alliances. Liberal idealism may be construed as high-minded moral adventurism in the cause of the citizen idea, coded as democracy and freedom under law. Moral ambiguity dogs all stances. Colluding in the interim with a Pinochet in Chile or a Karimov in Uzbekistan for a longer-term political 'good' is illiberal. Interfering at great cost for everybody in terms of blood and treasure in tyrannies like those of Sudan, Zimbabwe, Serbia and Iraq is also illiberal. To promote your liberal ideal you find you have to compromise it or deny it, whichever way you turn. You will be rightly pelted in the stocks of world opinion for being low, hypocritical and dirty in pursuit of your high-mindedness, whereas the explicitly low-minded are at least free from the accusation of hypocrisy.

I may seem to have strayed from the matter of the future of Christianity. That is because I am exploring dilemmas written into all human affairs and because the dilemmas of individualism and the innocent eye in the face of the dynamics of power and the collective life run in parallel with the dilemmas of universalism in the face of precisely the same dynamics. All the choices are costly and potentially tragic 'even unto death' and ultimate frustration. Pre-emptive war is properly condemned by political moralists as unjustified, and had it been unleashed in 1936 would have been condemned as aggression in the worst traditions of The Great Game. Yet it is difficult to avoid the conclusion that untold misery would have been pre-empted. All politicians walk on a moral razor's edge.

Christianity's Future: an Unscientific Postscript

I have tried to explore some of the options and constraints arising from the paradoxes of universalism and particularity, and of the collective and the individual, as they bear on the future of the United States and of Christianity. There is the post-Protestant potential for extreme individualism and the uncertain capacity of Catholicism to resist it. People may convert to Catholicism realizing it stands for the tangible as well as for the transnational, and for ritual and authority in any humane ordering of human affairs. But the outcome is uncertain. I have also hinted at the challenge of a re-absorption into Nature and the adoption in practice of a neo-paganism.

But what of the viability of the Christian narrative itself? Here I am openly theological, having suggested that the social sciences have been and remain covertly theological. For my theological purpose I revert to the Jewish master narrative from which Christianity originally emerged. Among the Jews a strain of thought arose from the frustration of exile and it turned on a salvation wrought through the figure of a collective Suffering Servant, even though Cyrus the Persian was also seen as a liberator in the hands of a divine Providence. History would, so to speak, come good this year or perhaps next year, in Jerusalem. The Gentiles would still make their way in God's good Providence to his holy hill, in spite of the later disasters that befell the Jews and Jerusalem in AD 70 and 135 at the hands of the Romans. What Christianity did was to shift the identification of the Suffering Servant from Israel as a group onto a peaceable Son of Man who set the vision of the Child at the heart of his fraternity and of his universal and invisible Kingdom-in-waiting.

The human face of monotheism was crushed on Golgotha by the dynamics of power and the power of evil, to be resurrected in an encounter with friends. Divine providence did not intervene to prevent the sacrifice of the Son of Man because victory had to be won at the point of total frustration engineered by the representatives of a holy people at its sacred centre and a representative of the politics of imperial Rome. At that moment the earthly Jerusalem and its holy temple were translated by Christians into the body of the Son of Man and the body of his followers, and Jerusalem translated into a universal city, home to all nations.

What therefore matters for the future of Christianity is whether a tent of salvation pitched in the vulnerability of the body offered once for all in the wilderness of history still invites humanity to come, and sit down and eat. Christianity under the pressure of events and the dynamics of power always bifurcates into the earthly kingdom or empire seeking to use the opportunities of power as well as being corrupted by them, and the peaceful transnational community of the common spirit. The options are not arbitrary but written into the logic of the sign of the cross. The future of Christianity turns on the viability of a narrative situated at the point where the justification of the ways of God to man breaks down and the wildness of history is unleashed. It has to take its chance of inevitable frustration with every other master narrative in finding its way through the paradoxes of universalism and individualism built into the recalcitrance of history.

One should never identify the moment of triumphant realization of the dream before time, except by simply making and enacting the sign of redemption here and now. Something like that gesture was made when Rostropovich played

Bach's Cello Suites on the Berlin Wall as it crumbled to dust. This is what Robert Browning called 'the Grand Perhaps' and it is precarious in the strict meaning of the word: standing in the need of prayer. In the positivist lexicon, it amounts merely to under-determined knowledge, but the Scripture teaches us that hope concerns what cannot be securely known, or else it is not hope. I would acknowledge, even with relief, that today hope cannot be bolstered or salvaged by the over-determined predictions of either a religious or a secular providence. That is why Browning also asks of Christianity 'Has it your vote to be so if it can?'

Chapter 4

Pentecostalism: Transnational Voluntarism in the Global Religious Economy

Pentecostalism is the most dramatic instance of a successful transnational and voluntary form of Christianity and many observers see it as a major wave of the future. I ask how true that might be, because Pentecostalism is certainly not all the future there is. It is in tension with older, profoundly resistant and sometimes resurgent forms of religion, whether Islamic, Catholic or even Buddhist, often rooted in the sacred union of a faith, a polity and a territory, or in the case of Anglicanism rooted in the idea of the parish, 'the church in a place', or in the case of Judaism, in ethnicity.

Christianity is distinctive in having derived part of its original repertoire from an ethnic group with an attachment to a territory, as well as a wider vision,[1] which it then revised to create a new social formation, the transnational voluntary association we call the early Church. This in turn acquired an attachment to a territory and a polity through the adoption of Christianity as the faith of the Roman Empire, East and West. Contemporary Pentecostalism reverts to the original voluntary form of the Church, and it is the most recent and large-scale realization of a long historical process of detachment from the state. This detachment from the state is associated with the process of social differentiation, and that process is always liable to partial reversals, as one can see from the role played by Pentecostalism and charismatic Christianity in parts of Africa and in Brazil. Even in the United States, where the break with the state was clean and took place early on, the pull of power, and national identity foster a generalized 'civil religion'. To use the economic metaphor, Pentecostalism is a series of fissiparous organizations, big and small, competing under the leadership of religious entrepreneurs, and a natural denizen of deregulated religious markets such as were pioneered in Anglo-American societies.

The immediate historical precursor of Pentecostalism is Evangelicalism, notably in its Anglo-American form, but also globally, and the two kinds of Protestant faith overlap in ways that make estimates of numbers problematic. The problem is that Pentecostalism is a charismatic movement stressing personal spiritual gifts in a way that has been partly paralleled and anticipated in Evangelicalism, notably the holiness movement initiated by Methodism, but also breaking away from Methodism in yet another protest against worldly compromise. Pentecostals

---

[1] Stephens, Randall, *The Fire Spreads: Holiness and Pentecostalism in the American South* (Cambridge, MA: Harvard University Press, 2009).

outflanked the American holiness preachers in their promotion of a style of radical primitive Christianity, attracting some of them, while repelling others. This pattern of overlap and fission has reappeared with every movement of Protestant reform, just as it has in movements of political reform. But instead of breakaways and divisions being a source of weakness for Pentecostalism it has allowed new charismatic leaders to form their own organizations. It promotes competition and constant adaptation to the environment. The only problem is finding yet another colourful and appealing name for each new initiative.

I begin with some broad comments on Pentecostalism, the future of Christianity and secularization. I then look at the problem posed by numerical estimates, before dealing with the qualitatively distinctive nature of Pentecostalism as a movement of world historical importance. The main section focuses on its modes of insertion in different types of socio-political order from the most plural and voluntary, like the USA, to the most territorial and involuntary, though varied, like Afghanistan. I conclude with some comments on the relation between the rise of Pentecostalism and the failure of politics and the state, and of the development narrative.

Pentecostalism and the Future of Christianity

What are the implications of Pentecostalism for the future of Christianity? Is it the last gasp of the Spirit before religious charismata sputter out as a spent social force, as secularization theory would suggest, or is it a harbinger of an expanding religious pluralism permanently active in the voluntary sector of global society? Those are the extreme possibilities, of course, and there are many intermediate paths. Nevertheless those stark alternatives dramatize the world historical importance of the issue, even if commentators in secular Western Europe dismiss it as a backward cargo cult or as what Eric Hobsbawm, with the condescension available to sophisticated posterity, has labelled primitive rebellion prior to proper political mobilization.[2] Pentecostalism unites the moral good with the material goods in a way that is both ancient and modern, even if in the past some anthropologists have thought Pentecostalism an inauthentic way to be ancient and some sociologists have labelled it a regressive way to be modern. In spite of that, it is so far the most effective form of autonomous religious mobilization for many millions in the two-thirds world and successfully realizes their aspiration for every kind of betterment.

Of course Pentecostalism offers many impossible promises and often expects implausible miracles of physical and mental healing and self-improvement, and its leaders can be exploitative, sexually and financially. After all, Pentecostals reflect as well as challenge the local environment and a lot is carried over as well as changed when the *brujo* in Latin America becomes a preacher and the Big Man or

---

[2]   Hobsbawm, Eric, *Primitive Rebels: Studies in Archaic Forms of Social Movement in the 19th and 20th Centuries* (Manchester: Manchester University Press, 1959).

Big Woman in West Africa becomes the Big Pastor. But it delivers enough to be the most immediate vehicle of hope for the hopeless. It offers a channel of advancement for a buried intelligentsia of energetic religious entrepreneurs. In many parts of the world the state has either failed, or ignored huge areas of distress in a corrupt and often violent pursuit of personal and sectional gain. Religious mobilization has taken over from, or run in parallel with, political mobilization, or, in the case of Islam, has itself become the vehicle of both national and transnational political mobilization. 'Primitive Rebellion' has acquired a very modern face, and has often displaced the 'sophisticated' doctrines and ideologies that were expected to supplant it according to the Marxist version of secularization theory. Sophisticated ideologies once in power find their power to mobilize drains away.

Much depends on how you understand secularization. If you understand secularization as depending in a major way on specific historical conditions, as I have done, and all those who embrace the notion of 'path dependency', then it may well be that the specific condition of religion in Western Europe has come about because the shocks of modernity were first encountered there. Religious responses to massive social changes in Europe were often inadequate, and very much affected by the way religion was built into regimes opposed to change and adjustment. Fear generated a religious reaction, particularly in the Papacy as it contemplated the long-term consequences of the French Revolution and anathematized 'liberalism'. Religious institutions were often organicist and *intégriste* in their reactions, though the collective and communal understandings rooted in a Catholicism broadly understood could re-emerge later to counterbalance the excesses of liberal individualism. What is temporarily 'recessive', to use the biological metaphor, often contains and protects latent potential for the future. Things were very different in North America where religious competition and separation from state power meant that the main kinds of religious group were voluntary and transnational denominations. In Europe these denominations failed to break down the close relationship of a particular Church to the dominant elites and state power. That was true even in England where they came closest to success in the mid- and late-nineteenth century and were associated with the demand for full civil rights by relatively excluded social sectors.

But just as the two English Revolutions of the seventeenth century, in 1642 and 1688, came to fruition in the American Revolution about a century later in 1776, so the voluntary denominations that failed to topple the Church-state system in England became the dominant form of religion in the USA. Pentecostalism is the final expression of this voluntary type of religion. It is now being propagated all over the world as a kind of revolution that works mainly at the cultural level. The Pentecostal Cultural Revolution first took off in Latin America, where the Church-state system was often weakened by the assaults of political radicals, as well as being syncretistic, and disorganized. However, disorganization also meant that radical elites mostly failed to gain ideological control over the mass of the people, as they did in the more centralized polity of France, and in the almost entirely European society of Uruguay. Pentecostalism created an open religious market even in Latin America, and in Africa it was not even necessary to do that, because religious monopolies only existed in the Islamic North. The question now is whether the breakthrough of the voluntary religious group in the two-thirds world can be sustained as it has been in North America, or whether it will falter as in Europe. The much debated question as to whether Europe or North America is an exception to the proper course of history has been transferred to the whole world. To some degree the future of Christianity depends on the answer to that question, though the future of Catholicism and Orthodoxy clearly pose rather different questions. One question concerns the compatibility of Orthodoxy and modernity, and provided you do not define modernity from the outset as excluding the kind of spiritual world found in the Orthodox East, the evidence suggests the issue remains open. If Asian businessmen can embrace Pentecostalism, or something very like it, then business people in Russia can embrace the spiritual benedictions bestowed by the Orthodox Church. Another way of expressing that is to say that the impact of rationalization in part at least depends on the cultural and historical context; Dallas, Singapore, Moscow and Buenos Aires are all part of the modern world and all actively religious.

How Big Is It?

In company with Islam, Pentecostalism represents the largest shift in the contemporary global religious economy. On the linguistic map of the globe it inhabits, and propagates itself within, lie two of the three great linguistic families: English and Spanish. It can be understood as the great awakening of Christianity today, taking place worldwide. Unlike Islam, it is fuelled primarily by voluntary conversion rather than demographic expansion. Maybe that adds up to a quarter of a billion people, though numbers depend on how you frame your categories. For example, it is difficult to ascertain where Evangelicalism ends and Pentecostalism begins, though it is clear enough that 'classical' Evangelicals believe that miracles ceased after the apostolic period and also that the stricter kind of Evangelicals accord much more weight to the letter of the text than the Spirit. One could not imagine including the Friday Apostolics of Southern Africa studied by Matthew Engelke in the Evangelical camp, but they do lie at the margin of Pentecostalism because the fire of the Spirit has not merely destabilized the text but actually devoured it in the white heat of prophecy.[3] Nor do the Friday Apostolics represent the only awkward problem when it comes to the demarcation of Pentecostalism. The *Congregação Cristã no Brasil* is the third largest Church in Brazil, numbering up to three million people, but it entirely confounds recent stereotypes based on more recent forms of Neo-Pentecostalism. This is a Church formed in what

---

[3]   Engelke, Matthew, *A Problem of Presence: Beyond Scripture in an African Church* (Cambridge: Cambridge University Press, 2007).

looks like a combination of holiness traditions and quiet Quaker-like fraternity.[4] It was founded by an Italian in 1910 and represents the older style of 'classical' Pentecostalism, apolitical and quietist. It is also distinguished from almost any other kind of Pentecostalism by its rejection of modern media. One simply has to use criteria based on some idea of 'family resemblance' to decide where the appropriate borders lie. Thus the two churches studied by Kristina Helgesson in South Africa, are both well within the Pentecostal fold, but the Olive Tree Church has adopted a stronger than usual version of Christian Zionism and one that includes some Jewish rituals and carefully fostered Israeli contacts.[5] You never know where reading the whole Bible will take you once you drop the hermeneutic spectacles provided by mainstream Christianity.

The expansion of categories can lead to much higher and seriously misleading estimates. Citations from figures offered in *The World Christian Encyclopedia* might well be given a rest, and any work like the *Atlas of Global Christianity* using categories like 'Great Commission Christians' approached with caution.[6]

Pentecostalism is part of a wider shift, including Islam, that has gained momentum over the last half century as social and geographical mobility also gained momentum, and as new media offering fresh perspectives and choices have brought everyone into a new proximity. People watch television in the poorest *favelas*, and Pentecostalism expands in tandem with newly available 'visions and revisions'.

When it first took off in Latin America in the mid-twentieth century, Protestants as a whole numbered only one per cent of the population, but they numbered well over ten per cent at the end, varying between three per cent in countries at one end of the spectrum and over 20 per cent at the other. About two thirds of these new Protestants were Pentecostal and about half of the Pentecostals were in Brazil, the largest country in Latin America.[7]

Pentecostalism took off in Africa a little later, and it is difficult to estimate the numbers because there is an overlap both with the mainstream churches and African-initiated churches. Christianity itself took off in Africa with de-colonization in the sixties, so that African Christians now number up to four hundred million. The Pentecostal proportion of the total population of countries from South Africa

---

[4] St. Clair, George, 'Building Purity', a paper given at the LSE anthropology seminar on the 11 December, 2009.

[5] Helgesson, Kristina, *'Walking in the Spirit': The Complexity of Belonging in Two Pentecostal Churches in Durban, South Africa* (Uppsala: DiCA, University of Uppsala, 2006).

[6] Johnson, Todd, and Ross, Kenneth, (eds), *Atlas of Global Christianity* (Edinburgh: Edinburgh University Press, 2010); I am responsible for a section on Europe 1910–2010, but *not* for a figure of 90 per cent cited for believers in God in Russia, which was interpolated without permission.

[7] Chesnut, Andrew, *Competitive Spirits: Latin America's New Religious Economy* (Oxford: Oxford University Press, 2003).

to Ethiopia and Burkina Faso hovers between three per cent and somewhere in the teens, with Protestants overall nearly one in five in Ethiopia, and there has been a rapid spill-over from English-speaking to French and Portuguese-speaking countries.[8] These percentages are not so markedly different from those in Latin America. A similar growth has occurred in Asia, particularly on the Pacific Rim, and in China and the Chinese diaspora, though here we are often talking about Pentecostal elements in mainstream churches and what might be called a form of Chinese Independency. There has been a smaller expansion in India and the Indian diaspora,[9] and even some modest penetration in Central Asia, for example in the fragmented and disorganized area of Northern Kyrgyzstan.[10]

Numbers are usually propaganda and predictions often precarious, but Pentecostals may well make up the largest single group of Christians apart from the Catholic Church. From the dangerous central area of Johannesburg to the poorer *favelas* of Santiago and São Paulo, and from Seoul to Accra, from the Roma of Romania and the Quechua of the Andes, one can see amazing networks of religious social capital, furnished with a myriad of colourful names, small and large hives of religious industry in every sense of the word.

Modes of Insertion and Locales

Pentecostalism is qualitatively new because it is voluntary, global and hybrid from the beginning. In locating the modes of Pentecostal insertion one begins by asking whether it was initially an American product and whether it is now largely an American export. As to how it began, there were many premonitions of Pentecostalism outside the USA, in Wales and India for example. In a way it is American simply because it is a voluntary organization, or a set of organizations, entirely free of the state even though it may sometimes cosy up to the state in places like Zimbabwe as described in David Maxwell's classic study, *African Gifts of the Spirit*.[11]

However, the issue is more complicated because the roots of Pentecostalism in the holiness tradition of Anglo-American Methodism, and Evangelicalism, meant that its dissemination followed global paths already laid down by missionaries in England and North America inspired by the holiness movement. Moreover, Pentecostalism fused black and white versions of Evangelical revivalism, and that gave it a potent transnational dynamic. As one would anticipate, the fusion of

---

[8]   Haustein, Jorge, Doctoral thesis presented in 2009 at Heidelberg University on Ethiopian Pentecostalism.

[9]   Bergunder, Michael, *The South Indian Pentecostal Movement in the Twentieth Century* (Cambridge: Eerdmans, 2009).

[10]   Pelkmans, Mathijs, (ed.), *Conversion After Socialism: Disruptions, Modernisms, and Technologies of Faith* (Oxford: Berghahn, 2009).

[11]   Maxwell, David, *African Gifts of the Spirit*.

black and white was partly reversed as the movement developed, when it came to the mingling of races. The white heat of revival initially melts down distinctions of colour, gender and class, but then they separate out again, leaving a potentially explosive memory of revolutionary fusion. The fusion eventually occurs again with renewed energy, in new conditions under new auspices.

The fusion of black and white revivalist *styles* was not reversed, and all kinds of new Pentecostal groups emerged, some principally white or black in their leadership or following, some mixed, and some including female leadership. The fusion generated in the heat of revival gives Pentecostalism a hybrid character, simultaneously ancient and modern, and enables it to cross any number of cultural species barriers in the two-thirds world hitherto blocking the global advance of Christianity. Unlike many mainstream Christians, Pentecostals accept the reality of the inspired world even while seeking to exorcize 'negative' spirits as demonic.[12] In the course of crossing these cultural barriers, especially in Africa, but also in Asia, the hybrid character of Pentecostalism enables it to adapt and become indigenous without losing its original character. Pentecostalism was pre-adapted from the outset to inspired cultures over the whole world, from the Australian aborigines to the Peke Ewe of Ghana, the Mapuche of Southern Chile, and managers of industry in the Chinese diaspora. This is not to say that Pentecostalism has entirely lost contact with its Anglo-American origins, or is unconnected with the global spread of English, or to deny that large numbers of Americans are globally active in its promotion. It is to say that Pentecostalism has an amazing capacity to become indigenous, and adapt to local cultures.

Elements in Pentecostalism, like the Neo-Pentecostal emphasis on health and wealth, have been pejoratively identified as typically American, but they are in fact widely present in the two-thirds world. They are persistent themes in the Hebrew Scriptures, the Christian Old Testament, and Pentecostals feed voraciously on the whole Bible. Unsurprisingly, given so many of them are 'the damned of the earth', they respond to an Old Testament emphasis on the good things God has in store for the righteous. Moreover, given they live in inspired worlds, they respond to the New Testament emphasis on baptism in the Spirit, especially the Pauline gifts of the Spirit. The specific modes of Pentecostal fusion make Pentecostalism recognizable wherever it appears, in spite of its adaptability, and also make it recognizably Christian, at least so far. Azonseh Ukah's useful coinage 'Pentecostalite' suggests a genuine problem at the margin.[13]

It is the good things Pentecostals believe God has in store for the poor and the faithful, together with the gifts of the Spirit offered to all and sundry, which enable Pentecostalism to be simultaneously ancient and modern, and to reach from the developed world to the developing world. Pentecostalism can be linked with North Atlantic spirituality at one end of the spectrum, as well as with African, Asian, and

---

[12]   Meyer, Birgit, *Translating the Devil*.

[13]   Ukah, Azonseh, *A New Paradigm of Pentecostal Power: A Study of the Redeemed Christian Church of God* (Trenton, NJ: Africa World Press, 2009).

native Latin American spirit cults at the other. At the same time Pentecostals have a discipline and an organizational form absent in contemporary western spirituality, and a global reach mostly absent from spirit cults. The discipline is crucial. Of course, from a western perspective it has been labelled authoritarian, but without any specification of a standard of comparison, say with western political parties, and without adequate analysis of what modes of authority are likely to emerge in strongly bounded social capsules protecting vulnerable people in their search for a new standard of life and living.

Modes of Insertion

In global perspective the expansion of Pentecostalism alongside the expansion of Islam might illustrate arguments for a linkage between monotheism and the emergence of one world, but that is too large a theme to be pursued here. Instead I begin with a generalized pen portrait based on my initial experience of the way a classical Pentecostalism made its way in Latin America. Pentecostalism inserts itself most dramatically amongst the aspiring poor of the contemporary megacity and amongst migrants making the Long Trek to the megacity. Pentecostals travel in a protective convoy from the countryside to the megacity, or form organizations for mutual help and spiritual support once settled in the poorer *favelas*. They are moved by the spirit and they are a movement of the spirit across all frontiers. Pentecostalism is about being moved, body and soul, and being ready to move. It is a call to change and it assures you that by faith and hope you are not a victim chained by circumstances but a victor capable of overcoming them. When people find themselves in the difficult world of the poorer parts of the city they may encounter a summons to redemption in the widest sense of the word, a rescue mission from chaos, and a message of hope and help arriving through modern means of communication. Modern technology encircles the globe, and if technology defines modernity then Pentecostals are very modern, in particular in their remarkable ability to create imagined communities crossing conventional frontiers, for example in West Africa.

Perhaps the message on the modern media invites people to make contact with a megachurch, maybe in a cinema, or maybe they hear it through personal contacts and street preachers inviting them to change their lives and circumstances by joining one of the thousands of small groups meeting in houses or shops. Either way Pentecostals are religious entrepreneurs setting up shop for themselves, and running their own show. They captain their own ship of salvation and sail away from the contemptuous hierarchies of the wider world. The hierarchies they then devise for themselves are at least their own and based on criteria which allow them to ascend in their own eyes and in the eyes of millions like them. Looking around at millions of similar people at mass meetings they feel they matter, and if politicians come along to address them and even learn their language they know for sure that they matter. They are no longer at the end of a long line of clients, but a collective voice to be attended to. Inevitably, that is also their moment of danger because they are being offered a share in the spoils.

They have on the one hand moved across frontiers and on the other hand they have drawn boundaries around themselves to protect and develop a new cell, strictly governed to ensure survival. People lash themselves together on rafts to survive in stormy seas. On that raft they adopt a regime of disciplined behaviour, shared learning and mutual assistance, otherwise they sink as rapidly as the millions floundering and foundering all around them.

Of course Pentecostals compete with each other for souls, and their cells divide as new leaders clash with old ones, or young Turks challenge old Turks. They learn on the job, and they learn quickly if they are to survive by their own efforts on an open religious market, which means they still speak the homely language of the people. Pastors are not separated from flocks by prolonged training in theological institutions.

Within the warm world of the Church Pentecostals assist each other, especially when in distress, and they acquire organizational skills and responsibilities that help them in the world outside. The most effective agents of Pentecostal conversion are not just modern modes of communication but person to person contact, which in Latin America might be the *visitadora*, the woman who calls to help, console and perhaps heal. Maybe converts learn to teach children, or acquire artisan and building skills, or join in a band or a choir.

The pastors who act as religious entrepreneurs are a remarkable group who find in the Church an avenue and an expanding arena for energies that might well be blocked in the word outside. I describe them as a buried intelligentsia, in part because they are so resourceful, and in part because their children often make their way up in the business or educational world. Given the explosive energies unleashed by the Pentecostal spirit, only resourceful and decisive leadership can prevent fragmentation and a loss of a sense of direction. The pastors are not dependent on the wider society, apart from needing to negotiate with local authorities in societies usually riddled with corruption. According to David Lehmann in his *Struggle for the Spirit* their most radical feature is indifference to sponsorship and to patronage from the intelligentsia.[14] They just do not care what metropolitan opinion thinks of them. Their reference point is not *The New York Times*, even though that paper has recently given them some notably understanding write-ups.

That is a pen portrait of the aspiring poor organizing themselves for every kind of betterment, moral and financial, and it approximates the classical mode of Pentecostal insertion in Latin America also present in Africa and Asia. But there are other modes of Pentecostal insertion, for example, among marginal ethnicities like the indigenous Maya and Quechua in Latin America, and among emerging middle classes in places like Singapore, Nigeria and Brazil. In Europe the main example of a marginal and depressed ethnicity affected by Pentecostalism would

---

[14]   Lehmann, David, *Struggle for the Spirit: Religious Transformation and Popular Culture* (Cambridge: Cambridge University Press, 1996).

be the gypsies, and there is also a Pentecostal presence on the geographical margin of Europe in Sicily.[15] It offers a despised or marginal group a reversal of stereotypes; gypsies cease to be regarded as work-shy and pride themselves on being respectable, meaning worthy of respect. The appeal to the middle classes in Europe is very modest, unless one counts charismatic Evangelicalism as a closely affiliated movement, but it finds vigorous expression in the so-called 'faith movements' at the heart of secular society, discussed by Simon Coleman, for example *Living Word* in Uppsala and a similar organization in Budapest.[16]

Pentecostalism can also penetrate a transitional geographical area where there is already some degree of religious and ethnic mixing, such as you find in Transylvania and the Ukraine. In Transylvania there is a kind of pluralism where each faith has an ethnic base, except for the voluntary denominations. The Baptists, for example, brought together Hungarians and Romanians in a major Church with a lively college attached, and the Pentecostals have a particular impact among the Roma. Baptists and Pentecostals alike offer a newly moralized, self conscious and transnational identity. Catherine Wanner has written an impressive ethnography analysing how Pentecostalism can work in the transitional arena and pluralistic culture of the Western Ukraine.[17] She shows how a megachurch of some twenty-five thousand in Kiev, led by a Nigerian, can offer better services to down and outs and druggies than the agencies of a corrupt state. I shall pick up the point about what the state fails to do or is ill-equipped to do in my conclusion.

There is no space here to give examples of all these different modes of insertion but I do need to look at very recent work illuminating some of the difficulties of analysis and categorization, beginning with China and the Chinese diaspora in South-East Asia in the context of the Pacific Rim.

Apart from Africa the most remarkable growth of Christianity has been in China and the Chinese diaspora. This growth energizes the mainline churches as well as the Pentecostals, which means analysis is *everywhere* complicated by the interchange between Pentecostals and the growing charismatic elements in mainline Protestant and Catholic churches. I need to sketch in the wider background of religion on the Pacific Rim.

The Pacific Rim from Korea and Japan to Singapore, including mainland China and the Catholic Philippines, offers a tempting subject for the comparative study of Christian expansion and the different ways Christianity has been adopted and adapted, or rejected, persecuted and expelled. Christianity has been most successful in South Korea because it became aligned with Korean nationalism

---

[15]   Cucchiari, Salvatore, 'Adapted for Heaven: Conversion and culture in western Sicily', *American Ethnologist*, 15 (1988): 417–41; Gay y Blasco, Paloma, *Gypsies in Madrid: Sex, Gender and the Performance of Identity* (Oxford: Berg, 1999).

[16]   Coleman, Simon, *The Globalisation of Charismatic Christianity: Spreading the Gospel of Prosperity* (Cambridge: Cambridge University Press, 2000).

[17]   Wanner, Catherine, *Communities of the Converted: Ukrainians and Global Evangelism* (Alberta: Cornell University Press, 2007).

against both Chinese and Japanese imperialism, and it has been least successful in Japan, where it has been aligned with western imperialism. In China Christianity has been attacked as linked with western imperialism, but at the same time it has been classified as a religion rather than a superstition. Moreover the western taint was forcibly purged by the communists so what eventually emerged was Chinese and autonomous. Currently Christians in China number between three per cent and six per cent, and in Taiwan perhaps less, since up to recent years the Taiwanese government was virtually as repressive as the government of mainland China. In mainland China there are now one or two cities (one, Wenzhou, known as New Jerusalem) where Christians make up perhaps 15 to 20 per cent of the population, with enough social clout and economic success for some to be known as 'boss Christians'.

When you look at these figures they are not so unlike the degree of penetration of Pentecostalism and Protestantism generally in Latin America, and there may well be an upper limit in both cases in the 10 to 20 per cent range. After all, success stimulates competition and emulation, with the result that Buddhists in this whole region have taken over some of the unique selling points of Christianity, including its social and educational outreach, just as Catholics in Brazil have incorporated some of the modes and methods of Pentecostals.

Clearly one key factor in religious success or failure throughout the region is whether a religion is aligned with national identity or with oppression, just as it was a key factor in Eastern Europe under Communism. One might add there are other similarities because communism in both China and Eastern Europe became hollowed out as a revolutionary faith seeking to mobilize the masses of the people. The elite ceased to be true believers and sought increasingly to achieve economic success in pragmatic ways while holding on to centralized state power. Notoriously they adopted state capitalism.

The Chinese diaspora in Malaysia and Indonesia, to be discussed below, offers a variation on the theme of ethnic identity and oppression because the Chinese are both feared for their economic success, and sometimes threatened as a minority, by the Muslim majorities. Christianity offered the Chinese of the diaspora what they saw as a modern form of ethnic identity. Moreover, the Chinese have an elective affinity with the Protestant work ethic. It can strike them as rational, and they can find in charismatic Christianity a promise of protection and a salve for strains in the family and corruption at work.

Singapore is distinctive because it has Malay and Indian as well as Chinese populations. A reformed Buddhism, sometimes mixed with a Confucian ethic, exercises some influence among the Chinese, as it also does in Taiwan, once again in response to the educational and social activism of Christianity. Christianity, much of it charismatic, but also mainstream, has made considerable advances in Singapore among the rising professional and business groups in a way familiar in many parts of the global religious economy.

I am sketching the background you need in order to understand the peculiar problems of analysing Pentecostalism/Charismatic Christianity in this very important area of the world. In Korea you have the most vital and missionary-minded kind of Christianity in the whole of Asia, and Korean missionaries, many of them Pentecostal, are to be found anywhere from the Philippines to Central Asia. They provide just one dramatic instance of the global phenomenon of lateral or reverse mission, which in Europe can be seen as the empire striking back, whether in London or Amsterdam. Pentecostalism in Korea represents an extremely energetic sector of a Protestant population of perhaps 20 per cent, in a country where Presbyterian Protestants have been largely responsible for the national education system, as they have also been in Taiwan. Korean Pentecostals have developed cell-like structures, often within vast megachurches that are in practice complete sub-communities, some of them numbering hundreds of thousands. These megachurches often preach a prosperity gospel with recognizable East Asian as well as American characteristics, and they have absorbed some of the spirit cults of Korea, particularly the spirits of the mountains and even, sometimes, the ancestors. You can describe this as the sanctification of local spirit cults by the one Holy Spirit or as adaptation to local culture. Either way, we meet again the confluence of the ancient and the modern.[18]

China itself poses the big question, and there have been enthusiastic prognoses of the conversion of China. It is here we run most obviously into the universal problem of the relation between Pentecostalism and other expressions of charismatic Christianity, both Catholic and Protestant. One avenue for the expansion of Christianity is found among the new professional and university elites of the big cities like Beijing. There you might find charismatic Christian cells openly active among IT professionals and the student population. I am not suggesting this is necessarily the dominant expression of religion in such groups, because I personally ran into highly educated professionals much engaged by a vast Buddhist theme park in the Shanghai region, and there is a significant sector of revived religiosity 'with Chinese characteristics' bringing together Confucian ethics with Daoist and Buddhist spirituality. Nevertheless, I visited an 'officially approved' charismatic Church in the university sector of Beijing, built by German architects in the style of 'state of the art' modernity, which had eleven choirs and six services on a Sunday, with attendances at each of over a thousand, mostly students.

The other side to this expansion is the growth of an indigenous Christianity in the countryside, which began in the Cultural Revolution, and sometimes picked up stray sparks from the earlier Christian missionary work eliminated decades earlier with the triumph of Maoist communism.[19] This growth represents the invention of primitive Christianity from scratch, stimulated by Bibles buried in the ground, but with a Chinese emphasis on the goods of all kinds delivered by faith.

---

18   Lee, Young-hoon, *The Holy Spirit Movement in Korea* (Oxford: Regnum, 2009); Anderson, Allan, and Tang, Edmund, (eds), *Asian and Pentecostal: The Charismatic Face of Christianity in Asia* (Oxford: Regnum, 2005); Buswell, Robert, and Lee, Timothy, (eds), *Christianity in Korea* (Honolulu: University of Hawaii Press, 2006).

19   Kao, Cheng-yeng, 'The Cultural Revolution and the Emergence of a Pentecostal-style of Protestantism in China', *Journal of Contemporary Religion*, 24: 2 (2009): 171–88.

It benefitted above all from the destruction of the temples along with the churches in the Cultural Revolution. The men were cut off from the service of the ancestors and the spirits through the temples, while millions of women were attracted to an underground Christianity working its way along domestic networks and providing solace, hope and mutual assistance.

I have not stressed so far the appeal of Pentecostalism to women, the space it creates for mutuality within the home in spite of patriarchal characteristics, or the scope it offers for female spirituality and, within limits, for female leadership. But the appeal to women is very evident on the global scene, and quite dramatically so in the underground spirituality that accompanied the Chinese Cultural Revolution. Today this kind of faith is often shunned by men, at least in public, on account of the predominance of women. For anyone interested in the appeal for Pentecostalism in a restored and mutually dependent family, and in the opportunities it offers and their limits, there is the work of Bernice Martin in Latin America, Jane Soothill in Ghana, Diane Austin-Broos in Jamaica, and Maria Frahm-Arp in South Africa. For a study of men, conducted in Venezuela, there is David Smilde's *Reason to Believe*.[20]

We are talking about the rise in China, but also globally, of a kind of cultural revolution of disciplined ways of being, mutuality and living which is self-directed and not dependent on the state and its initiatives, and also rejecting macho violence, as well as offering a haven to men not enticed by the romanticism of gun-toting guerrillas.

In China the government is uncertain how to deal with this parallel Cultural Revolution. When I met with those government researchers and officials concerned with the resurgence of religion in China, they were principally worried for obvious political reasons by ethno-religious enclaves in Buddhist and Muslim areas, but inclined to revise their overall attitude to voluntary associations, though with reservations about Catholicism. They could imagine harnessing religious groups to relieve pain, to support the family, to motivate aspiration and to create social capital, but not obscuring social realities, apart from the realities of control by the communist elite.

I turn now to the analysis of Asian Pentecostals and charismatics in the Chinese diaspora by Juliette Koning and Heidi Dahles.[21] There are three or four million ethnic Chinese in Indonesia (over one and a half per cent of the population), six million in Malaysia (26 per cent), and they are the pillars of both economies. The Chinese managers are treated with envy and suspicion as outsiders connected with western industrialized nations, especially the USA, and disliked as too mobile through education, and too reliant on their ethnic connections. They are also suspected for turning to a noisy charismatic Christianity from more staid Catholic

[20] Smilde, David, *Reason to Believe: Cultural Agency in Latin American Evangelicalism* (Berkeley, CA: University of California Press, 2007).

[21] Koning, Juliette, and Dahles, Heidi, 'Spiritual Power: Ethnic Chinese Managers and the Rise of Charismatic Christianity in Southeast Asia', *The Copenhagen Journal of Asian Studies*, 27: 1 (2009): 1–37.

or Protestant backgrounds or from a Buddhist or Chinese folk religiosity. Like the Chinese in Singapore they see Christianity as rational, and as a resource in a rationalized business environment. Their embrace of a charismatic/Pentecostal identity can be seen as an intense personal experience linked to moments of personal and professional difficulty, and as heightening a threatened ethnic identity. Whereas the converts previously lacked any active religious commitment they now have a sense of direction, of the community of mutual trust necessary to good business, of providential protection rather than unpredictable fortune, and of mastery. That sense of providence rather than random fortune, is found in entrepreneurial Pentecostalism all over the world, whether the business is large scale or in the informal economy. The Chinese converts rejoice in shared values and see their faith as 'the politics of the Lord' in a corrupt political and legal system.

The result is well-being, inspiration, solace and guidance. One woman professional spoke of having a tiny altar in her handbag which she set up in her office or in the room where she did her beauty treatment. Each day begins and ends in prayer and there is a preference for having fellow-Christians as colleagues. The networks of business professionals share testimony together and organize charitable activity, a practice also observable in Brazil. Business Christians in South-East Asia and Brazil alike organize help to the less fortunate.

My next example is very different, though it also shows something of the relation between Pentecostalism and the gaps in centralized state development. Uganda is, or was, regarded as a model of how development should be channelled, but in practice it mostly affects the urban middle class. Local religious changes, particularly in rural areas, have often been often ignored in the literature as irrelevant to serious outcomes. The development narrative extruded other narratives. In fact, according to Ben Jones, writing of rural Uganda, the Ugandan state is suspended in mid-air looking outward to international agencies.[22] In practice decentralization means that many local areas get on with their own organization. Jones' work on 'the church in the village, the village in the church' provides a vivid corrective to the developmental success story in the rural area of Teso in Eastern Uganda. As Jones points out, much of the research so far, apart from Laurent's study of the Assemblies of God in Burkina Faso,[23] focuses on large churches in urban centres or poorer congregations in peripheral urban areas, so that less is known about the way Pentecostalism can shape politics in poor rural communities. A quotation offers a first approximation to the theme of the study. Jones says that 'In the sub-parish under study, Pentecostal churches are part of the human and physical infrastructure of the village, dealing with a range of concerns also addressed by

---

[22]   Jones, Ben, *Beyond the State in Rural Uganda* (Edinburgh: Edinburgh University Press, 2009).

[23]   Laurent, Pierre-Joseph, 'L'Eglise des Assemblées de Dieu du Burkina Faso', *Archives de Sciences Sociales des Religions*, 44: 105 (1999): 71–98; Laurent describes how the Pentecostal message has spread through neighbouring countries through the trading links of the Mossi people.

government and customary institutions ... Churches are places where help can be found in the planting season, where one can build up support in an impending court case, or take the first steps on the path to becoming a "big man"'.[24]

Becoming born again is not inherently divisive, even though a clear line can be drawn between the behavioural requirements of church membership and customary mores. Pentecostals abjure the consumption of alcohol hitherto so central to village life and its frequent violence, they promote courtesy, they encourage women to negotiate improvements in domestic behaviour in the space of the Church, while insisting on HIV tests before marriage and forbidding alliances between those infected and others.

In post-independence Uganda political parties and local villages alike were regarded as either Catholic or Anglican, and projects were viewed through a confessional lens. Yet at the level of the local village, competition over access to state power is much less intense and churches provide the spaces within which potential leaders build up reputations and negotiate land disputes. The collapse of the cash-crop economy in the 1970s and early 1980s meant a decrease in state development, while civil violence in the late 1980s stimulated a spiritual revival as part of a process of reconciliation and communal therapy. That is also true in other conflict-ridden parts of Africa, but in this particular area of Uganda some widely observed characteristics of Pentecostal insertion, particularly in West Africa, do not apply. In West Africa the break represented by Pentecostalism renders the past a suspect category, and joining the brotherhood and sisterhood draws a line between the old network of extended kin obligations and the authority of elders, and the new community of the born again. This was not the case in Uganda.

During the chaos of the Ugandan civil war being 'born again' provided a legitimate reason for withdrawing from politics, while the radical moral demands of Pentecostalism meant one could be both an outsider *and* remain in the village. Membership increased. After the war however, this place of sanctuary ceased to be an isolated enclave and became an arena where villagers pieced together political actions without compromising the new approaches embodied in born again membership. Moreover Anglicans and Catholics gained better knowledge of Pentecostals during the violence, partly because they were all violently thrust together in concentration camps. They came to appreciate the spiritual revival and even to emulate it, despite losing some of their most diligent members to the Assemblies of God. Pentecostals also became involved in the remarkable efflorescence of burial societies to achieve a dignified closure following the violence. The state had not delivered on its promises, religious reform and local initiative did.

My final examples are New Life in Christ, in Tanzania, a charismatic breakaway from the Lutheran Church, and the Redeemed Christian Church of God in Nigeria. In his study of New Life in Christ, Martin Lindhardt emphasizes conditions in Tanzania: the retreat of the state, of socialism, and of the development narrative,

---

[24]　Jones, Ben, *Beyond the State in Rural Uganda*, 498.

and the need to cope with the consequences of neo-liberalism and the effects of war.[25] Lindhardt also sets his analysis in the context of the work of Birgit Meyer who showed how rupture was linked to continuity, in particular because a discourse focussed on the Devil included the old demonic forces of darkness as the shadow side of the forces of light. Charismatic Christianity was concerned with the problems of this life rather than the hereafter and it offered deliverance from evil through believers regularly stirring up the power of God by dancing and by passionate prayer. Christians are empowered to overcome depersonalized satanic power represented by witches, zombies and ancestral spirits. Experience of personal transformation enables believers to struggle and to distance themselves from occult forces impeding individual and social development. These experiences and these negative forces co-exist alongside modern technology and modern politics, and the Church offers a space for the moralization of money, for the exchange of gifts between man and God, and for expressions of hope and aspiration and reflections on the failures of modernity. There are many alternative kinds of modernity and the achievement of modernity is not some unilinear path but variable and fraught with contradictions and frustrations that are reflected in and challenged by Pentecostal-charismatic churches.

The Redeemed Christian Church of God enjoys the same kind of notoriety among other Christians and the same fascination for anthropologists as the Universal Church of the Kingdom of God in Brazil. Both have global ambitions and illustrate the extraordinary way such churches go out into the whole world, but especially to areas where they have natural resonance, which in the case of the Universal Church is Portuguese speaking Africa and Portugal, where it is now the second largest church. Asonzeh Ukah's study of the RCCG is focussed on the arrival of prosperity teaching in Africa.[26] The RCCG is one of the most successful of the new churches, in part because it combines the organizational format of an international corporation with an ethos rooted in Yoruba tradition. Ukah brings out its extraordinary ability to fuse deep roots in African spirituality, based on healing, protection against malign powers, prognostication, trance and visionary dreams, with a modern go-getting organization promoting itself through every marketing device.

The RCCG emerged from a much smaller, humbler and more ascetic body, the God's Glory Church, but when re-founded in the 1980s by Enoch Adeboye, a university teacher of mathematics, it sought out the rich and powerful and youthful cadres on university campuses. This shift was facilitated by the regress of post Civil War Nigeria towards a kleptocratic, and electorally corrupt, state and by the mass unemployment brought about by neo-liberal economic policies. The national hopes of a new and frustrated middle class shifted from politics to religion, so the RCCG became a venture in the autonomous creation of social capital, providing an all-embracing environment with educational resources, community banking, insurance, media enterprises and health facilities for members in return for their

---

[25]   Lindhardt, Martin, 'The Ambivalence of Power: Charismatic Christianity and Occult Forces in Urban Tanzania', *Nordic Journal of Religion and Society*, 22: 1 (2009): 37–54.

[26]   Ukah, Azonseh, *A New Paradigm of Pentecostal Power*.

investment in sacred bonds, divinely guaranteed. It also offered a protective trade union for women by stressing mutuality in a stable monogamous family, and an equivalent for the Big Woman of traditional society through the role of powerful women pastors. The teaching was what I call an Afro-Jewish amalgam, with an element of Christian Zionism. Jesus, as another organization, Winners Chapel, phrases it, is the Winner Man, and the role of the New Testament lies in a reading of the teaching of Jesus stressing prolonged prayer, fasting, healing and exorcism. Jesus became poor for our sakes that we might become literally rich. After all, as Adeboye put it, who actually wants to be poor?

Adeboye is also the chief actor in the choreography of worship during the monthly Holy Ghost Night held in the Redemption Camp, a 10 square kilometre site with an auditorium seating half a million people. This camp is a territorial strike to establish a colony of heaven on earth. So a movement that transcended territoriality goes back to the land, while a church that gloried in what Zechariah called 'the day of small things' rejoices in the arrival of the Big Time as well as the End-time.

Is It Halévy All Over Again?

There are various ways of looking at Pentecostalism. Peter Berger summed up one approach up by saying that Max Weber was alive and well and living in Guatemala City. Perhaps that should be amended to São Paulo or even Buenos Aires, because São Paulo is one of the great capitals of the Pentecostal world, and in Buenos Aires about a quarter of the actively religious population is attached to neo-Pentecostal churches floating free of the conventional denominational anchors. However, the invocation of Max Weber is both correct and misleading. There is certainly evidence of a vigorous Protestant work ethic, domestic discipline and willingness to look to the longer term rather than immediate self gratification. At the same time, the religious ethic is, in an important way, expressed in churches that are themselves economic enterprises rather than in economic enterprises governed by a religious ethic. It is true there is a myriad of such economic enterprises, but they are in the main closer to penny capitalism than Weber's Calvinist capitalists, and they often amount to shrewd negotiations and relations of mutual trust in the informal economy rather than large scale capitalist institutions. Small-scale economic miracles, with the accent on the miraculous and providential, are more in evidence than a western style of rationalized capitalism. Jean-Pierre Bastian, writing from a European Calvinist perspective, is even inclined to view Pentecostalism as a version of Latin American syncretism and spiritism, and from the evidence cited from Africa and Asia one can see how far that might apply and how far it does not.[27]

---

[27]   Bastian, Jean-Pierre, *Le Protestantism en Amérique Latine: Une Approche Socio-Historique* (Geneva: Labor et Fides: 1994).

For my part I prefer to see Pentecostalism as an extension of the 'free church' principle, represented in England and the United Sates by denominations like the Baptists and Methodists, and to be sparing with appeals to the classic Protestant Ethic as formulated by Max Weber. Instead I appeal to the French Jewish historian, Elie Halévy, who in his classic history of England in the nineteenth century pointed to Methodism as a form of mobilization of self-consciousness in the aspiring working and lower middle classes. Methodism promoted a work discipline that led many believers to rise socially and economically, and inculcated skills of organization, articulate speech and leadership that might assist either in business, or in the lower ranks of teaching, or in the formation of trade unions. Methodism, argued Halévy, saved England from the type of revolutionary upheaval that constantly overtook France and resulted in religion being viewed in all the countries influenced by the French model, including many in Latin America, as inherently conservative and bound up in obsolescent social elites and formations.[28] The significance of the rise of a voluntary associational faith like Pentecostalism in Latin America and elsewhere is therefore the replacement of the French model of inherent opposition between religion and change by an American model of religion as a cultural revolution of its own, forging ahead in particular where the state has been a conspicuous failure or shown itself incapable of meeting existential and moral need.

That world of voluntary association began within in the German Church in the form of a pietism that reached high up the social scale, and then emerged in Britain, especially England, as free voluntary religious associations capable of reaching people further down the social scale – and of pulling them socially upward at the same time – until it finally realized itself in the United States. There it proved capable of constant adaptation to different social sectors, and was able to engage people on the margin – black, white, and now Hispanic – and eventually to extend its scope and adaptability to the developing world. This sequence of stepping westward and engaging those on the move, from Kansas to Los Angeles, and those at the margins, was paralleled by an evolution from the slow congregational singing of chorales and psalms in Geneva and Leipzig to the lively hymns and massed choirs in Britain and the United States, and then to revivalist choruses with extensions into the worlds of Gospel music and jazz. Pentecostalism is a form of popular culture, and it partly spreads through catchy tunes. Put it that way and Pentecostals emerge as the great grandchildren of Martin Luther and his popular singing Church.

The Global Religious Economy and the State

From almost all the evidence cited, especially in sub-Saharan Africa, the failure of the state is clearly important in stimulating a shift from politics to religion,

---

[28]   Halévy, Elie, *The History of the English People in 1815* (Harmondsworth: Penguin, 1938, Book Three, chapter 1).

even though the shift is partial. I have already mentioned the greater ability of Pentecostal services to combat social disorganization and addiction in Kiev. I have also emphasized the capacity of Pentecostalism to reverse the negative stereotype of marginal groups, for example the Roma in Romania, and also in France and Spain, as well as indigenous peoples in Latin America. In Spain this autonomous regeneration was far more effective than the efforts of the state through its agencies. Moreover, among so-called 'first peoples', like the aborigines of Australia, hitherto regarded as impervious to conversion, a move to Pentecostalism begins as the welfare agencies provided by mainstream Christianity are withdrawn. There is something about the withdrawal of a state agency or a mainstream mission that stimulates autonomous action.[29]

If we return to the Chinese example we find an alternative cultural revolution parallel to what is now a centralized and technocratic revolution engineered by the state, often showing scant regard for personal concerns. It could benefit from voluntary associations to create or supplement the social capital needed to sustain large masses of people on the move and exposed to anonymous or anomic conditions. Among managers in the burgeoning industries of East and South-East Asia there is a need both for the virtues of the Protestant Ethic and for a place where workers in rationalized environments can be persons and can come together in small and personal groups. There they meet with people like themselves, sharing the same problems, and they find a space where executives can let go and cry. In Brazil such people need support in trying to cope with the amoral pressures and frequent corruption of the business world, such as is provided by a megachurch like Renascer em Cristo. In Chile, while Pentecostalism may flourish in the poorer parts of the city, charismatic kinds of Protestant Christianity provide a personal environment for the new middle classes, in which their need for a supportive and emotionally charged environment is met, and where they can meet with other people outside the traditional elites. Some of those in the more traditional business elites may want to find rest for their souls and their consciences in a charismatic Catholicism, or in the educational and social atmosphere provided by some of the newer Catholic orders. Among the poor, Pentecostalism offers a therapy for body and soul to those without access to professional assistance and often suffering severe psychic and somatic distress. Andrew Chesnut underlines the crucial importance of a healing ministry, of miracles of healing and of 'witness' to their efficacy.[30]

In many parts of Africa the same conditions are found in the cities that you find in Latin America and all over the so-called global South, but in a profoundly inspirited atmosphere where the conditions are often among the worst in the world. In the shanty town of Soweto near Johannesburg there is a vast megachurch close to the other great institution, the hospital, that used to be mainly white but now is mainly black. In Nigeria there are on the one hand massive charismatic

---

[29]   Brock, Peggy, (ed.), *Indigenous Peoples and Religious Change* (Leiden: Brill, 2005).

[30]   Chesnut, Andrew, *Born Again in Brazil: The Pentecostal Boom and the Pathogens of Poverty* (New Brunswick: Rutgers University Press, 1997).

movements among new professional classes and in the universities, and myriad small religious enterprises alongside vast entrepreneurial initiatives that provide services of every kind from the religious to the social and educational and create complete sub-communities. The Redeemed Christian Church of God is only one of these, and it restores a kind of spiritually animated tangibility that more clinical forms of Protestantism reject as irrational and Catholic. Though people dismiss these manifestations as exploitative and even as imported, whether in Nigeria, Ghana or Uganda, they appeal as an authentically African mode of spirituality. In this they are contrasted to some extent with the mainstream churches, which are often virtual NGOs doing what a corrupt state is unable to do for itself. In rural Uganda Pentecostals contribute to local social capital in a way that illustrates the highly selective nature of the claim that Uganda as a whole is a model of state initiated and internationally supported development.

What I am suggesting through all these examples is the existence of a cultural space of varying size, but present on a very wide scale in modern society, that is not catered for by the state, partly because the state is failing and or at any rate based on clienteles and corrupt to the core, and partly because some things are best done by voluntary associations positioned between the individual and the state. In the Pentecostal case the appeal of such associations is enhanced wherever a world of spiritual animation remains intact. In the United States the space between individual and state is so ideologically cherished and defended by vested interests that the state is inhibited from doing what it actually can do, especially in the sphere of health. Elsewhere, for example in much of Europe, the elites profit from centralized state action and are to some extent constituted by it. They are less well disposed to autonomous voluntary action and even actively hostile to schools of any kind with a distinctive religious ethos.

This brings us finally to the situation in Europe where more or less centralized bureaucracies exercise the kind of centralized control previously exercised by the Catholic Church in association with traditional elites and ruling classes. This association, also present historically in countries with Protestant state churches, though with a less militant political presence, has resulted in widespread alienation from religious institutions, reinforced by a generalized anti-institutional prejudice not confined to Europe but widespread in the developed world. This has led to a gradual attenuation of religious institutions, including those in the voluntary sector, and the rise of a free-floating spirituality without the resources needed for some kind of continuity, though agglomerations of people may come together for particular causes, like the threat posed by climate change.

The exceptions to this are countries, like Poland, where religion has been associated with national survival against oppression, though this association may not continue for ever once new generations emerge without that experience, and once the Church is exposed to attack by new elites in the media, particularly in countries where the Church has itself been partly corrupted by its alliance with state power, as the current situation in Ireland, and maybe in Austria, suggests. It has been reported that large numbers of people in Graz have 'resigned' from the Church on account of recent scandals. In Greece and Russia corruption is sufficiently endemic for the corruption of the Church not to seem exceptional, and certainly not bad enough to threaten the union of national flag and national Church. In any case a great deal of devotional activity takes place outside the immediate purview of the institutional Church. The inspirited world is present in a free market of healers and seers literally operating in the shadow of the Church, sometimes in the graveyard, just as the relatives of the dead visit and talk to them in the North of England. They break the monopoly of the clergy and partly evade their attempt to coral and institutionalize their activities in a more 'correct' dogmatic form. In that sense Russia already has its free-lance Pentecostals.

This is how I tentatively understand the exceptional character of the Western secularity, and in the case of France, an exceptional ideological secularism. But in the rest of the world, particularly where Marxism and politics in general have failed to fulfil their more grandiose visions, the religious impulse flourishes, either in relation to national and territorial consciousness, of which Islamism and Hindu nationalism are the most obvious instances, or else through the transnational voluntary association, of which Pentecostalism is the most energetic contemporary expression.

Chapter 5
Has Secularization gone into Reverse?

There are three areas where a case has been made for the reversal of secularization: the first concerns religious revival in terms of belief and practice, broadly understood, in regions where previously the trend had been in a secular direction, the second concerns the two-thirds world where in fact secularization had not made much impact anyway, and the third concerns the rather different issue of disenchantment and re-enchantment. I look at each in turn.

Regarding the first of these three areas, I consider the state of Christianity in North America and in Europe, including Russia. Some of what I argue may be surprising, given I have been and remain a long-term critic of many versions of secularization theory. However, I have never denied massive shifts in a secularizing direction in parts of Europe or major changes of attitude, even in the USA, especially since the sixties. I have tried to chart those shifts and I do not assume either a steady demand for religion on grounds of existential need or on account of supposedly inbuilt faulty perceptions of reality derived from our genetic make-up. When some commentators speak of 'post-secularity' I merely note they have overlooked the evidence of the persistence of religion on the ground, and ignored its continuous presence in public debate. They have belatedly rediscovered the presence of religion at a point where in the West of Europe one can cite evidence of steadily declining religious constituencies and reduced public influence. David Aaronovitch in *The Times* for 20 October 2009, noted the paradox quite precisely: he said we have never been more secular and yet the issue of religion looms larger. That is because there is increased institutional activity and concern about religious lobbies in the EU, aroused above all by the increased Islamic presence.[1]

All sinners are welcome at the penitence stool but they need not claim to be pioneers in a new country. The gratuitous rediscovery of religion, stimulated by the extension of the EU eastward, and even more by Muslim (and Christian) migration to Europe, takes two different forms. There is an exaggerated moral panic among some increasingly militant secularists, and there is a liberal attempt to include the supposedly new religious voice. In fact little has changed on the ground, certainly not in a positive direction, apart from the attitudes and interests of commentators, significant though these changing attitudes may be.

My second area for discussing de-secularization relates to the two-thirds world, and the varying applicability, or indeed the irrelevance, of the secularization thesis

---

[1] Silvestri, Sara, 'Islam and Religion in the EU Political System', *West European Politics*, 32 (6 November 2009): 1212–39.

in Latin America, Christian sub-Saharan Africa and Asia. I hope it is obvious why Islam and Islamism from Dakar to Indonesia is too big and problematic a subject to be included in this particular discussion, but perhaps I still need to indicate why. The problem is that secularization in Islam has meanings seen as imported from the West and, moreover, the axis is of discussion focuses more on public law than is the case in most other societies. I suspect there is a de-secularization in Islam, but I am not sure whether we are in a position to document any rise there may have been in religiosity or in practice. Some aspects of the issue relate to the quite distinctive case of Iran and others to the partial reversal of secularizations of the public realm originally imposed from above, for example in Tunisia and Turkey. The partial reversal that has happened in several Muslim majority countries is worth noticing for my purposes here because it parallels the partial reversal of secularization imposed from above in Russia and China, and also the attempt by religious nationalists in what have been post-colonial secular states, like India and Israel, to recover a religious character. All of these imposed secularizations had western roots and all the reversals have been in one way or another inspired by anti-western sentiments. Secularization has been imposed by western-influenced elites and de-secularization has come with the political mobilization of the masses and this is where we find the most plausible instances of secularization going into reverse. Indeed I would relate much of that reversal to the failure of the Marxist project.

My comments on the two-thirds world will focus on the spread of transnational religious voluntary bodies, above all Pentecostalism. Voluntary bodies challenge established religions based on birthright membership, occupying a territory or holding a holy land or city in particular reverence. I am particularly interested in the variable penetration of Pentecostalism, (and Evangelicalism generally), in the two-thirds world, and in the revitalization of the main established religions that helps to bring it about. I think, for example, of moves to stimulate a more lively and competitive Catholicism in Latin America and moves in Buddhism to take over some of the unique selling points of Christianity, such as social amelioration. This Evangelical penetration and the response of established religions provide a major axis for my discussion.

The third area concerns re-enchantment, a theme sometimes discussed in terms of an important and allied argument in favour of the growth of 'the holistic milieu' and the expansion of 'spirituality' in the global North at the expense of organized religion. Mainstream secularization theory has placed considerable reliance on the concept of disenchantment, and I ask what weight we might place on rival tendencies to re-enchant. Like secularization, disenchantment provides an example of a one-directional historical concept and I want to bring out just how complex the issue really is, especially when you remember that Judaism has been a secularizing agent in relation to sacred kingship, and both Judaism and Christianity have secularized nature by worshipping God as one and transcendent. To push enquiry further we need the kind of long-term historical assessment found in contributions like Keith Thomas's *Man and the Natural World*.[2] Moreover there are important discriminations to be made between different *kinds* of disenchantment and re-enchantment. The romantic attitude to the mystery of Nature is not the same thing as the apprehension of occult and dangerous forces threatening life in medieval times, or the personified natural powers of Greece, or Native American wisdom about the natural environment, or ecological activism related to notions like Gaia. The history of the idea of Nature and what is natural is one of the most important sites for thinking about secularization. I turn now to a more detailed examination of the three areas of concern just outlined.

Christianity in the Global North

First of all, then, I provide an overview of the Christian 'global North' from Los Angeles to Vladivostock. In seeking to understand what has been happening in the Christian 'global North' we lack integrated data about the incidence of different kinds of religious expression in particular regions, megacities and cities, just as, with one or two notable exceptions, such as the Bäckström and Davie study, we lack integrated comparative data on the links between religion, welfare and voluntary organization.[3] We feel able to comment on the gross figures for the highly secular Czech Republic but pay less attention to the difference between secularized Bohemia and Moravia. Within the Czech Republic there are huge variations by region as well as by size of town. Moreover Slovakia shows considerably higher degrees of what looks like a stable religiosity than the Czech Republic, in spite of increased moral permissiveness among the young. Intensely local variations have as much to offer analysis as very widespread trends in Europe and North America towards so-called self-actualization at the expense of commitment to public institutions as such, whether political or religious. We need a proper socio-graphic mapping because religion has to be explored in depth in different historic-geographical niches before our over-generalized data and our over-generalized theories can yield properly sophisticated understandings. Certain kinds of local religious ecology are relatively resistant to secularization and we need to know more about the conditions affecting a successful or a failed resistance, including topography, communications, size of towns, size of region and degree of regional autonomy among them.

Let me first say something about these resistant niches. In the United States they are found in the American South and South-West, and broadly in the extensive belt of what is geographically and socially Middle America. In relation to the 'liberal' North-East coast of the USA, and to the Pacific West coast, with

---

[2] Thomas, Keith, *Man in the Natural World: Changing Attitudes in England, 1500–1800* (London: Allen Lane, 1983).

[3] Bäckström, Anders, and Davie, Grace, with Edgardh, Ninna, and Pettersson, Per, (eds), *Welfare and Religion in 21st Century Europe* (Aldershot: Ashgate, 2010, vol. 1).

its experimental spirituality and Far East outcrops, the bastions of conservative religion are often related to ethnic concentrations, for example the Scots, so-called Anglos, and African-Americans in many parts of the South, together with major pockets of Hispanics, and in the Mid-West major concentrations of Greeks, Poles, Germans and Scandinavians. The South is more Protestant in a revivalist tradition and the Mid-West more Catholic and more Protestant in various Lutheran traditions. The pattern shifts with migration both to the North and to the South and the 'sunshine states', but the fundamental point relates to the juxtaposition of religious groups retaining some serious ethnic base, such as the Hispanics of Florida or the Germans in parts of Texas, all of them situated in a vast area of conservative and dynamic religion.

The USA as a whole has been known for the remarkably stable character of its religion since indices peaked in the mid-twentieth century, and that has remained true until recently, even if Americans have throughout reported a higher level of practice than was in fact the case. Since the 1990s however, there has been a significant increase in the proportion of Americans, up to about one in five, reporting no religious affiliation. Until now America has been the place where voluntary organizations thrived, religious organizations included, but the appearance of more young people without denominational anchorage, may signal an important shift, though this probably represents a more individualized (self-actualizing) religion than straightforward secularity, as well as the transfer of a Catholic pattern of disaffiliation from Latin to Hispanic North America.[4] The USA remains the most obvious example within the Protestant religious universe of a non-secular and indisputably modern society, but that does not mean one can describe what happens there as de-secularization.

Some commentators have claimed that the religious factor in the public sphere and in American politics has been much more in evidence over the last decade, but Jimmy Carter's presidency was some thirty years ago and the mobilization of the religious right behind the Republicans also goes back several decades. Much depends on whether you are referring to the relation of religious affiliation to voting behaviour, which has always been a factor, or the kind of controversy that arose over the Catholicism of Kennedy, or the covert or overt use of religious language. The significance of President Obama may lie in the mobilization of several religious groups, such as the Hispanics and the African-Americans, behind a charismatic, religiously committed and Democratic black candidate. That could, perhaps, constitute a break with the older alignments in the 'culture wars' and one which is paralleled by shifts among some Evangelicals out of the Republican camp, more particularly in the Mid-West rather than the South. We are talking therefore about some disaffiliation, perhaps connected to a perceived over-politicization of

---

4   For further discussion of this complex issue one can consult 'Who Has Religion?' by Christopher McKnight Nicolson in *The Immanent Frame* (www.ssrc.org/programs/the-immanent-frame), 21 Dec. 2009.

religion in the Bush era, and about a possible and partial breakdown of recent alignments in the culture wars. But we are not talking about de-secularization.

As for Canada it might be seen as a geographically enormous but thinly populated and relatively secularized 'periphery' of the USA. The Canadian Pacific coast and the Canadian Rockies, with their lower religious indices, continue the pattern to the South in the Pacific and Mountain regions of the USA. There is a strong Scots Presbyterian presence in the Centre and West of the country, and a Greek and Ukrainian presence in the Central regions that might be seen as mirroring the Greek and Polish concentrations to the South around Chicago. Toronto is arguably the most multi-cultural city in the whole of North America. Toronto apart, Canada has been described as more a mosaic than a melting pot. It has a smaller Evangelical sector relative to its overall population than the USA and the mosaic creates what one might call quasi-establishments in different parts of the country, which may help explain why it is has a somewhat less vital competitive voluntary religious sector than the USA.[5] At the centre of the mosaic is the vast province of Quebec constituting the largest stronghold of what would have been a French North America, stretching down in a long arc from Quebec city to Des Moines, Saint Louis and New Orleans, had the conflict with the Anglo-Americans from 1756–63 gone the other way. The situation in French Canada was one of rapid secularization, comparable in scale to what happened in Holland at the same time in the sixties. French Canada contains well over 40 per cent of the Canadian population and its distinctive and separate identity used to be defined by its Catholicism. Today Québécois identity is more defined by culture and language. At the same time Reginald Bibby has argued that a perception of a continuing movement downwards in religious vitality is merely what the media take for granted, not an inference from the figures, which have remained stable and quite high since the nineties: 25 per cent weekly attendance, 35 per cent monthly. Bibby goes so far as to suggest that organized religion has been making a comeback, in spite of the demoralization of some of its leaders by what they read in the press.[6] Still, if one takes the situation before the sixties as a reference point, Canada provides little evidence of secularization in reverse.

Supposing we now turn to the resistant areas of Western Europe to see how they have fared over recent years, before summarizing the evidence for Western Europe as a whole. There is nothing in Western Europe to compare with the vast reservoir of conservative religion in Middle America and that is partly because European countries are more centralized whereas the USA is more federal. Perhaps Germany is a partial exception to this on account of its federal structure, and maybe Italy also, because its elongated geography dictates vigorous regional

---

[5]   Stackhouse, John, *Canadian Evangelicalism in the Twentieth Century* (Toronto: Toronto University Press, 1993); Noll, Mark, *A History of Christianity in the United States and Canada* (Grand Rapids: Eerdmans, 1992: chapter 17).

[6]   Bibby, Reginald, 'Canada's Dateless Debate about Religion', *Implicit Religion*, 12: 3 (2009): 251–69.

politico-religious cultures, above all a sharp divide between North and South. In Western Europe as a whole the key media and intellectual elites in the national capitals have much more leverage than in the USA, particularly through the control of national education systems, and I would surmise that this greater nationwide leverage includes federal Germany.

One should never neglect the impact of elite secular control of an integrated educational system on religious culture, such as is found pre-eminently in France and has been increasingly evident over recent decades in Britain. Nor should one neglect the impact of comprehensive welfare systems and the ethos of the welfare professions. Both education and welfare have been historically suffused with Christian motivations and the transfer of both sectors to the nation state has transformed those Christian motivations into professional expertise, even though the welfare professions may be disproportionately represented in Christian congregations. The caritative impulse has undergone a partial bifurcation, with the priest being the one who comes alongside others in their joys and deep distress, and the welfare worker making appropriate and rule-governed dispositions for their better support and care. What the work of Davie, Bäckström et al. shows is the dominant role of the state in welfare in the Protestant North, with some delegation of functions to churches, and the dominant role of family and Church in the Catholic/Orthodox South, with overt cooperation between Church and state in Germany and more covert complementarity in France than one might expect.[7] In the group of examples following I shall underline the role of centralized media alongside the role of centralized education and welfare.

Brittany, Southern Holland (indeed perhaps Holland as a whole), and Ireland provide examples of regional niches once known for their resistant piety in Western Europe, and in all of them major secularizing trends have been evident, even though there are quite distinctive reasons lying behind those trends. Brittany is the kind of Celtic periphery found also in Ireland, but with a combined linguistic and religious base, now being eroded. Holland, in particular in Southern Catholic Holland, had integrated multi-confessional cultures organized around religion, which collapsed under the liberalizing pressures of the sixties, assisted by the impact of Vatican II and the attainment of Catholic cultural and political aims.[8] What happened in Holland provides just one very dramatic instance of the breaking down of the boundaries protecting homogeneous cultures in a bi-confessional society. Ireland is a self-defined 'Celtic' society which culturally defended itself in religious terms against incorporation in Protestant Great Britain and became a virtual theocracy for at least two generations after a period of initial political autonomy prior to independence. But then Ireland joined the EU, and prosperity followed, and in its wake there emerged an intellectual and media elite ready to take on a Catholic Church mired in sexual scandals and unused to the necessary arts of self-defence.

---

[7]   Bäckström and Davie, *Welfare and Religion in 21st Century Europe*.

[8]   Van Rooden, Peter, 'The Strange Death of Dutch Christendom', in Brown and Snape, (eds), *Secularisation in the Christian World*, 175–96.

Attendance dropped, especially among young people, though from a very high initial level, and vocations went into crisis.[9]

These exemplary instances of religious resistance undermined are worth setting against the case of French Canada mentioned above. In French Canada a European settler society defended itself against the rest of Canada and Protestant North America in religious terms, and achieved most of its aims. At the same time French Canada underwent a liberalization which combined with the effects of Vatican II to shift the basis of cultural defence to language. Modern media, above all television, exercised a major influence in all these cases.

It is worth saying something more about Britain because it provides an example of religious decline on a scale comparable to Holland. That can be judged by the recent work of Anthony Heath et al. in Britain, showing how religion retains the character of a serious reference group but one greatly reduced in size, and of De Graaf in Holland showing a greater divide in Holland than in Britain between a still quite large religious constituency and a seriously secularized majority.[10] Britain ought, in terms of the historic importance of voluntary organization, including competitive religious denominations, to have more resembled the USA. Religious adherence in Britain held up reasonably well in the immediate aftermath of the Second World War, as was also the case in continental Europe, but the sixties saw a rapid decline, as did the nineties, and the age profile of the churches is so weighted to the older age groups that the smaller voluntary religious bodies struggle to survive.[11] Indeed, the Methodists, now with less than 300,000 members, and with a tilt towards the elderly, have felt obliged to unite with the Anglicans, who suffer from a similar tilt. As in Holland Evangelical groups with a firm ethos and providing moral guidance, emotional expression, and friendly communal relations, have survived relatively well. Religion is a declining factor in voting behaviour in Britain, just as it is in Western Europe.[12]

The state of religion in Britain makes the condition of voluntary societies dedicated to the inculcation of values of service or cultural improvement in the country peculiarly relevant to the condition of the churches, for example bodies like Sunday Schools, youth clubs, the Mother's Union, choral societies, Village

[9]   Foster, Roy, *Luck and the Irish: A Brief History of Change 1970–2000* (London: Allen Lane, 2007).

[10]   De Graaf, Nan Dirk, and Te Grotenhuis, Manfred, 'Traditional Christian Belief and Belief in the Supernatural', *Journal for the Scientific Study of Religion*, 47: 4 (2008): 565–98; Heath, Anthony, Martin, Jean, and Elgenius Gabriella, 'Who do We Think We Are? The Decline of Traditional Identities', in A. Park, J. Curtice, M. Phillips, and M. Johnson, (eds), *British Social Attitudes* (London: Saga, 2007: chapter 1).

[11]   Voas, David, 'The Continuing Secular Transition', in Pollack and Olson, (eds), *The Role of Religion in Modern Societies*; R. M. Morris, 'The Condition of Modern Belief', in R. M. Morris, (ed.), *Church and State in 21st Century Britain* (Basingstoke: Palgrave Macmillan, 2009: 153–72).

[12]   Kellner, Peter, 'Dave's New Best Friends', *Prospect*, March 2010: 33–6.

Institutes and Townspeople's Guilds, the Scouts, Crusaders, and other groups, like the Boy's Brigade, that are virtually folk memories, if that. These organizations, in common with teaching in primary schools, were often chosen as spheres of activity by women, and the changes in the meaning of gender and of the role of females in employment have affected their character, and that may well have had a negative impact on religion.[13] The centralization and bureaucratization of education and especially of teacher training since the mid-twentieth century, has had a further negative impact on religion. To this one might add transformations in attitudes, not only to long-term organizational commitments but to personal responsibility, punishment, guilt and, above all, the concepts of ethical and aesthetic 'judgement' as those relate to any hierarchy of values. The interactions are very complex and not to be automatically swept under generalized concepts like rationalization. If I wanted to document the displacement of Christianity in Britain as a natural point of reference for believers and non-believers alike I would do so in terms of the assumptions that in the earlier part of the twentieth century can be discerned in the writing of good authors of the second rank like John Buchan, Elizabeth Goudge and Howard Spring, when compared to contemporary authors.

Exactly when the ethos of voluntary service or of personal responsibility underwent transformation is disputed, some observers pointing back to the thirties or earlier, others to the sixties, but the erosion of organizations lying within the penumbra of Church attachment, like Church teacher-training colleges and a shift in the attitudes of primary school teachers, is not seriously in doubt. In Britain there is a pervasive scepticism about almost everything, allied to an embarrassment about enthusiasm, especially religious enthusiasm, that is conspicuously absent in the USA, and may even have something to do with Britain's decline in the world. Attitudes were much more 'American' and voluntary organizations much more vital at the height of Britain's power in the nineteenth century. My main object in using Britain as an example of the variable fate of voluntary organization is to remedy the relative neglect of this penumbra of Church attachment, but it also relates to what I want to say later about the vast expansion of the voluntary principle in the world at large. It is a paradox that what was characteristic of Britain and in some ways a British (or Anglo-American) social invention linked to the churches is now expanding globally while contracting in Britain.

This is the point to refer parenthetically to Australasia because Australia and New Zealand both replicate the secular and secularizing tenor of religion in Britain, though the several ethnic groups that historically have occupied the British Isles are represented in different proportions: Irish Catholics are a major presence in Australia and Scots Presbyterians in New Zealand, especially the South of South Island. Both New Zealand and Australia are religiously plural societies, combining

---

[13]   Brown, Callum, *Religion and Society in Twentieth Century Britain* (London: Pearson, 2006).

local quasi establishments and ex-territorial churches, for example Catholic Italians and Orthodox Greeks, with numerous religious voluntary associations.[14]

Religion in the rest of Western and Central Europe also offers little evidence that 'God is back' or of post-secularity. The Scandinavian pattern of low practice and high identification has altered little and characterizes much of Northern Protestant Europe. People 'resign' from the Church in Germany, but the majority retain this minimal form of identification, even though the weight of numbers shifts in a Catholic direction, as it has also done in Britain, Holland and Switzerland.

Overall Catholic identification and practice have suffered less erosion in Western and Central Europe than the Protestant state or local churches, but Catholic countries have not escaped secular pressures. All European churches exemplify in different degrees the Westphalian principle of the dominance of a particular religion in a given territory, in spite of a trend towards voluntary belonging and to personal seeking rather than automatic quasi-uniformity. It may well be that the role of the state and of state religion operating as monopolistic service stations is responsible for Europe's exceptional secularity.

The Alpine region covering countries like Switzerland and Austria, has experienced major secularizing tendencies, but pockets of relative isolation have meant a continuing degree of majority identification and broadly affirmative belief, with comparatively little explicit atheism, while in Latin Europe the epicentre of secularity remains France, especially the Paris basin, with Spain semi-secularized in the wake of the demise of Franco, and Italy more stable, even though commentators refer to a fragmentation of belief. The polarization between Catholic and socialist regions has decreased, with Alpine areas like Western Austria and Bavaria becoming less actively Catholic, and socialist cities like Vienna and Bologna less actively anti-clerical.

The Catholicism of the Mediterranean littoral has more in common with the culturally embedded religion of parts of Eastern Europe, and the highest indices of religion are found in this region, for example in islands like Malta, Crete and Cyprus. Malta has one of the highest indices in all Europe of identification with Catholicism, of Catholic practice, and of belief in God. This is what I mean by a resistant niche. Whereas three in five people do not believe in God in the Czech Republic, two in a hundred do not believe in God in Malta. According to Joe

---

[14] There are major differences between Australia and Canada which cannot be discussed here, but focus on the major role exercised by the Canadian clergy in promoting a modest version of the Enlightenment, absorbing evolution and initiating nationwide systems of education and social welfare. These collapsed in the 1970s, but did not exist in Australia to the same degree, where a more straightforwardly republican and secular ethos exercised considerable influence. This difference is beautifully brought out in: Hilliard, David, 'Towards Secularisation and One Step back', in Brown and Snape, (eds), *Secularisation in the Christian World*, 75–92; Christie, Nancy, and Gauvreau, Michael, 'Secularisation or Resacralisation? The Canadian Case, 1760–2000', in Brown and Snape, (eds), *Secularisation in the Christian World*, 93–118.

Inguanez the trends in Malta are entirely characteristic of those found in other strongly Catholic countries, though starting from a level as high as that in Ireland.[15] Mass attendance each week involves about one person in two in Malta, three in four in Gozo, but the trend is downwards with each generation and there is a variation in Malta between 87 per cent and 35 per cent, the latter figure applying to the old dockyard area. Transmission from generation to generation has weakened as it has all over Western Europe. There is the same decline in polarization between the Church and politics found elsewhere and the same increase in consumerism, competition and greed. There is the same inclination to a spirituality of 'Me and God'. At the same time there is greater participation among those who do attend mass, greater personal involvement, more interest in prayer, scripture and spiritual direction, and increased lay initiative. As elsewhere liberal intellectual Catholics have some reserve towards popular devotions and what can be called the element of popular effervescence represented by rival village processions and fireworks.

Malta provides opportunity to remind ourselves of the kind of secularization found in shifts in the law away from specifically ecclesiastical norms to a form of regulation based on a complex amalgam of rights and broad agreements about the social good or utility. Malta does not legalize divorce or abortion, though there is increasing pressure for change. It may be compared in that respect with its nearest neighbour Italy, which legalized divorce in the mid-seventies and, at the other end of the continent with Holland, where a highly secularized society is associated with one of the most libertarian legal regimes in the world.

Clearly nothing in the evidence so far provides any colour to the idea of de-secularization or post-secularity. Eastern Europe provides examples both of the most secular countries in the Christian world and the least, and the startling differences between countries adjacent to each other depend on the positive or negative historic relation of religion to different nations faced by a forcible secularization by secularist elites mostly imposed by alien power. Poland, Romania, Slovakia and Croatia stand in one column while the Czech Republic, Estonia and the former DDR stand in the other. Romania is a special case because the survival of the Romanian Orthodox Church, as distinct from other churches, including those associated with the Hungarian minority, was linked to a continuing relation to the state under a communist regime asserting national autonomy.

I do not want to repeat my analyses elsewhere of the detailed variations in Eastern Europe, beyond saying that if there is evidence of de-secularization rather than a re-emergence of religion strengthened by trial, it is to be found in Albania, Bulgaria and the Russian Federation. All three countries were subject to severe anti-religious measures by secularist elites, and a vacuum was created with the evanescence of communism over the period from the mid-eighties to the early nineties, now partly filled by religion. Bulgaria is interesting because its nationalism is attached to the land itself and its religiosity more individualized

---

[15]   Inguanez, Joe, A., *'Pastoral Commentary' on Malta: Sunday Mass Attendance Census 2005* (Malta: Discern, 2009).

than institutional. Orthodox identification has increased but attitudes remain rather secular. Serbia is also interesting because the re-emergence of the Church is associated with a revived Serbian nationalism which expresses itself in the lighting of candles but not in the more 'intrinsic' aspects of an internalized religiosity. Like Poland it sees itself as a victim nation and one at an exposed frontier.[16] Both Bulgarians and Serbians anticipate a growth in the number of believers.

Adherence in Eastern Europe is not to be judged by criteria of weekly attendance but by expressions of religiosity embedded in culture, such as pilgrimages, the tending of the dead, the lighting of candles, and obeisance to icons. In Russia there is a genuine return of Orthodoxy and in some areas the young and rural are more religious than the old and rural. Religion has returned to the public sphere, even though separated from the state, as part of the aura of historic national continuity and power. Indeed churches throughout the sometime Eastern bloc have returned to the public sphere as accepted participants, and the political representatives of countries like Poland can express opinions about the public role of religion in the fora of the EU which Western Europeans find surprising. Ukraine is interesting and important because it was a part of the Soviet Union that retained functioning churches to a far greater extent than the rest of the country. It is also more pluralistic than any other of the now fully independent countries of the Eastern bloc, at least in the western half of the country, where Catholicism jostles with several Orthodox churches and also with Evangelical Christians. The voluntary principle, based on competition, makes only modest progress in the Eastern bloc as a whole, but it stands a better chance where there is already a degree of pluralism, which often occurs in border country, as in Transylvania and the Western Ukraine.

Nearly all Eastern European countries from Greece to Lithuania are characterized by an ethno-religious nationalism inimical to cultural, ethnic and religious diversity. Throughout the Balkan/Middle Eastern area minority religious communities, Christian on the one side and Muslim on the other, have experienced expulsion for the last century and a half at the hands of an exclusive nationalism, including the nationalism of the communists in Bulgaria. The Serbian attempt to extrude Muslims was only the latest episode in a very long history that includes Russian imperial expulsion of minorities, both Christian and Muslim, as it advanced southwards, and Muslim massacres of Christians throughout the near East. My sense would be that in much of this area, in particular in Turkey, Egypt and in the immediate near East, the shift to a secular nationalist politics at the elite level, sometimes under European, especially French, influence, has been reversed.

---

[16] Naletova, Inna, Tomka, Miklos, and Zulehner, Paul, *Religionen und Kirchen in Ost (Mittel) Europa* (Wien: Entwicklungen seit der Wende, 2008).

Religion in the Two-thirds World

That completes my comments on North America and Europe, and *both* cultural blocs can be seen as exceptional when compared to the rest of the world, to which I now turn, in particular Latin America and Africa. In doing so, I aim to bring out the expansion of the voluntary principle, except of course in North African countries with settled Muslim majorities. Throughout my argument I am contrasting the kind of religion based on birthright, territory and kinship with the kind based on a voluntary decision to join a fictive transnational fraternity – or sorority. Of course, it is true that religion in many parts of the world is now a matter of choice due to various kinds of mobility, and that voluntary associations inevitably bring children up as members of a denominational culture, but the analytic distinction still holds. In Christianity it is signalled by adult rather than child baptism.

Christianity includes both types of religion, because it grew out of a faith based primarily on birthright, as signalled by circumcision, and was then for three centuries a voluntary organization until adopted as the official religion of a territorial empire. Early Christianity placed great emphasis in its foundation documents on being embedded in Hebrew Scripture and drew many of its initial converts from diasporic Judaism, while at the same time using the Hebrew idea of the incoming of the Gentiles to power its universalizing message. In the geographically and socially mobile world of today, with its global communications, much of Christendom – and beyond – is characterized by a transnational voluntarism, of which Pentecostalism is the most dramatic example. That means that the spread of global communication, currently eroding the resistant religious enclaves in Europe, is elsewhere assisting the global spread of transnational voluntary associations such as make up the dominant form of religious organization in the USA. At the same time, as I have argued elsewhere, the territorial, or perhaps more properly the birthright principle, is very tenacious, and can maintain itself over many centuries in diaspora, as the history of the Jews and the Armenians shows. My discussion will focus on the two most potent forms of contemporary Christianity: Catholicism, with its roots in birthright adherence and strong links to the collective and the state, and Evangelicalism (in particular Pentecostalism) with its roots in voluntarism, separate from the state and associational in character.

I turn first to Latin America, where the spread of voluntarism at the expense of birthright belonging first became evident. The initial reaction of many observers was to see this dramatic shift as simply an extension of American imperial and cultural power in the religious field, and it is only as the shift has been documented in areas where the American link is implausible or remote that it obviously has its own autonomous dynamic. To note that voluntary religion has historically been most characteristic of the USA is not the same as tracing every case of its emergence, from Ethiopia and Uganda to China and Kyrgyzstan, back to American cultural power.

Lain America was until the mid-twentieth century regarded as religiously homogeneous and firmly rooted in the Latin Catholic mode of birthright Christianity associated with a canonical territory. Thus a Jesuit father once said to me that other religious bodies had no right to proselytize there, a viewpoint with which the Russian Orthodox Church might heartily agree faced in its own canonical territory by the same disconcerting 'incursions'. Of course, Catholicism in practice has taken many forms in Latin America. In the past it has served both to legitimate conquest and resistance, and in the late twentieth century it has legitimated and provided schooling for established elites, exercised an 'option for the poor', sought the kind of authoritarian modernization associated with Opus Dei and generated a form of charismatic Christianity rivalling Pentecostalism.

When it comes to the issue of secularization and de-secularization two features stand out. One is the reproduction in Latin America of the struggle between clericals and anti-clericals characteristic of Latin Europe, especially France. This struggle reached a climax in the Mexican Civil War virtually parallel to the Spanish Civil War, and one may say that the radical secularism this generated has by now greatly declined. The second feature is the failure of radical elites to mobilize what was a sclerotic system of control, however centralized in theory, to secularize the mass of the population. France largely succeeded in doing this through centralized education but the French-influenced elites of Brazil did not. The continent remained inspirited, apart from one or two places, like the European settler society of Uruguay, where a secular elite associated with a particular university succeeded in creating a society rivalling the Czech Republic in its secularity.

Pentecostalism was the product of all kinds of mobility and in particular created a portable identity moving in a protected caravanserai to the megacity, and a kind of popular mobilization indifferent to the patronage of erudite elites. So it represents two radical shifts: a portable identity free of the entanglements of social and ecclesiastical hierarchies, and an autonomous social space unencumbered by intellectual patronage from above. The effect of this shift is mainly to turn apathetic Latin American Catholics into active Pentecostals (or members of Evangelical churches 'in renewal') and in many places to stimulate a revivified Catholicism. This is neither secularization nor de-secularization but a major reconfiguration. I would add that the extent of conversion to a voluntary Evangelical religiosity varies from about five per cent to 25 per cent, with the average being about ten per cent. This seems to me to mark an upper limit of expansion likely to be followed by a plateau, a point that will acquire further relevance in the discussion of Evangelical/Pentecostal penetration in the Far East and the Pacific. I conclude that neither secularization nor de-secularization is relevant in Latin America.

If we now turn to Africa it is a continent even more inspirited than Latin America. It lacks the emplacements of established territorial religion over centuries such as one finds in Latin America, except in parts of the Muslim North, and the boundaries of national states are even more arbitrary than elsewhere, give that they enclose several tribal groups potentially in conflict with each other. The missionary Churches often have a history of European establishment and in sub-Saharan Africa can sometimes act as local quasi-establishments, for example the Catholics and Anglicans of Uganda. They can be in 'critical solidarity' with governments and they often provide the basic welfare and educational infrastructure of weak or failing states. As for African elites, they were often the products of missionary education, or secular education in Europe, or both, and they were inclined to create hybrid quasi-religions, owing something to Christianity and/or socialism, and infused with what was held to be an authentic African spirituality.

This phase of Africanization was accompanied by the increasing emergence of African independent churches, like Aladura in Nigeria, and then by the emergence of Pentecostal churches, many of which aspired to a global modernity and rejected Africanization as backward looking. The appeal of Pentecostal churches was paradoxical, because they not only aspired to modernity but absorbed elements of African spirituality in a way that led converts to regard them as more authentic than their mainstream competitors. Perhaps this potent capacity to be simultaneously modern and indigenous derived from a spiritual genealogy in the USA that in the early twentieth century fused African-American and white revivalism. Indigenization included both the 'holiness' traditions of classical Pentecostalism and the 'prosperity gospel' of Neo-Pentecostalism. The prosperity gospel of health and wealth fused easily with an African religious tradition that managed misfortune and at the same time sought God, the good and the 'goods', in what I have described as an 'Afro-Jewish' manner.

If we now turn to the Far East and the Pacific we find a very different contestation between the voluntary and the territorial or birthright principle, because the established territorial religions of Asia are non-Christian and often regard conversions made by voluntary religious organization as latter-day manifestations of colonial penetration. In India the extension of political participation to the mass of the people has meant that the secular orientation of the immediate post-imperial elites no longer defines the state and Hinduism has been politically mobilized as the authentic religious expression of Indian nationalism. Catholics form the largest Christian Church and have some territorial concentration in Southern India, for example Kerala, and it seems that Catholicism has adapted itself to India over time in several different ways.[17] Pentecostalism is also concentrated in the South, and it too has adapted to its Indian environment.

My main interest here is in the variable penetration of Evangelicalism and Pentecostalism in the countries of the Far East ranging from Singapore and Malaysia to Taiwan and Korea and (by far the most important) China. In this vast region, Malaysia and Indonesia are mainly Muslim, while the dominant established religion elsewhere is Buddhism. With regard to our theme of secularization and de-secularization we are dealing above all with a secularist Chinese communism and its attempt to wipe out religion and superstition. It is difficult to talk about de-secularization in other countries, unless one takes into account the violent destruction of the communist party in Indonesia and some recovery of religion, Catholic, Buddhist and other, in communist Vietnam.

---

[17]   Cannell, Fenella, *The Anthropology of Christianity* (Raleigh-Durham, NC: Duke University Press, 2006).

The variable penetration of Christianity in Far Eastern countries represents a major and fascinating problem of interpretation for comparative sociology: one per cent in Japan, five per cent in Taiwan, ten per cent in Indonesia, 15 per cent in Singapore, 30 per cent in South Korea. In Indonesia and Malaysia there is a major concentration of Christians in beleaguered Chinese minorities, as well as in several distinct local groups, for example in West Irian and Sarawak. Of course these Far Eastern nations represent very different kinds of society, but if we look at the Christian impact on modernizing or modern Buddhist societies and on the mixed religious economy of a highly modernized Singapore certain patterns emerge. A lot depends, just as it does in Europe or indeed anywhere, on the relation of Christianity to nationalism. In Korea Christianity, particularly Presbyterianism, lay at the heart of Korean national revival in the context of Japanese and Chinese domination, whereas in Japan Christianity was seen as foreign and threatening. In Taiwan it was held severely in check by an oppressive nationalist government, and in Singapore tightly controlled by a government that wanted all religions to provide order and cohesion. In all these societies, as in Africa, Christianity was associated with modern welfare and education, even when it was only the kind of small minority found in Japan. Scottish and Canadian Presbyterians provided the basis of the education system in Taiwan, and American Presbyterians helped create the education system of Korea. The pattern of response to the impact of both Christianity and modernity is also fairly clear: Buddhism reforms itself in what is sometimes known as a humanistic form, to provide the kind of social benefits associated with Christianity, and creates its own versions of voluntary religious organization. One could describe these changes under the rubric of the consequences of competition, similar to the consequences we noticed in Latin America of competition between Catholicism and Pentecostalism. A more, or less, large secular sector emerges, 15 per cent in Singapore and 45 per cent in South Korea, though that is a complex issue where there is large scale participation in folk festivals. None of this, however, can be organized as evidence for or against secularization, though the emergence of a secular sector such as one finds in Korea should count in favour of a modest version of the secularization thesis.

For the evidence that is most dramatically relevant to secularization and de-secularization we turn to the massive programme of forced secularization in China, following the same impulse to wipe religion out that animated secularist elites in Russia and Eastern Europe. In short our main evidence for de-secularization, relates to the aftermath of militant Marxism, an aftermath that is also relevant to Islam, since what were once Marxist elites in Muslim countries turned later to an anti-colonial Islam.

What patterns, then, do we observe in a society comprising one in six of the world's population, keeping in mind that China bids fair to share hegemonic status with the USA. There is a revival of Buddhism, some of it popular, some of it of the 'humanistic' cast already noticed elsewhere in the Far East. There is also some interest in a revival of Daoism as the one kind of religiosity indigenous to China and a parallel revival of Confucianism as an ethical system capable of securing the social order and harmony central to the policies of China's communist elites, as it was also to imperial China. The issue then arises as to how far the expansion of Christianity and the resurgence of Islam are compatible with this elite programme of social order and harmony.

As for Islam, the main anxiety amongst the Chinese concerns separatist tendencies in some border areas in the West of the country. These tendencies are regarded as more threatening than parallel Buddhist movements in Tibet, though both kinds of separatism are countered by the mass movement of Han Chinese in to disputed areas to swamp local populations. As for Christianity, it is overwhelmingly voluntary and without the kind of territorial base occupied by Muslims and Tibetan Buddhists, though Catholicism has historically related itself to complete local communities, and arouses concern on account of international control from elsewhere. Protestantism once had a strong relation to imperial powers, notably Britain and America, but contemporary Protestantism appears fully indigenous. One has to ask about the social locations of an expanding Christianity, about the likely policy of the government towards a movement that now rivals the communist party in size, and about the implications for any thesis positing de-secularization.

Protestant Christianity, much of it reinvented from scratch in a form that has some Pentecostal characteristics, has various social locations. One is in the modern business, IT and student sector of the burgeoning megacities, including Wenzhou where the proportion of Christians may be as high as one in five. In the megacities one finds the dynamic megachurches of registered Christian bodies and lively unregistered house churches. The other location of Christianity is mainly in rural areas. It seems that the Cultural Revolution in China physically uprooted the emplacements of folk religion and that Christianity moved into the vacuum, particularly among women, who combined a new access to a high God with traditional concerns about the management of misfortune. As the Muslim West and Buddhist Tibet are now multi-ethnic areas, they too are infiltrated by Christianity. Some of those responsible for policy towards religion are inclined to shift the understanding of the meaning of 'the opiate of the people' towards a medical metaphor referring to the relief of pain. Provided religious bodies are not associated with ethnic separatism or foreign influence they may well be left alone, and the old policy of repression intermittently abrogated. There may well be some gain to the state in harnessing religious bodies to cope with costs, especially in the spheres of welfare and social dislocation, of breakneck modernization. In the expansion of some religious bodies and the relaxation of elite hostility one may reasonably see a measure of de-secularization, although much depends on the arbitrary predilections of local bureaucratic cadres.[18]

---

[18]   Madsen, Richard, 'Pre-modern Religious Policy in Post-Secular China', unpublished paper delivered at the International Sociological Association meeting in Gothenburg, July 2010.

Clearly in all that I have argued de-secularization has relevance in two spheres only: the mass mobilization of peoples unhappy with secular modes of governance seen as western-inspired, and the partial reversal of the consequences of the communist attempt in Russia and China, and also in countries like Ethiopia, to suppress religion. In the highly specific case of Western Europe there is no evidence of de-secularization and in Latin America and sub-Saharan Africa secularization was always an elite affair and today one observes various kinds of religious revitalization in social worlds always inspirited. In the USA we have yet another highly specific case, where the crucial secularization relating to the state occurred very early as part of an increasing plurality of voluntary religion. This increased in vitality with modernization, and with minor exceptions remains dynamic to this day. However, to remain religious is not to experience de-secularization.

Re-enchantment and Disenchantment

Disenchantment is a notion closely tied to rationalization, and insofar as we are considering scientific approaches to the manipulation of natural phenomena I would have thought it far advanced and synonymous with modernity. Americans may believe all kinds of nonsense about channelling or aliens but that is solely matter for private fantasy. The Iranian government may believe this or that about the future course of history and eschatology but its procedures for obtaining enriched uranium are identical with those of the Americans.

In the same way Britons may harbour all kinds of notions about the meaning and source of illness, just as they conventionally talk about the weather in terms benign or malign forces, but they rarely believe in curing illness by witchcraft or manipulating the weather by spells. Appeal to the miraculous with regard to natural processes is either figurative or a strategy of last resort. There is a widespread interest in alternative medicine of course, but on the assumption that there are understandable natural potencies untapped by conventional medicine. In a discussion of 'cool occulture' Christopher Partridge refers to a vogue for paganism, pagan mythology, occult powers and witchcraft in the popular culture of young people.[19] He suggests young people also find spiritual resources in 'pagan' narratives. Partridge concludes that popular artefacts contribute to the construction of 'new sacralised plausibility structures' and that this counts as re-enchantment. My response would be that this vogue for enchantment in a fantasy world is probably continuous with all kinds of inchoate belief attributing animation to the inanimate or meaning to meaningless events. But when the chips are down people hang on desperately to what the next scientific advance promises in medicine, welfare, hygiene or warfare rather than trying to conjure responses by resort to the occult. I see no serious de-secularization here in the wake of a vogue for 'occulture'. That there is 'a cultic milieu' or that there is some resort to holistic

---

[19]   Partridge, *The Re-enchantment of the West*; Gibson, *A Re-Enchanted World*.

understandings of some consequence I do not doubt, though I do not see it as filling a gap left by the decline of organized Christian religion or fulfilling criteria of serious de-secularization. What the holistic milieu may illustrate is the triumph of the therapeutic principle.

But that is not the end of the story because there is also the question of a revolution in our attitudes to nature. Such a revolution has been largely influential in middle rather than working class milieux, so that the natural world has now become an object of reverence, even worship, and the environment sacralized. Arguably we have lost any sense of transcendent purpose in history or a historical narrative of redemption from evil, in favour of a return to a monism (which of course can be atheistic) or to a mystical pantheism mostly undertaken as part of a personal experiential quest. There is what Ernst Troeltsch called a 'parallelism of spontaneities' in pursuit of purity, especially the purity of Nature as embraced by 'green' causes. Hans Kippenberg has traced in scholarly detail the extent to which Christianity in the nineteenth century was criticized for cold rationality and lack of affect in its approach to Nature and the mystical.[20]

All this involves a rejection of a personal God and of organized churches, as well as a turning away from doctrine, patriarchal authority, and male violence, including the violent exploitation of the natural world and the animal kingdom. Exploitation is associated with industrial capitalism, even though some of the worst polluters have been societies in the sometime 'Eastern bloc'. To some degree the ethical yields place to the aesthetic, to a sense of pan-human communion and the union of the self with others, with animals and Nature. Much of this might be assimilated to the category of personal mysticism and gnosis.

Again, my initial reaction to this is puzzlement, because as someone brought up in the nineteen thirties in an evangelical sector of the world's first industrial nation, all these 'novelties', including the care for animals, the delight in the natural world and even the interest in vegetarianism, are perfectly familiar to me. I was early familiarized with Scripture but never encountered an exegesis of the now much-quoted text giving man dominion over nature. If you look at the hymns of the period one of the most ubiquitous was a hymn by Mrs Cecil Frances Alexander, wife of an Evangelical bishop, called 'All things bright and beautiful', and one of the most quoted poems was one that claimed 'You are nearer to God in a garden than anywhere else on earth'. Historically the place of landscape in art goes back at least to Dürer in the sixteenth century, and I recollect a vein of responsive love for the natural world as the arena of God's Creation that goes back to writers like Thomas Browne, Milton, Marvell, Vaughan and Traherne in the seventeenth century. If the eighteenth-century Deists have been, and are currently, indicted as casting a cool scientific eye on Nature they also delighted in its majesty and intricacy. The longer tradition of what is now renamed 'creation spirituality' reaches back considerably more than two millennia through St. Francis and the

---

[20]   Kippenberg, Hans, *Discovering Religious History in the Modern Age* (Princeton: Princeton University Press, 2002).

Celtic saints to the idea of the paradisal Garden of Eden found in the second creation narrative in Genesis. One also finds celebrations of the works of the Lord in the first creation story in Genesis, in Psalm 104, in the peaceable kingdom of Isaiah, and in the book of Job.

If the exploitative attitude to nature is going to be blamed onto Protestantism and capitalism, it is surprising that the influence of a care for the natural world and the animal kingdom has most of all been characteristic of Britain, Australia, Canada, and the United States. Christianity and Judaism have both been deeply opposed to dualism, though there is in the history of the Church a spiritual struggle against what are seen as carnal lusts, which sometimes takes extreme forms, as well as against inordinate self-centredness, pride and greed. For this kind of discussion one needs an exploration in depth of notions like nature and the natural, not simply snapshots of recent trends in California, however interesting these may be.

In the course of a learned discussion, Christopher Partridge quotes the historian Keith Thomas on the rise and fall of witchcraft but does not mention his equally important book on *Man and the Natural World* which deals with our problem, more particularly in England. This book includes the narrative of a major change in attitudes to nature dating back half a millennium with significant episodes in each successive century. But Thomas also invokes a much longer historical backdrop and documents contrary tendencies which qualify that narrative in a major way. I want to use Thomas's analysis and deploy extended comments by Alan McFarlane, to reflect on numerous paradoxes.[21]

Alan McFarlane summarizes one major thrust of Thomas's argument as documenting the theme of disenchantment from 1500 to 1800 and hailing it as just the kind of revolution that would enable one to regard re-enchantment as a counter-revolution. But then, like Thomas, he also draws attention to a broader and historically much longer horizon that throws disenchantment into doubt, apart from the magical manipulation of occult forces operative in Nature. Here Christianity itself can be cited as a secularizing influence over many centuries, which was operative well before the Reformation. It may also be salutary to recollect the revolt against Christian rationality in relation to Nature that took place in the mid-nineteenth century long before the recent re-enchantments. If one is thinking about affective attitudes to Nature rather than magic and witchcraft then it may well be that the incidence of disenchantment does not offer us anything like a straightforward picture of change in one direction. The same holds true of the incidence of anthropomorphism, which is sometimes cited as a parallel development. The Bible asked 'What is man that thou art mindful of him?', the Renaissance made 'Man the measure of all things' and Alexander Pope in the eighteenth century assigned man a 'middle state, both greatly rude and rudely great'.

I pick up McFarlane's argument at the point where he is stressing the difference between the 'Anglo-Saxons' and the French when it came to the number of

---

[21]   McFarlane, Alan, *The Culture of Capitalism* (Oxford: Oxford University Press, 1987: 77–97).

major regional cities in France compared to England, as well as the power of local potentates and the lack of centralization. He argues that the relative political security provided by a small but powerful and early nation-state created the conditions for a well controlled economy. This economy was distinguished by an individualistic capitalist mode of production that both put a price on every thing and could afford to regard certain aspects of nature as priceless. Late medieval and early modern England was a society that had the wealth and leisure to treat Nature, trees, flowers and animals as intrinsically delightful. The spread of literacy was so widespread that it helped undermine the distinction between urban civility and rural idiocy. It was also possible in an individualistic kinship and marriage system for the English to be great meat eaters *and* devoted to particular animals *and* opposed to cruelty to animals. Indeed studies of the origins of vegetarianism point to religious noncomformity and its negative attitude to rural sports.

Both Thomas and McFarlane bring out the religious factor. They refer to the paradoxical relation in Christianity between the goodness of God's ordered creation, free of magical presences, given as a paradise garden for our delight, and the divine mandate constantly to labour upon it for its improved use-value and for human wealth, health and betterment. Ascetic Protestantism picked up and emphasized an ascetic attitude that had long predated it, which combined with other factors to bring nature under control and allow 'a sentimental re-integration on Man's own terms'. By 1500 and even more by 1650 attitudes to the world of nature were in place that may even go back to Germanic rather than Roman 'civic' origins. They were later to be preserved and flower ever more luxuriantly in the course of the Romantic Movement from the 1780s on, with the onset of the world's first urbanization and industrialization. We are dealing therefore, not with a revolt against individualistic capitalism but varying tendencies within capitalism itself at play now all over the world. In this sphere de-secularization and secularization exist in a dialectic relation with each other, not in some unilinear fashion understood as a definable sequence towards the secular. As for de-secularization in general I have indicated that the most obvious cases relate to the world-wide collapse of the Marxist functional alternative to religion: a constituency of more than one and a half billion people. Elsewhere we have continuing secularization in the special situation of North-Western Europe, a fairly steady religious state in the special situation of the USA, and in Latin America and Africa the persistence of largely inspired universes for which secularization and de-secularization are alike largely irrelevant.

Chapter 6
Religious Responses to
Modes of Secularism

I want to reflect critically upon the very idea of 'religious *responses*' (or *reactions*) to 'modes of secularism'. In itself the notion of religious responses carries no particular implications since it simply provides a useful starting point. However, a critique of the partly invisible mind-set often lurking behind it allows me to clarify my own approach to questions I tangled with over forty years ago in *The Religious and the Secular*.[1] In my conclusion below I also situate the dichotomy of the religious and the secular within the tension between faith and 'the world' because that tension belongs to specifically Christian language. The specificity of Christian language is crucial to a wider historical understanding of the secular. The secular is an initially Christian category rather than simply the opposite of what is after all the 'essentially contested' concept of religion, and one needs to understand both the positive and negative Christian evaluations of the *saeculum* to grasp the varying characters of such Christian incursions into it as monasticism and Evangelicalism.

Nevertheless, in most of what follows I seek to clarify my problem with a notion like 'religious responses' and to suggest why it can sometimes be far from innocent.[2] I want to excavate why it seems 'natural' to refer to 'religious responses' to modes of secularism rather than secular or secularist responses to religion. In the course of my critique I shall canvass some of those secularist modes, and their long-term genealogies.

My problems begin not only with some of the broad assumptions lurking behind 'religious responses' but also with some of the linguistic usages now apparent in the term 'secularism'. 'Secularism' used to have an established and delimited signification in sociological writing as denoting an anti-religious ideology putting forward a programme, minimally designed to restrict religion to the private sphere and maximally to eliminate it altogether. Maybe I overestimate the stability of that usage even among sociologists, but the current use of secularism blurs important discriminations. Secularism understood in a restricted sense is not at all identical with secularization. Secularization has been used by sociologists and others, as the governing noun for a set of social processes, which may or may not include the programmatic ideology of secularism, but usually include other nouns of process

---

[1]   Martin, David, *The Religious and the Secular* (London: Routledge, 1969).
[2]   Marty, Martin, and Appleby, Robert Scott, (eds), *Fundamentalisms Observed* (Chicago: University of Chicago Press, 1991).

like privatization and rationalization. Unfortunately, sociologists have not been able to protect their usages against a journalistic use of 'secularism'. Nowadays secularism popularly denotes an amalgam which includes social movements and ideologies which have the conscious intention of restricting the influence of religion, *and* secular changes and processes with the net effect of doing so. One cannot deal analytically with such an unstable amalgam.

'Secularism', understood as an anti-religious ideology and/or movement, emerges under specific social conditions, most significantly in world-historical terms as a *response* to the particular kind of religious formation obtaining in pre-revolutionary Catholic France and pre-revolutionary Orthodox Russia. It was then transferred in mutated form to non-Christian contexts, for example the Kemalist ideology informing the Turkish Revolution of 1922 and the Maoist ideology animating the Chinese Revolution of the late 1940s. Of course, secularization understood as a process, occurred in various forms long before that. It occurred, for example, when the Church was 'nationalized' in the early modern period by monarchs and emperors from Henry the Eighth to Louis the Fourteenth, Joseph the Second and Peter the Great. Karl Marx might well have approved of such a usage in writing of the state religion in Germany, and the particular historical example of 'nationalisation' illustrates the complexities of the whole issue because it involves the partial transfer of the aura of the sacred from the Church to the institution of monarchy and later to the nation as a whole. It suggests that the history of the sacred is distinct from the history of Christianity and even in opposition to it, given that Christianity was in its origins and even from time to time in its history a movement removing the aura of the sacred from lands and cities, kings and emperors.[3]

The secularism of today, which has presumably stimulated and reinforced the current journalistic usage, stems from a variety of sources. One source lies in a polemical exhumation of a Victorian debate over religion and science. The polemicists often seem influenced, knowingly or not, by the restrictive protocols about meaningful statements promoted by a philosophical positivism reaching back through A. J. Ayer to the Vienna Circle, though an earlier and different nineteenth-century positivist movement also proposed a 'mode of secularism' reaching back to Comte and especially influential in France and Brazil.

Another source can be located in the attitudes of leading cadres in the European Union. These attitudes are perhaps most obvious within the Franco-Belgian political axis, but they are also widely disseminated in the various intellectual and media elites of Northern post-Protestant Europe. These elites characteristically insist on a certain ideological conformity, in particular conformity to the notion that religion is a private matter excluded from the public forum, though the demand is much more a prescription than a description of what is or has been the case. That is particularly obvious when one considers the crucial contribution of religion, especially the Catholic Church, to the formation of what became the European Union, as well as

---

[3]   Martin, David, *Does Christianity Cause War?* (Oxford: Oxford University Press, 1997).

the long-term dominance of Christian Democratic parties within it. Of course one may well argue that such parties underwent an internal secularization, conceding primacy to a profane consumerist dynamic, but that shift cannot be subsumed under the history of secularism as an ideology. Internal secularizations are, of course, historically endemic (the fourth century establishment of Christianity by Constantine, the sixteenth century Papacy, American Civil Religion) because the criteria for identifying internal secularizations go back to the primitive Christian category of 'the world' and 'the worldly' I discuss in my conclusion.

It is important to distinguish between situations where the official norms of the Church, more particularly in matters of sexual morality, contraception and family regulation, exercise a decreasing influence on secular law, and the ability of religious bodies to make contributions to public debate, for example on small business, war, housing, race, minorities and migrants. If one makes such a distinction it begins to look as though the specific influence of the churches is more and more in the public realm by comparison with its decreasing role in the private realm. The acceptance of divorce in Italy in the mid-seventies or recent changes in Germany and the USA regarding stem-cell research can be seen as instances of secularization in particular sectors of public regulation, though many Christians undoubtedly feel that certain kinds of ecclesiastical rule on sexuality ought not to be enforced as a matter of national policy. As the birth rates of European Catholics clearly indicate, the views of Christians and the views of some ecclesiastical institutions are far from identical. One does not need to be a secularist to reject the imposition of ecclesiastical *rules* as distinct from the promotion of Christian values in the public sphere, and in the USA the wall of separation between Church and state ensures that most Americans have come to reject any close relation between an ecclesiastical discipline and public law-making.

The specific role of *secularism* in bringing about changes in the public realm, especially law, can be traced back to the radical anti-clericalism of the nineteenth century, and to the secularism of radical liberals and republicans, responding in some degree to the kind of claim embodied in the Catholic Syllabus of Errors (1864) and the pronouncement that 'Error has no rights'. Such *responses* go back in one way or another to the French Revolutionary and French Enlightenment tradition. By a reversal of positions, the suppression of error emerged in the twentieth century as the principle that *religion* had no rights, enforced globally by militant communist secularists from Ethiopia to North Korea, and by no means dead in contemporary secular polemic.

There is then a long-term genealogy in the history of secularist ideas and movements reaching back to the Enlightenment. Both the positivist (or scientistic) polemic, and the ideological positions required by influential intellectual and media elites, claim that genealogy, and proponents and opponents alike recognize the role of what is simplistically labelled 'the Enlightenment Project', as though that were a unitary source. Maybe the regular citation of 'the Enlightenment Project' owes something to the influential work of Jürgen Habermas and Alasdair MacIntyre, but I am not equipped to identify what role these major thinkers may have played in disseminating the idea of '*the* Enlightenment Project' based on reason and human autonomy.[4] Historically, of course, there were numerous enlightenments arranged along a spectrum from an often vigorous hostility to religion in the French case to varying degrees of overlap with religion in the American, English, Scottish, Dutch, Swiss and German cases.[5] The point is substantial given the vast contemporary influence exercised by the heirs of the American Enlightenment all over the globe, and the diminished influence of the heirs of the French Enlightenment, notwithstanding the continuing influence of the latter in the global academy.[6]

Not merely does elite opinion mistake the role of religious bodies in the public sphere, by assuming the prescriptions and restrictions advanced by elite opinion correspond to an empirical state of affairs, but it also mistakes the actual state of religious belief and practice. Clearly there are large areas of Western Europe where religious constituencies are declining and religious political influence diminishing, and these trends have been visible for some time in voting behaviour and the decline of Christian Democracy. Such trends are to some extent linked to political re-compositions following the extensive collapse of a secularist western communism. The decline of religion has a very complex relation to the decline of some of the older kinds of militant secularism, as well as to a further, but only marginally related, decline in long-term organizational attachments, including political and religious grass roots organizations.[7]

It is therefore really odd that there has been a shift of intellectual opinion *away* from the notion that religion is unimportant. It now appears religion is considered alarmingly resurgent to the point where it endangers programmes designed to restrict it to the private sphere, or alternatively that it is of sufficient importance to be reconsidered as a candidate for contributions in the public sphere. As religion has constantly made such contributions even in the places where the intellectual opinion formers actually live, it needs some explanation, and I would cite the increased salience of Eastern Europe with the expansion of the EU, and the impact of Muslim minorities in Western Europe and Islamism elsewhere. As for Eastern Europe, the major role of religion in public debate is not so much a matter of resurgence, as of the end of secularist persecution and suppression, in particular since 1989. Only the increasing public presence of Muslim minorities has much to do with religious revitalization, though it is also related to levels of migration and a differential birth rate. The revival of religion and the restoration of its public role in the Russian Federation and Ukraine lies outside the EU and only figures marginally

---

[4]   MacIntyre, Alasdair, *After Virtue* (Notre Dame: University of Notre Dame Press, 1981); Habermas, Jürgen, *Between Naturalism and Religion* (Cambridge: Cambridge University Press, 2008).

[5]   Sorkin, David, *The Religious Enlightenment: Protestants, Jews and Catholics from London to Vienna* (Princeton: Princeton University Press, 2008).

[6]   Himmelfarb, Gertrude, *The Roads to Modernity: The British, French and American Enlightenments* (New York: Vintage, 2006).

[7]   Davie, Grace, *The Sociology of Religion* (London: Sage, 2007).

in the European debate. I attribute most of the change in intellectual opinion to the influence of Islam, in spite of some other global influences mentioned below.

Greece affords an interesting example of the problems which can follow from the idea of 'religious responses' to secularism. Greece is marked both by the Byzantine tradition of a *symphonia* between Church and State and by a strong ethno-religious sentiment stimulated by resentment against an alien Muslim imperialism. Very many Greeks, whether religious or not, have been glad of a long standing membership of the European Union but also resentful towards what they perceive as the imposition of western secular norms by Brussels. The Greek Church mobilized opinion against what were widely regarded as alien intrusions on Greek culture. In that limited sense the Greeks of South-Eastern Europe were rather like American Republican Southerners protesting against the intrusion of Supreme Court rulings from 'the centre' on local culture. They were 'responding' to rulings that attacked the idea that membership in an ethnic community and Greek citizenship could be identified legally with a particular religious tradition. However, the legal shift required by the EU is unconnected with a wider secularization and Orthodoxy remains profoundly embedded in Greek culture. As for Greek secularism, it is in part a *response* to the political influence of the Greek Church. More than that, Greece has historically cherished a secular and Hellenistic as well as a Byzantine heritage, and both are built into Greek nationalism.

Thus far I have suggested we are not dealing simply with religious responses to secularism but also with secularist or secular *responses* to religion in a historical spiral of interacting responses. Religion is a potentially interacting variable, and not necessarily a dependent (or epiphenomenal) variable. What then are the other global influences on the debate mentioned above and what kind of debate is it anyway? The global influences are quite varied, and they go beyond the revitalization of Islam to include the kind of ethno-religion found, for example in India, associated with the BJP and propagating Hindutva. The emergence of such movements is associated with the mobilization of masses in the two-thirds world, the role of newly educated middle classes in that mobilization, the backwash against colonialism and the end of an era when many newly independent countries were ruled by secular elites trained by or influenced by the West. These changes can be put together under various colourful rubrics, for example Gilles Kepel's *The Revenge of God* published in 1993 and *God is Back* by John Micklethwait and Adrian Wooldridge published in 2009.[8] These books influence elite opinion more than the kind of careful survey of the continuing role of religion in the public sphere over many decades in Casanova's *Public Religions in the Modern World* published in 1994.[9]

So far I have not highlighted the situation in the USA, but apart from Islam it provides the example most often cited of a 'return of religion' in the 'public

---

[8]   Kepel, Gilles, *The Revenge of God: Resurgence of Islam, Christianity and Judaism in the Modern World* (Cambridge: Polity, 1994); Micklethwait and Wooldridge, *God is Back*.

[9]   Casanova, *Public Religions in the Modern World*.

square'. Yet the mobilization of religiously conservative constituencies in the USA is now decades old and has arguably undergone the same kind of diminution in influence experienced by religion in Europe. This is an instance where one might reasonably speak of a response to secularism since the democratic mobilization of religious conservatives was stimulated by decisions of the Supreme Court and by the cultural and moral revolution of the sixties and seventies, though that was itself not without important religious motifs. At the same time the developments of the sixties were themselves defined as responses to the stifling religiose conformity of the post-war period. Once again we are dealing with continuing and complex interactions, and interactions that are by no means exhausted by simply parsing them as alternations between religion and secularism. One should remember that the religiosity of the immediate post-war period was analysed by commentators as internally secularized, and that the Civil Rights Movement in the sixties represented an unprecedented mobilization of religious opinion.

The mobilization of the Religious Right is, therefore, hardly the kind of recent novelty that should lead to current reorientations of intellectual opinion, whether by way of arousing alarm about a recrudescence of religious influence or by a more positive reassessment of the public role religion might properly play.[10] In any case Americans have rarely impugned the right of voluntary religious bodies to contribute to public debate. Voluntary associational life is an unchallenged part of the dynamic of American democracy and routinely cited by way of contrast with some parts of Europe. For example, the Catholic Church in the USA has over decades contributed to discussion on the economy and on peace and war in major and much debated official statements. Abortion and euthanasia are not the only religious concerns.

Perhaps the idea that religion has become more important in the public realm in the USA has less to do with conservative mobilization since the 1970s than with the publicity accorded the religious views of George Bush, reinforced as that is by a desire to establish the same kind of equivalence between the moral status of the USA and militant Islam as was earlier held to exist between the USA and the former Soviet Union. This postulated moral equivalence was the mirror image of the huge moral disparity assumed on the American political right in the Reagan era between the USA and the 'evil empire' of Soviet Russia, and in the Bush era between the USA and an 'axis of evil', including 'fundamentalist' Iran. Some Americans saw this Republican attitude as an illegitimate politicization of religion, and the recent increase in Americans with no denominational address expresses this resentment without necessarily involving a change in attitudes to religious belief. I suspect we are being dragged along on the coat-tails of American culture wars, especially their increased intensity during the Reagan and Bush eras, and by rival attempts made by the combatants to gain the higher moral ground. In culture wars, as in other wars, truth is the first casualty and political righteousness and victory the prime considerations.

---

[10]   Bruce, Steve, *Politics and Religion* (Cambridge: Polity, 2003).

The same holds true with regard to the role played by the category of 'fundamentalism' in American, and by extension, European culture wars. Fundamentalism has been constructed as a moral panic whereby movements defined as non-liberal, or as non-liberal Christian, are swept together to occupy a shared fundamentalist category, and one in which American conservative Christianity is portrayed as playing an analogous role to Islamic fundamentalism, to demonstrate how religion per se is the principal source of contemporary reaction, conflict and social oppression. Those who promote this view locate a root source of malignancy in the 'dualistic' separations of good and evil held to characterize religion though they substitute instead a dualism between good secularism and bad religion. Clearly competition over what is factually and empirically the case in the disputatious area of religion and 'secularism' is linked in a very complicated way to moral competition over claims to superior righteousness (and/or civilization). Attempts to establish what the philosopher Gillian Rose called the 'broken middle' are liable to go unheeded.[11]

Matters are made more complicated when it comes to the issue of religion in the developing world, not merely by the definition of religious cultures as not *really* modern, but also by the vocabulary of 'orientalism' and the labelling of discourses as 'colonialist'. Orientalism can be deployed to counter critiques of Islam, and colonialism can be deployed to ward off critiques of the cultures and the political corruption of ex-imperial territories, notably in Africa. In the field of Pentecostalism, which is principally a phenomenon of the 'two-thirds' world, an anti-colonialist discourse is used to criticize it by the governing elites of that world and by some anthropologists defending the integrity of culture against exogenous change, especially religious change. Increased religious multiculturalism is far from universally welcomed. The vast expansion of Pentecostalism is therefore defined as an American imperial export. That this is historically dubious makes little difference, because the charge is integral to the claim that Western Christian religion in particular was damningly implicated in the movement of Western imperial expansion. For a discussion of that issue one might turn to Norman Etherington (ed.) *Missions and Empire* (2005) because it shows in what ways Christianity and empire were aligned and also opposed.[12]

In fact Pentecostalism was nurtured in a fusion of white revivalist and African-American religion that pre-adapted it to cultures in the two-thirds world. It is carried by people of any number of ethnic groups moving around that world and shows a quite extraordinary capacity to indigenize. It is worth adding that the social aetiology of Pentecostalism is sometimes rooted in 'responses' to poverty, as is suggested by the plateau in its expansion in Chile during the period of rising living standards in the Frei era, and sometimes rooted in the search for

---

[11]   Rose, Gillian, *The Broken Middle: Out of Our Ancient Society* (Oxford: Blackwell, 1992).

[12]   Etherington, Norman, (ed.), *Missions and Empire* (Oxford: Oxford University Press, 2005).

autonomous social space in the face of other dominant religions. Perception of a secularist threat is rarely if ever a serious factor.[13] It is true that Pentecostals in Brazil have been aware of hostile secularist reactions in the Worker's Party but the massive expansion of Pentecostalism in Brazil is not a response to that hostility. Pentecostal churches and the Worker's Party have inevitably had to respond to each other, largely by making appropriate accommodations, including substantial Evangelical support for Lula in some recent elections.

The alignments of opinion constantly shift making it difficult to get one's rhetorical dispositions right, especially when addressing more than one reference group. For example, liberal opinion is divided about Islam because liberalism simultaneously demands respect for other cultures at the same time as liberal imperialism 'crusades' (sic) against regimes of which it disapproves. Liberals note, sometimes sotto voce and on occasion very loudly, that Islam offends most obviously in those areas it cares most passionately about. One effective strategy is for liberal secularists to concentrate on the criticism of Christianity on account of its lack of respect for other cultures while holding in reserve the contention that Islam, like all religion, is backward because it is not infiltrated and tamed by secular liberal modernity like Christianity. Another secularist strategy is to lambast Islam as currently the most prominent case of false beliefs and inhumane practices, while reminding one's readers that Christianity, like all religion, has in the past exhibited precisely these objectionable features. At the same time as this goes on liberal Christians and Muslims can cooperate in a common cultural defence of a religious mode of life (and/or minority cultures in Europe) against militant and 'culturally insensitive' secularist criticism. Tariq Modood, for example, as a cultural Muslim, makes an interesting case on Oakshottian grounds for the established Church of England as a helpful vehicle of Muslim cultural defence. Or again, some conservative Western Christians and radical western secularists can agree that indiscriminate respect for cultures and for the 'Other' can serve to hide tyranny and political corruption and to defend the indefensible. This is a quite likely combination when it comes to cultures with the kind of anthropological 'integrity' that condemns women to legal and cultural inferiority. Secular feminists and missionaries are here aligned together, at least pro tem.[14]

Occasionally a cross-bench viewpoint makes itself heard, for example Austin Dacey's argument in *The Secular Conscience*, that religion belongs in public life, in part so that its feeble arguments can be better rebutted by the secular conscience.[15] Roger Trigg, a philosopher and a Catholic, argues that religion should be attended

---

[13]   Martin, David, *Tongues of Fire: The Explosion of Protestantism in Latin America* (Oxford: Blackwell, 1990) and, *Pentecostalism: The World Their Parish* (Oxford: Blackwell, 2002).

[14]   Keane, Webb, *Christian Moderns. Freedom and Fetish in the Mission Encounter* (Berkeley, CA: University of California Press, 2007).

[15]   Dacey, Austin, *The Secular Conscience: Why Belief Belongs in Public Life* (New York: Prometheus Books, 2008).

to in public debate because it is rational and therefore fulfils liberal criteria of acceptability.[16] Both Dacey and Trigg appear to be arguing against proposed restrictions, but neither stresses that this debate is in several bad senses academic, because people can, will and should voice their views publicly as fellow human beings and citizens.

Arguments in this area are judged not simply on their merits but on the stances and alignments those who promote them are presumed to exemplify. That poisons debate. Moreover, the stances people adopt in these contestations, especially when they turn significantly around contestations between religion and secularism, are influenced by their social location and experience, including their historical experience as a group. For example, Israelis with an historical experience of central Europe and Russia, are likely to view religion through a perspective shaped both by the restrictions of the religious ghetto and by the persecutions instigated by their neighbours. They may also be worried by the part played by the religious parties and Shas in Israeli politics.[17] Secular Zionism is partly a product of a central European experience and of the historical context provided by secular European nationalism with attendant ethno-religious cleansing. However, Israelis with an American experience as their historical hinterland may have a rather different view. American Jews quite often gravitate from a left-wing secularist attitude derived from a European experience to a far more sympathetic position based on their American experience, and influenced by unhappiness about left-wing hostility to Israel.

It is axiomatic that intellectuals approach issues of secularism and religion through their national experience. French intellectuals have an historical hinterland which includes radical secularism while German intellectuals may remain exponents of *Kultur-Protestantismus* and Polish intellectuals may recollect the rigours of secularist persecution more than the cultural dominance claimed by the Catholic Church. All the different attitudes just canvassed have varied historical experiences of different types of religious formation behind them and cannot be herded together under the head of 'religious *responses*' to secularism. They belong to the spiral of religious-secular interactions.

I referred earlier to the assumption that religion is reactive rather than active, a notion deriving in part from the idea that religion is epiphenomenal and socially reactionary. That further implies it blocks progress to a fully secular modernity, and one that is defined normatively, not in terms of social scientific criteria. Once religion is excluded by definition and as a matter of social ontology from any properly constituted modernity, things become difficult for anyone analysing religion as a continuously active part of the transition to modernity. At best it is likely to be regarded as a transitional phenomenon en route to modernity rather than something capable of acting as a constitutive aspect of 'the modern' in all

---

[16]   Trigg, *Religion and Public Life*.

[17]   Lehmann, David, and Siebzehner, Batia, *Remaking Israeli Judaism: the Challenge of Shas* (London and New York: Oxford University Press, 2007).

its different manifestations. Once we *assume* that religion is only transitional, we effectively revert to the unilateral and universal version of secularization theory hatched in the particular circumstances of Europe. Yet that is precisely what needs to be determined by middle range theorizing rooted in comparative evidence. A universal secularization excluding religion by ontological fiat from any properly constituted modernity should not be our starting point.[18] Methodism was an *active* element in the modernization of Anglo-American culture, and has been credited with a major role in inhibiting the kind of revolutionary secularism characterizing parts of Europe.

Of course, as the example of Methodism illustrates over the period from (say) 1740 to 1940, religion changes in the course of modernization even as it also affects the course of modernization.[19] It responds to its environment and to circumstances just as the varying modes of secularism do. One example of a response to circumstances might be contemporary changes in communist China, including the reformulation of policy regarding resurgent religion. Religion in China may soon be officially regarded, if current debates go in a more tolerant direction, not as a dangerous opiate but as a useful medicine to sustain the health of the body politic. One might well discuss such prospective changes in China under the head of secularist responses to religion, except that I am not interested in inverting misleading assumptions. I want only to establish an interactive model instead of a one-sided model of interpretation betraying some indebtedness to an ontology dismissing religion as epiphenomenal and re-actionary.

After all, even the rather aggressive style of contemporary positivist atheism assigns weight to the stimulus of the events of 11 September 2001, and in that sense it too is 're-actionary'.[20] Of course in this case religion is credited only with a negative capacity to wreak havoc whereas the ongoing redefinition of religion as a health-giving medicine credits religion with a positive capacity. That too is important because there is a distinct asymmetry in defining religion as impotent and at the same time raising a public hue and cry about its remarkable power for negative purposes. A further influential assumption holds that 'fundamentalist' religion is inherently reactive, and reactive specifically in response to secularism, sometimes with the additional corollary that this hard kind of religion is the dominant and potent mode rather than the soft and impotent variety.

From a social scientific viewpoint we have to be sceptical and cautious when it comes to characterizations about what religion, treated generically, does or does not do within the ensemble of influences present in our contemporary word.

---

[18]   Stoeckl, Kristina, *Community and Totalitarianism: The Russian Orthodox Intellectual Tradition and the Philosophical Discourse of Political Modernity* (Frankfurt: Peter Lang, 2008).

[19]   Hempton, David, *The Religion of the People: Methodism and Popular Religion c.1750–c.1950* (London and New York: 1996); Abrahams, William, and Kirby, James, (eds), *Methodist Studies* (Oxford: Oxford University Press, 2009).

[20]   Eagleton, Terry, *Reason, Faith and Revolution* (London: Yale University Press, 2009).

All the forms of solidarity in developed society, whether religious or political/ideological (communism, socialism, liberal imperialism, nationalism and so on), can under given circumstances and in varying combinations of elements (economic, demographic, geopolitical, amongst others) lead to violence and conflict. It follows that any identification of religion as the main *active and negative* factor in contemporary violence is likely to be superficial and unscientific. I want therefore to establish not only that the religious and the secular are interactive but that any given nexus of events comprises numerous levels and interwoven strands, sometimes occluded by labels like the media usage of 'sectarianism'. The identification of a particular type of source as the malignant factor in human affairs has to be rhetorical. To stress this point about the attribution of largely negative consequences to religion is by no means to stray from the main issue, because there is a widespread assumption, not at all confined to active secularist polemicists, that 'religious responses to secularism' are last-ditch attempts to halt the liberation of humankind from *the* major illusion blocking the path of progress towards a less violent world order. To adapt and invert Shakespeare: take but religion away and hark what concord follows.[21] It is an assumption seriously implicated in state engineered mass murder.

Conclusion: Back to the Sources of the Religious/Secular Dichotomy

A further problem relates to the sources of the dichotomy between the religious and the secular and therefore to the whole discourse in which we operate. I have already suggested the notion of internal secularization is parasitic on Christian criteria, but that is only one element in what I want to argue. The genealogy of the secular, as Talal Asad has pointed out, has specific roots in Christianity.[22] Primitive Christianity and Buddhism both set up a tension with 'world'. They are therefore the pre-eminent forms of religion belonging to 'the Axial Age' as a period roughly covering the first half of the last three millennia and exhibiting a 'reserve' towards the world and the worldly. By contrast Islam and Confucianism are much less inclined to quarrel with the world order, wanting rather to subject it to law in the case of Islam, or to elicit a potential harmony of relations in Confucianism. Judaism, as the source both of Christianity and Islam, bifurcates into an acceptance of the world provided it is subject to moral precept and the law of righteousness, and a rejection of the world as contrary to God's perfect will and therefore awaiting transformation. Christianity mostly picks up the latter, along with some partial anticipations of universalism present in the later prophetic tradition of Judaism, even though it increasingly modifies its hope and expectation in the direction of law and mundane adjustments to wealth and power once it is adopted by the

---

[21]   *Troilus and Cressida*, Act 1, scene 3, line 109.

[22]   Asad, Talal, *Formations of the Secular: Christianity, Islam, Modernity* (Stanford: Stanford University Press, 2003).

Roman world and becomes 'worldly'. These are broad characterizations, of course, with the sole object of establishing the greater salience of the secular/religious dichotomy in two of the world's great religious systems and of underlining the special case of Christianity as a faith which makes a claim *over* the secular by expecting its transformation as the Kingdom or rule of God when the secular/religious dichotomy is abolished because 'God is all in all'.[23]

The angle of eschatological tension in Christianity is lowered or heightened according to circumstances, notably the presence or absence of crisis. The important point here is to recognize that the Christian religion in its foundation documents sets up the heightened angle of tension between faith and the secular, between the Christian Way and the Way of the World, which is written into cultures influenced by the Christian repertoire to this day. I use the term 'repertoire', because elements in that repertoire are taken up and emphasized, or alternatively half forgotten, according to circumstances and the kind of society in which they are disseminated, Roman, feudal, mercantile, capitalist or whatever. In primitive Christianity the violence of the world, with its greed and false objects of worship, is under judgement and shall at some point give place to a different order. That religious/secular tension, and the linked but not identical faith/world tension, is expressed and from time to time heightened in any number of ways up to the present day, in the sectarian undertow, in the movements of monks and friars, and in the Radical Reformation, Puritanism, Evangelicalism and Pentecostalism. It includes associated tensions and themes very much present in contemporary culture, such as the need for a change of life, the stress on mature choice rather than birthright membership, penitence and apology, the primacy of inwardness, sincerity and trustfulness (faith) over externalities, the essential fraternity and equality of human beings (expressed in Christian liturgy above all in the common meal), the redemptive role of the innocent and the victim, the supremacy of self-giving sacrifice in compassion and love, the integrity of the created order, and so on. Some Christian themes, like the remarkable rejection of 'honour' in the New Testament, have rarely succeeded in achieving more than a very partial penetration of social mores, as the honour code of chivalry in the Catholic Middle Ages indicates.

So the salience of the secular/religious dichotomy informing our current discourse specifically inheres in Christian civilizations and gives a distinctive character to the salience and meaning of secularization in Christianity, though it does not confine secularization to Christian cultures or define it as an exclusively Christian phenomenon. The religious-secular dichotomy is just one of those many elements that have partly lost their original marks of identification, but continue to inform our thinking. However, I am not engaged mainly in the retrieval of sources, which are usually numerous, but enquiring rather into what happens to our patterns, and to our conventional ages and stages, if we go back to basics and to the elevated tension between faith and the secular characterizing the developments of the

---

[23]   1 Corinthians 15:28.

Axial Age. I am interested in how the return to base lines permits us to revolve the fundamental parameters of the secular/religious distinction to create historical patterns significantly different from those generated by standard secularization theories as these are rooted in a pattern of historical advance whereby humankind makes a transition from darkness, oppression and ignorance to knowledge, liberation and enlightenment.

En-lightenment is a metaphor shared by the secular and the religious.[24] It follows that the particular transition just described exemplifies a pattern parasitic on the Christian transition from the time of ignorance and darkness to the liberation and light of Christ. But it is only one among several that can follow from taking a base line in the notion of 'the world'. These alternative patterns include the idea of internal secularizations whereby worldly motifs take over within religious institutions and stimulate extra-mural reactions outside the purview of official Christianity, or the idea that Christianity makes periodic incursions into the secular and then becomes itself internally secularized, for example under Constantine, or the idea that there is a continuous secular practice, for example with respect to the exercise of power and violence in society, which is only given secular articulation in Machiavelli, or a parallel violence in Nature only given secular articulation in Darwin, or the idea that the order of nature is secularized for empirical scrutiny and enchanted for reverence by turns, each return of enchantment being different. This is not the place to show how one may revolve fundamental dichotomies to achieve varying historical patterns. I want merely to underline their importance.

---

24   Davie, Donald, *Dissentient Voice* (Notre Dame, IND: Notre Dame University Press, 1982: chapter 2).

Chapter 7
Science and Secularization

In this chapter I discuss the relation of science to secularization with regard to the sociological frameworks of rationalization and social differentiation in the context of cross-national and cross-cultural comparison. I suggest there is no consistent relation between the degree of scientific advance and a reduced profile of religious influence, belief and practice. The crucial factors are sociological and historical, in particular the relation of religion to power and to the role of the intelligentsia in promoting radical social change. It is also argued that mental space constitutes a manifold so that there is in principle no zero-sum relation between science and religion.

That there is such a relation derives from the Enlightenment master narrative and it acquires much of its emotional power not from the logical consequences for religion of science as from a putative relation between religion and moral evil and the legitimation of oppressive regimes. However there are indirect consequences of science for religion through the social consequences of technological change. In practice the consequences of historical studies, for example biblical criticism, are probably greater than the direct consequences of science.

This issue is bedevilled by the way people talk about 'religion' and 'the secular' (and latterly 'secularism') as if they knew some essential meaning attached to those terms. The same is true for 'science'. It is also bedevilled by the way some educated people talk about what they believe *ought* to be the case rather than what actually *is* the case. That is because certain historic crises between science and religion have acquired an almost mythic status, in spite of recent revisionist history, for example the writings of John Brooke at Oxford. I am thinking of the Galileo controversy, of what Paul Hazard called the crisis in the European mind from the late-seventeenth to the early-eighteenth century, and of the controversy over Darwin.

I might be expected to revisit the philosophical issues involved, for example about the status and freedom of humanity, whereas I shall be for most of the time simply a sociologist. Being simply a sociologist is not as simple as it seems because I have to begin by explaining what we do and do not take seriously about theories of secularization. That involves a rapid dive into the inwardness of sociology with respect to concepts and procedures. It has to include a ragbag of different kinds of explanation from the advent of the car to the political alienation of the working class to the long-term processes of rationalization. There is also the distinction between science as a mode of understanding and the indirect consequences of science and technology for our everyday lives. My brief is to discuss the former yet sociological theories of secularization are more concerned with the latter.

The classic procedure of sociology in the absence of controlled experiment is cross-cultural comparison, so the core of what I argue has to turn on something so obvious, so crucial, and to my mind so compelling, that it is a sociological question why educated people do not take it on board. In terms of cross-cultural comparison, countries at roughly the same level with regard to scientific advance have religious profiles pretty well across the complete range. That means such general tendencies to secularization as may exist (other things being equal) have to be set against the contingencies of history and the particularities of culture where things are hardly ever equal. I also have to speculate about mental space. Do we, or some of us, entertain mental spaces where there is an either-or, as between science and religion, or is mental space a manifold where we call upon different kinds of discourse and understanding according first, to our individual context, and then to the degree of openness or closure of mental space made available to us by our culture.

I have to touch on the kind of religious mutations brought about by modernity, apart from straight secularization, such as the recent re-emergence of magic, the current interest in spirituality and the process Paul Heelas and Linda Woodhead call re-sacralization.[1] Finally, I have to open up a theme implicit throughout, which is the power of master narratives, especially the Enlightenment master narrative, to cloud over the sociologically obvious in favour of an 'obvious' but false hypothesis about religion receding as science advances. The French may think master narratives have had their day but in my view that only tells us they have lost the plot. Enlightened intellectual histories of the relationship of science and religion, especially their dubious assumptions about the avant-garde, obscure the actual data about secularization and mandate a principled ignorance about our global reality. That is why it keeps surprising us. Waiting for the world to play catch-up with us is a mug's game.

As I have hinted, my colleagues in the field of the sociology of religion, for example Grace Davie, Steve Bruce, Linda Woodhead, and James Beckford in the United Kingdom, might well regard rebuttal of so crass an idea as misspent time and energy. This is what the late Imre Lakatos, philosopher of science, would have called a 'radically deteriorating research programme'.[2] Once upon a time, somewhat before Darwin, many social scientists had their own evolutionary schemes where such ideas about science and religion were seriously entertained. The notion that there was a particular incompatibility between science and religion, and one that was of central importance in the decline of religion died in the fifties.

What then *do* sociologists of religion take seriously? They take seriously a positive relationship of some kind between religious vitality and vulnerability, whether on account of poverty, or the absence of support from a welfare state, or

---

[1]   Heelas, Paul, and Woodhead, Linda, *The Spiritual Revolution: Why Religion is Giving Way to Spirituality* (Oxford: Blackwell, 2004); Flanagan, Kieran, and Jupp, Peter, (eds), *A Sociology of Spirituality* (Aldershot: Ashgate, 2007).

[2]   Lakatos, Imre, *The Methodology of Scientific Research: Philosophical Papers* vol. 1 (Cambridge: Cambridge University Press, 1978).

both. They take seriously the privatization of religion, although not everybody is convinced about it, for example, José Casanova in his impressive rebuttal, *Public Religions in the Modern World* (1994).[3] The privatization of religion refers to its declining social significance for public rhetoric, legitimation, debate and policy. It has become inappropriate to invoke God in the performance of a public role. A former Downing Street adviser, Alastair Campbell, warned the then Prime Minister, Tony Blair, about to address soldiers destined for Iraq: 'We don't do God'. However, President Clinton was happy to invoke God even when welcoming the advent of the human genome project, so much depends on cultural context.

Sociologists also take individualization seriously, as linked to privatization. It is argued that we put together our own personal bricolage of religious attitudes and ideas and build our own individual spiritual pathway. So much for the Church. An example of this might be a comment by one of the Beatles: 'Why should ten thousand people believe the same thing?'

At this point I have to tip the ragbag of theories on to the floor. There is the effect of geographical and social mobility in breaking up dense communal relations, permeated by religion, and in breaking up the unity of the generations. There is consumer hedonism hostile to long-term commitments of any kind and unwilling to invest time and energy in maintaining institutions, religious or otherwise. There are the rival attractions of a picnic in the car, or Sunday morning football for the under-thirteens, or week-end entertainment in front of the television. There is the impact of secular control of education and the media, so that even personnel employed by the Church or in Church schools make pre-emptive strikes in favour of secular criteria and values alien to religion. Then, in the longer historical perspective, there is the displacement of religious solidarity by national solidarity or the claims of party political ideology. It is not easy to turn these assorted ideas and influences into joined-up sociological narrative, but they clearly have little to do with the impact of science, apart from the indirect consequences of scientific invention. Science as a technical procedure, available in this context or in that, is not the same as science as a mode of understanding. The philosophy of science, as practised by Feyerabend, Popper, Fodor and Hesse amongst others, hardly enjoys mass sales.

Sociologists take seriously their empirical indices and such basic organizing frameworks as rationalization, social differentiation and (already mentioned) privatization. As for empirical indices, religious belief and practice are routinely correlated with age, generation, gender, status, occupation, education, urbanization and so on to produce patterns of change. However, the crude data are not entirely self-interpreting, so that you have to put questions to them, such as how far a decline in female practice is due to changing female life-styles. How is it that, according to Andrew Greeley, any association between advanced education and irreligion has virtually disappeared in the youngest European generation.[4] If we

---

[3] Casanova, *Public Religions in the Modern World*.

[4] Greeley, *Religion in Europe at the End of the Second Millennium*.

find that natural scientists and technologists are more religious than practitioners of the humanities and social sciences that probably nudges us away from any idea that hard science is exceptionally incompatible with religion.

I turn now to our two crucial organizing frameworks: rationalization and social differentiation. You will notice we have entered an intellectual world dominated by schemata and nouns of process ending in '-ation'. Nouns of process have a way of implying movement from state A (religious) to state B (secular). So do schemata like the shift from Community to Association. That way we find ourselves tilted on a historical slope where any particular religious present is pregnant with a secular future. Michael Wheeler, in his study of the religion of John Ruskin, complains of precisely this way of thinking and shows how unjust it is when trying to understand Ruskin.[5] Another version of this approach, and one which still influences how we understand change, was the notion of progressive enlightenment associated with writers like Macaulay and criticized in 1931 by Herbert Butterfield in his *The Whig Interpretation of History*.[6] I discuss these kinds of master narrative later, only pausing to notice there are other master narratives of rotation, such as Sorokin's ideational and sensate periods, or narratives of decline such as Oswald Spengler's *The Decline of the West*.[7]

Rationalization is a concept we owe to Max Weber, and in his work it is more part of a narrative of decline towards what some people translate as the 'iron cage' of rational bureaucracy than of progress. It does not refer to the advance of abstract reason but rather to the consequences of increasing technical efficiency in rendering our world impersonal and disenchanted. Here we enter some of the indirect consequences of science, for example when we consider the increasingly rational and bureaucratic way in which we today organize health. Once there were hospitals named after St Bartholomew or St Thomas, but that religious frame has now been hollowed out, and the sense of a vocation to heal is now confined to the private motivations of individual carers and doctors. Clearly health is a sphere where the white coat of medical science is most pure and respected. On the other hand the grey suits of health bureaucrats and administrators are less pure and less respected.

The advance of rational bureaucracy was a theme developed by the late Bryan Wilson, and for him it belonged very clearly to a narrative of bleak decline.[8] As a major theorist of secularization he envisaged a regression from the personal, communal, religious and conscientious to the impersonal, fragmented, irreligious and de-moralized. Again this has little directly to do with the advance of science, at least of natural science. But I do find it interesting that an agnostic like Bryan Wilson should so bravely enter this contentious area to risk the coals of fire prepared

---

[5]   Wheeler, Michael, *Ruskin's God* (Cambridge: Cambridge University Press, 1999).

[6]   Butterfield, Herbert, *The Whig Interpretation of History* (New York: W.W. Norton, 1965).

[7]   Spengler, *The Decline of the West*.

[8]   Wilson, Bryan, *Religion in Sociological Perspective* (Oxford: Oxford University Press, 1982).

for anyone linking the decline of religion to the decline of morality, personal responsibility and conscientiousness. The counter arguments are obvious. Is the contemporary United States so obviously virtuous? Was the England portrayed in Hogarth's *The Rake's Progress* or in Jacobean drama so obviously responsible and clean-living? The criminologist and sociologist of morality, Christie Davies, has important things to say on this issue in his impressively documented *The Strange Death of Moral Britain* (2004).[9] He plots the indices of the decline of religion against moral and criminal indices, fully alive to all the caveats and personally conscious of both gains and losses. His focus is the same as Bryan Wilson's, and he charts the rise in nineteenth-century Britain, alongside modernity, of a personally responsible and conscientious kind of religion, propagated by the Sunday School, and by voluntary charitable organizations and voluntary youth organizations. This was a religious mutation rather than secularization, and it accompanied modernization and rapid advances in science. It does not fit a thesis linking either modernity as such or the advance of science to the decline of religion. Different observers argue about the moment this religious mutation took a different course, or if you like went into decline, but there is considerable agreement about a parallel rise and fall occurring all across Europe. Any correlation between fewer enrolments in Sunday Schools and greater knowledge of the Special Theory of Relativity is adventitious.

Christie Davies also relates these parallel changes to a shift from moral to 'causalist' understandings of human behaviour that owes something to social science and maybe genetics, as well as to a utilitarianism shifting from principles of moral justice to principles of minimum harm. Again these are gains and losses but I do not think anyone can be unaware of what has happened. Even criminals themselves have become expert manipulators of: 'We are sick, we are sick, we are sick, sick, sick; we are sociologically sick'. The social scientific translation of a Christian vocabulary relating to forgiveness and victimage is also pretty clear. I recently heard the family of Herod the Great cosily characterized from the pulpit as 'dysfunctional'. So much for mired in sin.

Yet sociology should maintain its usual reservations about the seemingly obvious here, where it is sociology and psychology rather than natural science that is to be blamed for the corrosion of religious language. When I hear young people referring to the apparently demoralized worlds in which they so often live, I hear expressions and judgements about 'bastard' and 'inappropriate' behaviour saturated in morality. Even my social work relatives and friends resort to moral judgements outside the immediate environment of what for them is clearly a moral vocation. As for the close neighbours of 'dysfunctional' families, their comments are downright theological. These are families from 'hell', and going to 'hell'. Therapeutic language may have triumphed but there is a persistent gravitation back to moral evaluation. The adjective 'pathological' is a judgement posing as a description.

---

[9]   Davies, Christie, *The Strange Death of Moral Britain*.

Of course, morality can be separated from religion both with respect to individual behaviour and in the context of moral philosophy. That is not at issue. Nor am I suggesting that just because there may be an inherent limit on the erasure of moral language there may be a linked and similar limit on the erasure of religious language. I am saying, however, that religious language is bound at the hip to moral language *and* that moral language of itself throws up analogues of religious understandings, such as the gratuitous, the redemptive, the salutary, and the justified, as well as locutions implying vertical as well as horizontal dimensions. Personally, I doubt whether either social or genetic determinism can erase the links between religion and morality implied by linguistic usages.

My discussion of rationalization has, following Bryan Wilson, included the role of technically efficient and impersonal means, in relation to morality. I now turn to 'social differentiation', which is my own primary framework for analysing secularization, though you will notice how it overlaps the framework of rationalization. In my view, social differentiation, while bringing about certain convergences on the secular, also allows room for a stress on historical particularity and cultural contingency when it comes to posited links between advances in science and declines in religion.

The concept of social differentiation has roots in the increasing division of labour and refers to the increasing autonomy of semi-discrete sectors of social life. One by one these sectors, for example law, social control, social legitimation, communication, health and education, acquire their own proper autonomy from ecclesiastical regulation and influence and from religious modes of thinking. Theology is no longer the automatic queen of sciences. Just as we are all aware of the impact of rationalization so social differentiation is part of every day experience regarding the autonomy, even conflict, of teacher with priest and of secular therapy with the priestly cure of souls when it comes to the dilemmas sometimes faced by health professionals in Catholic hospitals. If I wanted a small example with large implications of autonomy I might choose the partial edging out of the theologian on public bodies concerned with bio-ethics by philosophers or theologians talking philosophically. That change is part of a liberal claim to exercise universal objective jurisdiction as against all particular modes of thought and interest. That claim must be wrong, but it is not clear what the alternative might be, especially given that liberalism is so often a Judeo-Christian mutation, as both John Gray and Charles Taylor have argued.[10]

Since I believe social differentiation allows for historical and cultural contingency and variability I need to offer an illustration. The order in which different cultural sectors are differentiated varies historically, and the partial and then absolute separation of Church and state in the United States had momentous positive consequences for religion from 1790 to the present day. By contrast, the late separation of Church and state and/or Church and elite in Western Europe

---

[10]   Gray, John, *Heresies: Against Progress and Other Illusions* (London: Granta, 2004); Taylor, Charles, *A Secular Age* (Cambridge, MA: Harvard University Press, 2007).

had momentous and continuing negative consequences for religion. I also happen to believe rationalization is equally inflected by history and culture, having lived in Dallas, Texas, which is simultaneously one of the most rationalized and most religious metroplexes in the world. At the same time rationalization is patient of a much more universalizing treatment at the expense of historical particularity. There are those who, perhaps rather ethnocentrically, see post-Protestant Sweden and post-Catholic France as templates of the universal future. It might be nice but I suspect 'ought' and desire have once again run ahead of 'is' and historical plausibility. There is a way to go yet before Iraq approximates to Sweden.

So far, we have looked at some of the variables sociologists take seriously, at empirical indices and interpretative frameworks like privatization, rationalization and social differentiation. We have insinuated worries about historically tilted slopes, Whig interpretations of history, and the extent to which we are working within master narratives, particularly Enlightenment ones, and even, maybe, Kuhnian paradigms.

The way should be clear for my presentation of cross-cultural and cross-national data showing no consistent relation between the degree of scientific advance and a reduced profile of religious influence, belief and practice. However, in a way all too typical of my sociological tribe, I need first to step back for an essential point about sociological interpretation, at least as I position myself in the tradition of *verstehen* or understanding, and *Geisteswissenschaften* or cultural sciences. I emphasize understanding of signs as well as the explanation of indices. For our purposes I do that in the context of the depth and ambiguity of signs, in particular language, and the expansive manifold of mental space. There are emergent properties of action in the human universe not present in the physical or biological universes. I find them illustrated in the structure of motives in drama, including the constraints of options and alternatives for action in plotting, and the freedom of interpretation based on the way mutual anticipations are built into cues and scripts. This can be called the dramaturgical approach; and the point is to locate the right kind of scientific intentionality for any given problem not to transfer what works in one sphere of knowledge to another where it is inappropriate.[11]

Clearly the depth and ambiguity of symbols, signs, especially language, and the manifold character of mental space, bear quite directly on any notion of a zero-sum relation between science and religion. In mental space there is no such necessary either/or, because many different modes of ideation and discourse can be entertained simultaneously and selectively drawn upon according to context. Beyond that, the degree of openness and the degree of closure in mental space itself varies culturally, as between, for example, the constricted one-dimensional space of the former DDR, where either/or prevails, and the rather conspicuously wide open spaces of the United States, where angels, UFOs, and aliens happily cohabit with rocket science.

---

[11]   Duncan, Hugh Dalziel, *Symbols and Social Theory* (New York: Oxford University Press, 1969).

Allow me to press further this matter of the nature of mental space and to illustrate our recourse to different *kinds* of concept and discourse according to context. There is, for example, no difficulty about saying 'Your life in their hands', emphasizing the autonomy of medical science and the doctor, and 'He's got the whole world in his hands', emphasizing our dependence on profound spiritual resources. Consider also the difference between 'Great is truth and shall prevail' and 'You shall know the truth and the truth shall set you free' or 'I *am* the way, the truth and the life'? Here we enter into the phenomenology of being and freedom. I am not initiating a discussion of being and freedom or of the autonomous nature of language games here, but only stressing how sensitive we have to be about kinds of discourse to do justice to social complexity. There is more to sociology than causation, correlation, jargon, inverted commas and cultural relativism.

Now for my cross-cultural data: I am going to stay in the main with three revolutionary, scientifically advanced and rationalized societies, each with a widely different religious profile. I shall make one or two further observations, in particular about two other scientifically advanced and rationalized societies, Uruguay and Singapore, one where Christmas does not happen, except privately, and the other where everything happens in public and in private.

From a socio-historical perspective, the United States, founded on the basis of an Anglo-Protestant pluralism, experienced a relatively friendly relation between religion and Enlightenment, for example, the overlap of Episcopalianism and Masonry. Subsequent migration brought yet more Lutherans, Catholics, Jews and others, for whom religion was a residual anchor of distinct and sometimes regional identity in the American melting pot. Popular religion and elite Enlightenment mostly cooperated to support an inclusive civic nationalism. This was progressively based on common citizenship rather than an organic exclusive nationalism of ethnicity and language. That process came to an interim conclusion in the 1960s with the Civil Rights Movement. But the culture wars since the 1960s have not severed the ties of a common culture, for black and for white, for Hispanic and Anglo alike. By European standards American culture wars, however hot, are mere skirmishes, and the divides can be crossed, as they clearly have been in the person of President Obama.

In France and in Québec matters have been quite otherwise. In Québec an organic, ethno-religious and linguistic nationalism emerged, persisting up to the sixties when religion and linguistic nationalism to some extent went their separate ways. Religious practice dropped as dramatically as it did in Holland over the same period. In France itself a civic and linguistic nationalism established by revolutionary violence warred against a religiously informed organic nationalism. The climax came after 1870 with the Third Republic. Religious practice began to fall, Church and state were separated in 1905, and *laicité* has been dominant ever since. I need only mention one more difference, which is between the decentralized governance of the United States, and the centralization, particularly of education, in France. Decentralization inhibits attempts at ideological monopoly by secular elites in the United States, where they are relatively unimportant. Centralization assists monopoly by secular*ist* elites in France, where they are important. Where else could the term *bien pensant* have come from?

As for East Germany, (the former DDR), centralization reached its apogee under the enlightened and secularist dictatorship from 1945–89, following the pagan interlude of blood and soil, 1933–45. Modernization was dramatically held back and active religion reduced to a small minority, in spite of the fact that a Stasi-infiltrated Church was everywhere the springboard for bringing down the dictatorship in 1989.

What now of irreligious Uruguay and riotously religious Singapore? Uruguay is a fairly simple case given that the reds more or less beat the whites, and the maximum immigration from Europe coincided with maximum Church-state tension in the sending countries, Spain and Italy. A secularist university was created producing an elite for a 'Latin' country that does not even acknowledge Christmas. Uruguay is also 80 per cent urban.

Singapore is clearly one of the most urban, multicultural and rationalized countries in the world. Religion in Singapore has been state-controlled in a rather neo-Confucian manner to underwrite the values of national cohesion and development. The mutations in religion coming with modernization include some separating out of the rich syncretic and animistic mulch from classical Buddhism, an expansion among the socially mobile of a personal, close-knit, almost cellular form of Christianity, and straight secularity.

I stress again how this process of separating out and this rise of a consciously personal religion characterizes many modernizing societies, as it characterized a modernizing Europe. One finds similar changes in Brazil, Turkey and Indonesia. In an 80 per cent Muslim country like Indonesia, highly educated women adopt the hitherto rare practice of wearing the headscarf as a sign of modernity and a protest against syncretism. Unfortunately the concentration in our western media on fundamentalism as a reaction against modernity neglects this alliance of Islam with modernity, as well as a similar alliance throughout the developing world between Christianity, hygiene, education, technology and transnational connections. Only in our traditional ex-Christendom or among nationalist intelligentsias elsewhere, is that connection not understood or else condemned as an inappropriate disturbance of traditional life-styles. The assumption is that one can opt out of change and the global reality, keeping traditional culture intact for the tourist gaze and the gaze of the anthropologist. As one aspiring and teetotal Pentecostal in Ecuador said to the anthropologist: 'Did you expect me to wear feathers, Miss?'

I also stress the crucial variable implicit in all the considerations so far put forward. That is the role of the Church and/or religion in relation to degrees of cultural distance and disparities of political power and establishment. This brings us back to the standard contrast between Western Europe and the United States. I want to illustrate how that works out with respect to a couple of related contemporary developments. They are the return of magic and the rise of spirituality that Paul Heelas and Linda Woodhead characterize as 're-sacralisation'.[12]

Régis Debray in his extraordinary biography of God over the last three thousand years claims that 'The Twilight of the Gods is Morning for the Magicians'.[13] That is a phenomenon present both in Western Europe and the United States. However, in Western Europe there is a negative relation between Christianity and magic, indeed a further separating out of the two by modernity, at least north of the Mediterranean littoral, whereas in the wide open spaces of the United States the gods and the magicians enjoy high noon together. The same applies to spirituality. In Western Europe spirituality is often encountered outside the churches, with art and music playing a major role as further sources of consolation and inspiration. Spirituality tends to offer an alternative to faith, as it does, for example, in Germany. However, in the United States spirituality and faith mostly move together. That difference I put down quite simply to my key variable. Religion in the United States adapts to every cultural level in the context of a pervasive reliance on voluntary association, federalism and a religious pluralism with no specific institutional connection between *a* church and *the* state or between elite power and culture. The contrast is clear between the United States since 1790 and more than a century of established Christendom in retreat in Western Europe.

Eastern Europe, for complex reasons connected with Ottoman domination and the secularist dictatorships imposed in the late forties by the Soviet Union, has been patchily different. The dictatorships successfully suppressed religion in the DDR, the Czech Republic and Estonia. However, in Greece, Romania and Serbia, and now in Russia, the revival of Eastern Orthodoxy is very evident, in spite of quasi-monopoly and a de facto or de jure establishment. The ethno-religious sentiments of repressed nations are very powerful and a long history of repression or defeat can for quite a while cancel out the effects of religious establishment on the achievement of independence. Islam's reaction to defeat as a religion programmed for victory is a large-scale instance of the same principle. In Russia it is not a matter of repressed nationhood but of a failed ideology giving place to an age-old union of faith and nation. The mutation separating out magic and religion with the onset of modernity is not exactly evident in Eastern Orthodox Europe. In Greece one finds a startling degree of iconic protection and spiritual insurance available, together with a belief in the devil only rivalled in the United States. Given Greek history it is not difficult to see why, but the advance of science is hardly the most evident factor.

I suggest the pictures I have offered of modern (and rapidly modernizing) societies, from the United States to Russia, do not say much for any hypothesis about the decline of religiosity with the advance of science, at least so far as science is received by the people at large. What matters is the *reception* of science and technology with respect to religion, not some intellectual and sometimes mythic

---

[12]   Heelas and Woodhead, *The Spiritual Revolution*.

[13]   Debray, Régis, *God: An Itinerary* (London: Verso, 2004).

history of the relationship generated in the academy. The key lies in reception theory and it is notable that hardly anyone, even Owen Chadwick in his splendid *The Secularisation of the European Mind in the Nineteenth Century* (1975), has brought together the social or popular history of religion and the intellectual history of ideas. Charles Taylor is a rare exception.[14] In the academy, too many of us, including theologians, rely on the intellectual history of ideas to understand religion and secularization and on the debates in the tiny world of intellectuals who have this particular interest. Only this can explain why my late and admired colleague, Ernest Gellner, sometime Professor of Anthropology at Cambridge, should publicly upbraid me for describing the United States as 'religious' given that in his view its intellectual representatives were people like Richard Rorty and John Rawls. On every conceivable criterion the USA is more religious than Western Europe.

Intellectual history remains affected by a master narrative treating religion as inchoate and backward superstition or as pathetic froth obscuring the surface of the real until blown away by revolution. Intellectual history is also too closely wedded to what John Weightman analysed in his *The Concept of the Avant-Garde*. It is not that the concept of the avant-garde never applies but that it's dangerous when taken for granted, as it is almost daily in the press.[15] It seems to me that the avant-garde in the romantic and antinomian 1890s has gradually extended its influence down the social scale, first between the two world wars, and then in the sixties. On the other hand, Louis Menand's account, in *The Metaphysical Club*, of the secularization which was inaugurated in the United States by the move to philosophical pragmatism, is only an irrelevant fifth wheel as concerns the religious history of Americans as a people.[16] Theirs is a religious practicality not a philosophical pragmatism.

There is one particular and virulent version of the Enlightened master narrative that has had some modest popular success, though I think it even more implausible than the idea that religion recedes as science advances. This narrative couples the idea of scientific truth and scientific innocent virtue in dispersing religious error coupled to culpable vice. The appeal of this coupling comes less from any popular dismay about inadequacies in the argument from design than from a popular unease about a seeming association of religion with violence and intolerance. The *damage* caused by religion is what people worry about and hear about, not esoteric if important issues about design flaws in Creation. How many of those who may vaguely have heard of the Selfish Gene and its author think about the vivid popular language in which the idea is couched other than as an invitation from science

---

[14]   Chadwick, Owen, *The Secularization of the European Mind in the Nineteenth Century* (Cambridge: Cambridge University Press, 1990).

[15]   Weightman, John, *The Concept of the Avant-Garde: Explorations in Modernism* (LaSalle, IL: Library Press, 1973).

[16]   Menand, Louis, *The Metaphysical Club: The Story of Ideas in America* (New York: Farrar, Straus and Giroux, 2001).

itself to let rip your genetic constitution?[17] The link between religious error and evil, whether promoted by scientists in the public eye, or over pints in pubs, seems plausible, and could take more time to disperse through sociological analysis than is available here. That is because it depends on a naïve and simplistic pointing at facts in Northern Ireland, the Middle East or wherever, backed up by a studied neglect of the all too complicated question of the way religion does and does not mesh with power and the dynamics of power. There is an equally studied neglect of an obvious process whereby a society partly converted (say) to Christianity, in turn partly converts Christianity to its own social structures, whether they are feudal, mercantile or capitalist. People who are scientific in relation to their own subjects, become carelessly opinionated about issues in the public world or the human sciences. It happens that there is no continuing Enlightenment institution in secular contexts comparable to the Church in religious contexts to take the moral flack hurled at the corruptions of power. Torquemada can be held up as a *real* Christian exemplifying faith deploying political power, whereas Joseph Stalin cannot be held up as exemplifying secular Enlightenment in power because he was *not really* enlightened. Again Christianity can be blamed for what happened when adopted as the faith of the Roman Empire, whereas Darwinism can innocently wash its hands of what happened when converted by capitalist society into Social Darwinism or deployed by Nietzsche. Yet the metaphors of Darwinism are decidedly more susceptible to malign conversion than the metaphors of Christianity. They appear well 'designed' to serve the purposes to which they are inappropriately put.

Claims to historical innocence are always suspect. If this sort of analysis does have any resonance, promoted as it is by biologists and geneticists skiing off-piste in the human sciences, it raises the possibility that religion might recede, however mildly, not with the advance of scientific truth but with the promotion of scientific error. It is worth adding that those scientific theories, which build religion into our mental basement as a neurological programme acquired in remote pre-history to assist our survival, appear to restrict secularization rather severely – on scientific or pseudo-scientific grounds. In Pascal Boyer's rendering of continuing emissions from the mental basement, only the hyper-intelligent can escape religion: an idea with obvious attractions for members of the faculty club. Religion remains immortal, at least among the *Untermenschen*.[18] It is natural, and easily come by, given our evolved 'instincts', whereas science is unnatural and hard to come by. Boyer does not define religion, and seems curiously uninterested in the major difference between pre-axial and post-axial religion, as well as making no attempt whatever to 'explain' the absence of religion. One thing at least is clear: the advance of science on this hypothesis does not entail the decline of religion. Lord Winston, the eminent gynaecologist, has also written a book about God, sympathetically attempting to bridge the gap between science and religion,

---

[17]   Midgley, Mary, *The Myths We Live By* (London: Routledge, 2003).

[18]   Boyer, Pascal, *Explaining Religion: The Human Instincts that Fashion Gods, Spirits and Ancestors* (London: Heinemann, 2001).

but he too aims to show how religion has been built into the psyche for our better adaptation and survival.[19] For him the religious urge stems from the desire to be united to something beyond ourselves. However, he also notes, and quite correctly, that if that were so we ought all to be religious. It follows that it was only half built in as a kind of side effect. Whether that explains why the neuro-transmitters of religion have been turned off in East Germany, or are blazing away in the United States or are strongly on for over half the population of South Korea and simply off for the rest, remains mysterious. It is even more mysterious if there is anything in studies claiming to show a genetic influence for religious tendencies, based on similar tendencies to religion or irreligion as between identical twins, and one which apparently includes the culturally and historically delimited phenomenon of fundamentalism. My assumption would be that most of the observable variations in religiosity, including fundamentalism, are explicable on the basis of culture and history, and the neglect of easily available evidence showing that to be so is nothing short of astonishing. It is some indication of the relatively closed mental worlds in which many 'open minded' academics and journalists operate.

Sociology is a humble affair and definitely not constructed after the model of rocket science or quantum mechanics. That is because it is a subject with a human *subject* matter. It does, however, operate within certain evidential constraints on matters where mere opinion is supposed to be king, and I hope that within those constraints I have offered considerations undermining the idea that religion recedes as science advances.

---

[19]   Winston, Robert, *The Story of God* (London: Transworld Publications, 2008).

PART 2
Case Studies of Secularization

Chapter 8
An Eastern European Pattern of Secularization?

Sometime in the 1970s the first delegation from China came to the London School of Economics, and one of the delegates took me aside to ask whether I agreed with Cardinal Koenig that European Christianity might benefit from the kind of persecution mounted in China. So far as the history of Eastern (and Central) Europe goes it all depends. In some circumstances persecution is successful, while in others it is not, and it is the task of the sociologist, in particular the historically minded sociologist, to analyse what those circumstances are. In my *A General Theory of Secularisation*, published about thirty years ago, I suggested that the degree and kind of secularization depended on the historical experience of particular countries, which included whether or not religion was positively associated with the origins and myth of the nation, as well as the relation of religion to the class structure, to power and to the state.[1] I also suggested that the type of religion made a difference: Protestantism was more vulnerable than Catholicism. What I then suggested about secularization in general applies equally to the very varied degrees and kinds of secularization in Eastern Europe over the years from the late forties to 1989.

Religion and the National Myth

If, for example, the relation of religion to the national myth is negative or in some way compromised then there is a good chance that state-sponsored secularization will have some success, as it did in the former East Germany, the present Czech Republic, Latvia, Slovenia and Estonia. Both Catholicism in the Czech Republic and Slovenia, and Lutheranism in Latvia and Estonia, were associated with Germanic dominance, while in East Germany the myth of the nation itself had been so undermined by the Nazi experience that it had to be exchanged for the communist myth and the atheism that went with it. Indeed, national pride and religion in East Germany are both at low ebb. Where the relation of religion to the nation is positive then religion may even be strengthened, as it was in Poland and Romania, and to a lesser degree in Lithuania, Slovakia and Croatia. Given the widespread presence in Eastern and Central Europe of an ethno-religiosity stimulated by subjugation by an alien empire of a different religion, there are more countries where religion was strengthened rather than weakened, thus giving the

---

[1] Martin, *A General Theory of Secularisation*; Martin, *On Secularization*.

impression that persecution is good for religion, and creating what looks like a common Eastern European pattern. It is worth noting that according to the survey of religion in Eastern Europe in 2007 by Tomka and Zulehner people in most countries believed that religion had gained strength overall since 1989, except in the countries where it had become very weak, like East Germany, yet most of the trends point downward if one traces the profile of religious belief and experience from the oldest generation to those in their twenties.[2]

So it is at one and the same time true that the range of consequences in particular countries of state-sponsored secularization is very wide, and that most countries have had an ethno-religious history rendering them resistant to secularization and creating some semblance of a common pattern. The point about ethno-religiosity is a relatively simple one, and hardly needs further emphasis. Most observers assume that the high levels of religiosity in Poland have a great deal to do with the way the Church has carried the national identity, and the first question anyone has to ask about variations in levels of religiosity turns naturally on variations in the role of religion with respect to national identity. In South-East Poland the Ukrainian Greek Catholics were mostly expelled in the early stages of communist rule but today the community maintains its ethno-religious traditions, supported by the intelligentsia, partly out of nostalgia for a peasant existence that barely exists any more.[3] In Hungary, however, there is a certain ambiguity in the relation of Catholicism to national identity, partly because the national myth has important roots in Calvinist Protestantism, which, after the Counter-Reformation was restricted to a minority, largely in the east of the country. The result is conflicting cross-currents and a relatively weak religiosity.

Variations in Secularization and Type of Religion

However, I want here to take the relation of religion to national identity as a given and concentrate rather on the key provided by the type of religion, whether it be Orthodox, Islamic, Catholic, or Protestant. I want to ask whether there are differing strengths and varying vulnerabilities associated with different modes of religion, so that, for example, one might locate a specific kind of resistance to secularization in the Orthodox countries of Eastern Europe different from that found in Catholic and Protestant countries, and even maybe having some affinity with the resistance found in Islamic countries. That is why I want to focus to some extent on Romania, which is overwhelmingly Orthodox, and has some claim to be one of the most religious countries in Europe in spite of, or even because

---

[2]   Tomka, Zulehner and Naletova, *Religionen und Kirchen in (Ost) Mittel Europa*.

[3]   Lehmann, Rosa, 'From Ethnic Cleansing to Affirmative Action: Exploring Poland's Struggle with its Ukrainian Minority (1944–1989)', *Nations and Nationalism*, 10: 2 (2010): 285–307.

of, many decades of persecution. The contrasting case here is Catholic Poland. I also want to say something about Greece, precisely because it remains a highly religious country, and one in the Orthodox tradition, while not having undergone a period of persecution. The contrasting case in this instance is Ireland. So we have in our sights two Orthodox countries, both highly religious by criteria proper to Europe as a whole, one having suffered persecution and one not, and two Catholic countries, both highly religious, one having suffered persecution, and the other not. My object is to tease out whether there may be differences in the Orthodox and Catholic responses to secularization that are relevant to the variations in the responses to secularization in Eastern Europe.

If we assume there are differences in the response to secularization according to whether the religion concerned is Islamic, Orthodox, Catholic or Protestant, our discussion can be organized in two different ways. One way would be to construct an evolutionary scale, or more modestly, a scale of comparative modernity, with Protestantism at one end and Islam at the other. If one took that route it might be thought natural enough that Protestantism, as the most individualistic form of religion, was most vulnerable to secularization, and Islam the least. That is precisely the scale of modernization deployed by Steve Bruce in his work on *Politics and Religion*, where Islam is least amenable to democracy and Protestantism the most, and Steve Bruce would relate this scale to a parallel scale of individualization.[4] Steve Bruce would go on to suggest that it is perfectly possible many countries will not proceed from a rather organic kind of collectivism to individualization, and thus neither to democracy nor secularization.

That possibility of permanent or at any rate of long-lasting resistance to secularization introduces the other way of conceptualizing the problem. Instead of a scale of modernization, one might think in terms of alternative forms of modernity. There may be several different modes of modernity, in which case Orthodoxy is a candidate to be one of them. One might place Orthodoxy alongside Islam, and imagine two major cultural blocs which are also cultural barriers in the path of the specific western kind of secular modernity, particularly with regard to the relation of religion to power and to a whole organic society, as well as a sense of ritual efficacy and the inspirited character of the world. Both are large enough and self-conscious enough to set themselves against western individualistic modernity, and to reject it as the kind of fragmentation that can only end in destruction. That is certainly a major theme in much contemporary Russian discourse. Both Orthodoxy and Islam reject the kind of separation of religious and political power that was implicit in Protestantism from the start, and that had some purchase even in Catholicism on account of the space created by the doctrine of the two swords. It is worth recollecting that it was only quite recently that Western Christianity, in particular Western Catholicism, ceased to be suspicious of democracy, and adopted the distinctly American view that Christianity and democracy were joined at the hip from the start. Even in Protestant

---

[4]   Bruce, *Politics and Religion*.

Britain it was for a long time maintained that parliamentary institutions were compatible with a relatively restricted franchise, while in famously democratic Protestant Switzerland female franchise had to wait till the second half of the twentieth century. So far as Orthodoxy is concerned, the struggle in Russia between Westernisers and Slavophiles, and between St. Petersburg and Moscow, is an old story, and there are influential voices today suggesting the Russia has now returned to its traditional axis of autocracy and Orthodoxy.

One does not have to accept that particular formulation to wonder whether there is an Orthodox cultural bloc resisting assimilation to the kind of secularity represented by Western Europe, and more explicitly by the European Union. Greece has been in the EU for some time, but it remains resistant to the kind of secularity the EU explicitly promotes. One aspect of that secular thrust would be the full acceptance of religious pluralism, and in most Orthodox countries there is a powerful current of opinion, by no means restricted to the ecclesiastical hierarchy, and including non-believers, that defines pluralism as a form of cultural invasion. In Russia the initial trend towards pluralism after 1990 was reversed, and in Romania the bridgeheads created by new religious movements have been tiny and marginal. The only serious exceptions are found in Evangelical movements, some of them of long-standing, with constituencies concentrated in the transitional territory of Transylvania and the pluralistic religious field of the Ukraine. The resistance does not come simply from cultural nationalists in the intelligentsia but has strong popular roots.

One may well feel that the mental map implied by this way of conceptualizing different kinds of modernity is rather too familiar, and reminiscent of the famous or infamous 'clash of civilizations'. Such a map reproduces ancient fault-lines, one in the Balkans, and the other at the border with Turkey, with Turkey poised uncertainly between the West and the Middle East. Ruthenia and the Western Ukraine are other important borderlands marked by constant tensions over nationality and religion, and by struggles about which religion represents the nation. As the words 'border' and 'map' imply this mental picture relates not only to physical geography, but also to geo-politics.[5] One does not need to take on board all the geopolitical implications of this map to explore the possibility of a different mode of modernity in the sphere of Eastern Orthodoxy. Nor does one have to assume an adamant resistance to democracy, since most Balkan states are to this or that degree democratic, while in 2008 a pro-western party gained a narrow victory even in a Serbia emerging from a strongly ethno-religious phase associated with conflict and eventual defeat in Kosovo. One needs only to think in terms of a popular adherence to the intimate relation of a particular dominant religion to local communities, and to the national community, and retaining the traditional *symphonia* of Church and state.

---

[5]   Bremer, Thomas, *Religion and the Conceptual Boundary in Central and Eastern Europe: Encounters of Faiths* (Basingstoke: Palgrave/Macmillan: 2008).

Contrasting Models: Orthodoxy and Protestantism

How then might one construct a model of the alternative modernities on offer in Europe taken as a whole, running from Orthodoxy to Protestantism, and maybe implying that the Orthodox type of resistance is found in an even stronger form in Islam? Perhaps the model should first be set out in general terms of a sharp contrast between Orthodoxy and Protestantism, before filling in the specific cross-cultural evidence about contemporary Orthodoxy, with some asides on how that evidence indicates significant differences between Orthodoxy and Eastern European Catholicism. This is where the contrast and comparison earlier indicated between Romania and Poland is relevant. Once that is completed I can proceed to the other contrast and comparison indicated earlier between Ireland as a Western Catholic country and Greece as an Eastern Orthodox country, neither of which suffered persecution under Communism.

I can put the broad Protestant/Orthodox contrast as a proposition complementing the standard proposition about the positive relation of religion to national identity where there is domination by an alien power with an alien religion or a militant atheist ideology. Perhaps at this point I could focus what I want to say about Orthodoxy as a whole on Russia, because it is such a dominant and brooding presence over the whole area of Eastern Europe. Of course in the case of Russia the relation of religion to national identity is not stimulated by external domination but by a pan-Orthodox sense of the historic and threatening 'Other' represented by Rome and the West generally, as well as the historic 'Other' represented by Turkic Islam and the lurking presence of 'the East' so often invoked in Russian poetry and music. Thus the relation of religion to a nation can survive in dormant form and then revive where it is co-extensive with and focused in culture, quite independently of the condition of a specific religious institution. For that matter there is in Russia a long-standing tradition of spiritually minded counter-cultures, often among the intelligentsia, opposed to state control and manipulation of the institutional Church, as well as a dislike of the clergy on account of their ignorance and poverty.

Here, however, I am thinking of the Church as a resource for, but not the necessary locus of, a layer of communal religiosity centred on the family, and rooted in a sense of generational continuity between the living and the dead not unlike the popular reworking of the feasts of All Saints and All Souls in Mexico. This kind of undifferentiated devotion focuses on tangible objects to be reverenced, touched or kissed, which may have numinous or therapeutic or quasi-magical properties. Of course, the Church can provide a haven of consolation in time of trouble, as well as sacred sites for festivals and pilgrimages, some of them offering a physical as well as a spiritual therapy. But these surges and rhythms of popular devotion, including the omnipresence of icons in the domestic icon corner, is not to be confused with active church membership, and certainly not with frequent recourse to the Eucharist, which is in any case not the prescribed Orthodox norm. Moreover, the meaning attached to faith is not so much personal in the Protestant manner, or dogmatic as dogma would be defined by the Catholic Church, as it is reverential before the mystery, almost one might say the effulgence of the divine. It is also actively conscious of omnipresent powers for good or ill, for beneficence or maleficence, and aware of the need for ritual purification to gain access to the good and the holy, and for gestures to protect the self against what is calamitous or deadly. Thus even businessmen support pilgrimages, expiate guilt by giving to monasteries and ask for a blessing on new building projects. The world itself is not a neutral theatre or stage for purely human action, but impregnated with divine manifestations and malign infestations. Evil is not simply a disposition of the infected personal will but an active presence to be shunned and exorcised, even though belief in a personal Devil is relatively rare. Perhaps one might summarize these varied characteristics of communal devotion as holistic in that everything takes place and coexists in an undifferentiated world containing a positive and a negative pole.

It can also be described as 'imagistic', which is how it survived under communism, though the Church is now attempting to regularize these imagistic devotions, and even sometimes to bureaucratize them, according to correct doctrinal norms, though of course realities constrain it to adapt. Certainly there is a strong thrust to recover the pre-revolutionary world, and to commemorate the martyrs of the communist period, even while there is also a certain moral continuity between revolutionary idealism and a revived Christianity. That continuity expresses itself autobiographically in how people account for their belief and through attendance in church by people of very varied forms of commitment, including 'Orthodox atheists'. Moreover, the Church is respected for its attempts to ameliorate some of the consequences of a kind of bandit capitalism, through social activities, such as assistance for orphans, drug addicts and sufferers from AIDS, and campaigns against alcohol abuse. Since Putin the state has given the church a higher public profile, allowed religious education in schools, financed church rebuilding as 'architectural heritage', discouraged foreign missionary activity, and restored Orthodox feasts and fasts in the Kremlin.

The pressure exerted in the Orthodox Church towards a renewed doctrinal orthodoxy can also be found among the Uniates, severely repressed in Russia, and indeed in every communist country except Hungary. At the same time all the different traditional churches (barring the Calvinists) which jostle with each other in the pluralist areas of the Western Ukraine and Transylvania, share a common devotional world based on imagery, pilgrimages, seers, and a practical spiritual therapy. There is also a tolerant atmosphere of mutual assistance and commonality between the different confessions, at least in Western Ukraine, and the Ukrainian state keeps its distance from any particular religion, given the precarious balance of religious power.[6]

---

[6]   Naumescu, Vlad, *Modes of Religiosity in Eastern Christianity* in *Halle Studies in the Anthropology of Eurasia*, vol. 15 (Berlin: Lit Verlag, 2010).

Less amiable than the imagistic faith of everyday believers, according to Juraj Buzalka, is the emergence of what he calls a post-peasant populism.[7] He says that historically populism has been the midwife of modernizing projects, but he is not entirely sanguine about the political trends it might represent, whether in Ukraine or the Russian Federation. Even in a city like Odessa, which prides itself on a long tradition multicultural co-existence, deep-laid forms of xenophobia and anti-Semitism can revive.

I have devised a model of a kind of religion resistant to secularization, as well as contributing to nation-building, and animating a major power bloc and civilization in the Byzantine tradition. Many of its characteristics are shared with folk Catholicism, but Catholicism is infiltrated by other, more differentiated elements, in particular a potential distinction between the international Church, and community and nation, as well as a rationalized articulation of the organization of the Church and dogma. Much depends on which part of the vast Catholic world one is talking about: folk Catholicism in Latin America shares much in common with Orthodoxy, and so does the Catholicism of the Mediterranean littoral. Austro-German Catholicism is by contrast more differentiated, more susceptible to individualization. It makes more sense therefore to create a model of religion in general in Eastern Europe, in particular Orthodoxy, by a comparison with Northern Protestantism, in particular voluntaristic Protestantism. I shall, however, also say something about the kind of Protestantism that becomes co-extensive with the nation, and retains communal aspects, such as you might find in much of Scandinavia. Just as there are Judaic elements in Orthodoxy, with regard to ritual and taboo, so there are Judaic elements in Protestantism, with regard to ethnicity and territory (and maybe prosperity also). The territorial principle, like the ritual principle, is persistent, if not perennial, globalization notwithstanding.

One of the key features of Protestantism is the purification of the heart rather than purification by ritual action, including authoritative priestly absolution. The inspirited world of the late Middle Ages was partly erased. All the tangible objects of devotion have been downgraded as interfering with divine-human communication rather than facilitating it. There is no mediation between man and God except through Jesus Christ. Priestly power is abolished and converted into the functional requirements of pastoral leadership. Potentially this leaves individuals to make their own personal decision to commit themselves to faith, ideally when of an age to do so. This places an immense pressure on the good faith of believers, and generates continual introspection as to how good and genuine that faith is. Simply to perform is not enough, and mere performance is under constant suspicion of being hypocritical. The outward comportment and the inner disposition must be one and indivisible. Whereas ritual is associated with honour and shame, inner purification is associated with sincerity and hypocrisy, and this difference is

---

[7]   Buzalka, Juraj, *Nation and Religion: The Politics of Commemoration in South East Poland: Halle Studies in the Anthropology of Eurasia*, vol. 14 (Berlin: Lit Verlag 2010). I am diffusely indebted to the *Halle Studies*.

manifest in every social sphere, notably politics. All external support has been removed, beyond an introspective scrutiny of the scriptural text with its promises and admonitions. External images have shifted location, and taken up their abode in the imagery of the text and the imagination of the individual. Ideally the text is able to do the talking directly, communicating within the solitary soul, although, of course the preacher of the Word may urgently press upon the believer the need for a personal decision in front of the congregation of the faithful. The Protestant cannot rest secure in the knowledge that the Church has all these difficult matters in hand on his behalf.

These pressures can easily become intolerable, because the psyche lacks all external support and is thrown back on its own resources. The high demands prove too high and it is easy to give up and rely on a proverbial wisdom for the transactions of everyday life. Moreover the high demands can be lowered and secularized into a rather generalized requirement that people be sincere and a general suspicion of all ceremonial as make-believe and false show. Protestant cultures are profoundly influenced by the secular deposits left by the evanescence of what was once active devotion. Evangelicalism mutates into high-mindedness and seriousness, and the Noncomformist Conscience into noncomformity and conscientiousness.

Obviously these Protestant characteristics are at the opposite end of the spectrum from Orthodoxy. I am suggesting, moreover, that they are prone to mutate into a secular utilitarian morality or a reliance on proverbial wisdom, the proverb rather than the divine Word, at least after a couple of generations. The dissolution of the tie between religion and the natural community, and of the bonds of the religious association, leads to a re-composition and fragmentation of the religious field very different from the holism found in much of Eastern Europe. In Eastern Europe, for example, magic resides within the overall sacred canopy, and is positively associated with belief, while the reverse is true in Protestant Northern Europe. Evil in Protestantism is not so much a presence or infestation, as it is in Orthodoxy, as an inward infection of the will. Thus beliefs in the Devil and evil in these very different religious universes need to be understood differently. The negative pole sensed out there has migrated inward. The spirituality which manifests itself inside the Orthodox universe, for example in ecstasy, in Protestantism wanders inchoately on its own, responding to the stimulus of individual need. That is what is meant by fragmentation, and it includes a fragmentation of the tie between generations, since on the one hand so much weight has been placed on mature and sincere choice, while on the other hand a spirituality dependent on individual need disappears as another generation is moved by needs of quite a different kind. The union of living and dead in Eastern Europe is attenuated in Protestant Northern Europe, and was one of the major breaks initiated by the Reformation.

What remains, however, in Protestantism and Orthodoxy alike, is a primordial territoriality: the basic geography of religious belonging. This survives whether or not the ecclesiastical institution is vibrant and active. In Denmark, for example, where the church is not conspicuously vibrant, a respondent asked why he should go to church on Sunday when he could be in Denmark all the week. In Bulgaria, where regular ecclesiastical activity is rather dormant, there remains a religiously toned attachment to the land, to Bulgaria, which may express itself in pilgrimages and holy places marking a sacred territory, the monastery at Rila for example. Indeed quite a lot turns on this relation of territory and holy place. Belarus is poorly defined territory without natural borders and it lacks a holy place or a sacred capital, like Kiev or Moscow.

The Evidence

Having set out a model based on a contrast between Orthodoxy and Protestantism we now need to turn to the evidence about religion in Eastern Europe, and the differences I hinted at earlier between Orthodoxy and Catholicism. Here, as in other places in this essay, I mainly rely on the data and analysis of Naletova, with some further reference to Greeley and Tanase.[8] A particularly useful focus will be provided here by the remarkable religious situation in Romania and its immediate neighbour, Moldova. We need to begin with some basic facts and some indications of why certain countries, Serbia, for example, have very distinctive characteristics.

Belief in God is high in all Orthodox countries, if somewhat lower in the Russian Federation and Belarus, and belief in God holds up irrespective of the state of the Church. Of course, in the case of Russia the range of cultures, including a Muslim minority of one in ten, makes judgements a little precarious. That the organizational state of the Church matters relatively little is interesting, because it is associated with optimism about religion, and associated also with confidence in the Church, even in Russia where confidence is expressed by over seven in ten. This ability of the Orthodox Church to inspire confidence is greater than the ability of the Catholic Church in Eastern Europe, and it encourages one to speculate that the undifferentiated character of the Orthodox universe inhibits a specific judgement about the Church as a distinct organization, rather than as the religious expression of the people as a whole. It seems that Catholics are more uneasy about the social role and value of the Church, and when not positively affiliated set themselves at a greater distance form the mental universe of belief. Evidence from Croatia, cited by Zrinka Stimac, shows not only that there is a high level of popular religiosity, and a vigorous assertion of the Catholic Church in the public sphere as guardian of national identity, but also a negative attitude towards

---

[8]   Naletova, Inna, 'Orthodox Religiosity in Eastern Europe: an Analysis of Six Countries', in Inna Naletova, Miklos Tomka, and Paul Zulehner, (eds), *Gott nach dem Communismus* (Wien: Pastorales Forum, 2008: 1–34); Greeley, Andrew, *Religion in Europe at the End of the Second Millennium* (London: Transaction, 2003); Tanase, Laurentiu, *Pluralisation Religieuse et Société en Roumanie* (Bern: Peter Lang, 2008).

the Church regarding its attempted regulation of personal morality and its ability to help with mundane problems.[9]

With regard to Orthodoxy I am laying stress on the unity of Church and community, above all the intimate sphere of culture, and suggesting that this unity is congruent with a strong conservative nationalism throughout most of the Orthodox world, though there are three countries, Bulgaria, Belarus, and Ukraine, where, for various reasons, the Church is less salient as an expression of the nation than elsewhere in the Orthodox world. The situation in the Ukraine has deep historic roots which make the role of the various competing forms of Orthodoxy, including the Greek Catholics, very problematic in the process of nation building. That helps explain why in parts of Ukraine Evangelical mission has been very successful, so that some five to six per cent of the total population is now Evangelical, even after a massive migration of Evangelical believers to the USA, while in the eastern parts of Ukraine Orthodoxy is not so much a belief as a confused sense of affiliation with Russia. All churches, with the exception of the Orthodox affiliated with Moscow, strongly supported the Orange Revolution. In Ukraine and Belarus the number of religiously non-affiliated is apparently increasing, in spite of the fact that Ukraine always maintained a higher degree of religiosity than Russia when part of the Soviet Union and today sends out Evangelical missionaries to what is now the Russian Federation.[10]

Bulgaria is an interesting case. In Bulgaria belief has recovered from a low point in the communist period, if investigations in that time are to be believed, but that recovery has not fructified in the active life of the Bulgarian Church. I have already mentioned how in Bulgaria religious feeling attaches to the land and expresses itself in pilgrimages to holy places. It has often been observed that Bulgaria, for historic reasons, identifies with, and in many ways reflects, Russia. For that matter, many Bulgarians migrated to Russia in the late nineteenth century and maintain their religion and customs to this day. Romania, by contrast, defines itself over against Russia, militantly so during much of the Soviet period. Maybe the clues about the different state of the church in Bulgaria and Romania lie somewhere here, and this perhaps is the appropriate point to draw attention to the high level of religiosity and the high prestige and influence of the Orthodox Church in Romania, and to reflect on a curious difference between Romania and Poland with respect to belief in life after death: one in two in the former and three in four in the latter. It is interesting that Poland and Ireland are virtually the same with regard to a very high belief in God and a high belief in life after death. Romania has an equally high level of belief in God, but not in life after death, and one notes that there are comparably lower levels of belief in life after death in both Russia and Bulgaria.

---

[9]   Stimac, Zrinka, 'Catholic Tradition and New Religious Movements: What is new in the Present Religious Landscape in Croatia?' in Thomas Bremer, *Religion and the Conceptual Boundary in Central and Eastern Europe*: 215–23.

[10]   Wanner, *Communities of the Converted.*

The Romanian Case

What then of religion in Romania? Romania has a claim to be one of the two or three most religious countries in Europe, even though, as in Greece, active religious practice according to ecclesiastical norms is patchy. After four decades of communism the number of atheists is minute. In the two provinces that originally made up Romania prior to 1918, Wallachia and Moldavia, there is a quasi-uniformity of religion, and this manifests itself in a lively monastic life, in spite of the partial suppression of the monasteries under communism. Transylvania, as a province acquired in 1918, is a transitional area, with a Hungarian population divided between Catholics and Calvinists, a largely Romanian Uniate Church, and quite numerous communities of Baptists and Pentecostals. To that extent Transylvania is religiously pluralistic, and has indeed enjoyed centuries of tolerance under the Austro-Hungarian Empire. The crucial point here, however, is that Romania is a Latin island in a Slav sea, and has been threatened on three sides, by Russia to the north-east, Turkey to the south-east and Austria to the west. In those circumstances, notwithstanding the communist attempt to indoctrinate and infiltrate the clergy, and extensive plans culturally to uproot the whole society by destroying thousands of villages and driving peasants into new towns, the Church was the one vehicle of a continuing Romanian identity. That was true all over the Eastern Orthodox world, but conspicuously so in Romania, so that the revolution of 1989 was accompanied by remarkable expressions of religious feeling. Crosses mark the places where people were shot down by the *Securitate*, rather than the kind of nationalist monuments that marked the revolution of 1848. It comes as no surprise that dedications of churches since 1989 have been disproportionately to Sts Constantine and Helena.

How then to make sense of the very high levels of belief in Jesus Christ and in God, and the fact that only half the population believe in life after death, whereas in Poland the proportion believing in life after death is three out of four? The Poles are closer to the fundamental norms of Catholic belief than any other country. There is maybe a similar phenomenon in Serbia, where belief in God is held by four in five, while on many other points belief is fragmentary and infiltrated with a kind of pagan hero-ethic consonant with the conception of Serbia as a victim nation stationed at threatened frontier. How do these relatively fragmented beliefs, beyond what may be regarded as the Christian core represented by God and Jesus Christ, fit in with the other differences between Orthodox and Catholics observed with respect to confidence in the Church? The short answer presumably lies in a difference between the Church as a vehicle of identity and a continuing holistic cultural tradition, and the Church as a distinct institutional entity, teaching specific doctrines. There is nothing inherently contentious about life after death, and teaching on that point is accepted, but the Catholic Church for example has other specific teachings about women, birth control and abortion which arouse scepticism about its institutional wisdom and are clearly ignored, if the low birth-rates throughout Eastern Europe are anything to go by. The Orthodox Church does not place equivalent store on this kind of moral authority and social control, which is a point to which one can return below in making a comparison between Greece and Ireland.

A Comparison of Greece and Ireland

In her comparison of secularization in Greece and Ireland Daphne Halikiopoulou argues that while Ireland and Greece are among the most religious societies in Europe, in part because they both have an historic experience of oppression by an alien power of a different religion, and stand at a religious frontier, there are nevertheless significant differences in their recent trajectory with regard to religion.[11] These differences are consonant with the differences noted with regard to Catholic and Orthodox experience in Eastern Europe during and after the communist period. In Greece there was considerable resentment over the EU ruling that it was unacceptable for Greece to require a statement of religion on identity cards. Indeed there was a more generalized resentment about the secular agenda of the EU as Greeks saw it, which was not confined to actively religious Greeks. Many Greeks also sympathized with Serbia over the issue of Kosovo, and saw themselves as part of a pan-Orthodox group of nations led by Russia. In other words, some of the ancient alignments associated with Balkan religious nationalism, once so important with regard to the Eastern Question, emerged again on the political scene. Of course, there is a range of opinion within the Greek Church, and there are many who seek a less nationalistic, triumphalist and monopolistic approach, including the new Archbishop of Athens, but traditional attitudes are deeply entrenched. At any rate the late Archbishop of Athens raised the flag of the Lavra before a vast concourse to remind everyone of how the union of Church and people had (purportedly) sparked off the war of Greek Independence against Turkey. Nothing like this happened in Ireland, where the long conflict with Britain is finally being brought to a resolution, and where the EU connection had clearly been of great benefit to Ireland. At the same time a new prosperity and an opening up of Irish society, particularly with the revolution in communications, presaged a new attitude to the authority of the Church, above all in the intelligentsia. The structure of the Church, and its ingrained habit of authority, especially over sexual ethics, brought on a crisis, not so much of religious identity as of confidence in the institution. Problems over priestly abuse of children further eroded ecclesiastical authority, adding to the crisis, No such crisis occurred in Greece, in spite of widespread concerns over ecclesiastical corruption, maybe because corruption is everywhere in Greek society, but also because the Church did not seek to exercise a moral censorship over national mores. What needs underlining here is precisely the unproblematic and undifferentiated nature, thus far, of the relation of Orthodoxy

---

[11]   Halikiopoulou, Daphne, *Patterns of Secularization: Church, State and Nation in Greece and the Republic of Ireland* (Aldershot: Ashgate, 2010).

to national identity. Culture and religion, in Greece and Orthodox Eastern Europe generally, are woven without seam throughout. Moreover, that helps explain why in many Orthodox countries, at least in the ex-communist ones, the young and the urban are just as religious as the old and the rural, if not more so.

I would add two further considerations to the above. One is that in parts of Eastern Europe, Russia and Central Asia, there are reversions to paganism and to the cult of heroic warrior figures such as Timur the Lame and Genghis Khan. These reversions parallel similar developments in Mexico and Guatemala which look back explicitly to pre-Hispanic heroes and customs. In the case of parts of the Baltic States the Church can be seen as a foreign imposition, so that the cultivation of folk traditions is another way of asserting national identity. The other consideration relates to geography. The vast expanses of Russia, including a potent Asiatic backdrop, exercise an influence on Eastern Europe, both negative and positive. These negative and positive influences radiate across an ill defined frontier, from Tallinn to Odessa, with a western salient in Western Ukraine. There are regional religiosities as well as national ones: the Catholicism of the Alpine region and of the Mediterranean littoral centred on Rome, the jagged frontier between confessions running through the mountainous Balkans, the protective ecological niche provided by the Carpathians for Romania, the Protestantism of the Baltic Sea both to its north and to its south.

Conclusion and Summary

I began this enquiry into the existence of a distinctive Eastern European pattern of secularization, or of resistance to secularization, by asking whether state persecution and suppression of religion had relatively uniform results. I concluded that a great deal depended on how far there was a positive relation between national identity and religion and on the nature of the religion itself. With regard to religion and national identity many of the countries in Eastern and Central Europe share a common experience whereby national identity has been carried by religion as part of a resistance to alien domination, but this common experience is not universal. Where this historic experience is present persecution can even revitalize the Church, and make it a vehicle of protest against tyranny and the suppression of the truth. That was conspicuously the case in Poland, and the Polish Catholic Church played a major role in bringing down the whole communist system, particularly after the Pontificate of John Paul the Second. However, even a seriously weakened and state-infiltrated Church was able to perform this role, as for example in the collapse of the former DDR. The point remains that there is a scale of resistance to secularization dependent on the role of the Church in relation to national identity and alien rule, negative in Czech Lands, in Estonia, and (for very complex reasons) in East Germany, ambiguous in Hungary, positive in Croatia, Slovakia, Serbia and maybe Bulgaria, and very positive in Poland-Lithuania and Romania-Moldova, though Lithuania and Moldova are less securely religious than

Poland and Romania. The Polish case is very well known, so it seemed to me worth concentrating on Romania. The Romanian Church has, according to Lucian Leustean, successfully carried the highly specific Latin identity of Romania under any number of regimes, and the communist regime was no exception, even though the regime attempted physically and on a massive scale to root out traditional culture.[12] The Church was aligned with identity to such an extent that it fitted in to the communist regime's policy of creating a national form of communism resistant to its Russian neighbour. Bulgaria, by contrast, was Slavic, and had a long historic tradition of regarding Russia as an elder brother.

That, then, recapitulates some standard observations about religion and national identity. The bulk of my argument has turned on the other major influence: the kind of religion involved in different cases. Here I have constructed a model running from Orthodoxy, with the minimum differentiation at the communal or the national level, and Protestantism, with the maximum potential for differentiation at every level, even though it readily recuperates the territorial principle assisted by its reading of the Hebrew Scriptures. Whereas Orthodoxy recovers the ritual principle in Judaism, Protestantism recovers the territorial principle. I argued that a religion focussed on ritual acts, and maintaining itself in the home, for example through reverential acts towards the icon corner, or through raising one's hands in the Muslim manner before meals, can easily survive the state appropriation of Church or mosque. The same is true of rituals for the burial of the dead, for paying visits to graveyards, or simply lighting candles. Physical acts of alignment do not require assent as in Catholicism or personal commitment as in Protestantism. Moreover when one surveys religion beyond the bounds of Christianity, in modern India, for example, or even in China, it seems likely that a ritual religion simply requiring acts of alignment, in particular uniting the living and the dead, represents a stratum capable of resisting secularization more successfully than what we take to be more developed, because more differentiated, forms. It is also quite likely that an inspirited universe is more palpable as one moves south and east, with Orthodox Eastern Europe being part of the inspirited world.

Perhaps Christianity, on account of its origin as a voluntary association, is exceptional in the potential it possesses for differentiation and individualization, so that medieval Catholicism as an all-embracing universe including a negative and a positive pole, as well as magical elements, and Orthodoxy, can be seen as reversions to a type of religion that all over the world can coexist with modernity without the historic lesions characteristic of the West.

---

[12] Leustean, Lucian, *Orthodoxy and the Cold War: Religion and Political Power in Romania 1947–65* (Basingstoke: Palgrave/Macmillan, 2009).

Chapter 9

East Germany: The World's Most Secular Society

Post-Secularity?

For some while there has been a keen debate in the sociology of religion about whether the three hundred million or so people of Western Europe (in particular North-Western Europe) or an equivalent number of people in the USA, presage the future of religion. The debate involves some major theoretical stances in the subject, and in particular it activates a long-term issue about the presumed effects of modernization on religion, given that both regions have been foremost in the process of modernization. A long time ago I wrote that it all turned on whether or not you thought that France, as the model for the clash between Enlightenment and religion, gave us a preview of the global future, or reserved that honour for Scandinavia, as the model for an internally secularized Protestantism. The oddity is that the USA, which is in its origins and development a quintessentially Protestant culture, presents an alternative to the French version of the Enlightenment. Yet it is the most religious of modern societies, unless you take seriously the argument that it is secularized from within. Inevitably a debate of this kind involves some scholars writing about incipient signs of secularization in the baby boom generation in the USA, and citing evidence for disaffiliation among young people today, while others canvass what Andrew Greeley has called 'Unsecular Europe'.[1] A phenomenon like the amazing spread of Pentecostalism in the developing world does not count with some observers because the societies in which it expands are not properly modern. You can even dismiss it as a premonition of secularization if you take Protestantism to be just the first step on the way to the secular future.

More recently the debate has taken on a seemingly new form with the popularity of the notion of post-secularity. One version of this hails a return of religion to the public square, even in Europe. The most recent expression of this is a book entitled *God is Back* (2009) by Adrian Wooldridge and John Micklethwait which might be paired with Steve Bruce's *God is Dead* (2002).[2] José Casanova argued against the supposed privatization of religion in his influential *Public Religions in the Modern*

---

[1]   Greeley, Andrew, 'Unsecular Europe: the Persistence of Religion', in Detlef Pollack, and Daniel Olson, (eds), *The Role of Religion in Modern Societies* (London: Routledge 2008: 141–62).

[2]   Micklethwait and Wooldridge, *God is Back*; Bruce, Steve, *God is Dead. Secularization in the West* (Oxford: Blackwell, 2002).

World (1994), and this points up a major oddity of the current debate about post-secularity, given that religion has been a consistent public presence in the public life of Europe throughout the post Second World War period.[3] After all the Church was central to the emergence of Christian Democracy and the diminution of its influence is a continuing process that bears none of the marks of post-secularity.

I suspect we are witnessing a largely intellectual return to the consideration of the role of religion, for example in the book by Jürgen Habermas entitled *Between Naturalism and Religion*, which is as sociologically naive as it is philosophically sophisticated.[4] This intellectual interest is not prompted by anything new in the evidence, in Western or even in Eastern Europe, but by the impact of Islam, including the sizeable migrant populations of Muslims in Europe itself, and by the inclusion of highly religious ex-communist countries like Poland, Romania and Slovakia in the European Union. There has been a religious revival in Russia and Ukraine of major political significance but that is hardly the centre of the debate. Moreover the debate proceeds as if the challenge to secularization theory were quite recent whereas the present author initiated it as far back as 1965, interestingly enough just at the time when 'the death of God' was at the height of its intellectual popularity.

In 1969 I also put forward the idea that the course of secularization, (understood most plausibly as a process of differentiation whereby major functions like socialization and welfare are transferred from religious to secular agencies), was significantly channelled by national histories ('path-dependency' in recent parlance), in particular by the type of Enlightenment experienced (French, British, German or American), and by whether religion played a positive role (as in Poland) or a negative role (as in France) in the emergence of the nation. Recent writing about *the* Enlightenment project too easily leads us to suppose enlightenments were all of a kind and to ignore its religious roots as recounted in David Sorkin's *The Religious Enlightenment*.[5]

Whether or not the concept of post-secularity has any purchase outside intellectual debate, the current discussion has some genuine interest since it turns on some major theoretical approaches to religion and secularization. These include classic secularization theory, rooted in the relation of religion to modernity, in particular meta-processes like rationalization, or even the advance of reason and science. Then there is the individualization thesis, which is not necessarily incompatible with classic secularization theory, but shows itself in a very partial shift from religion to spirituality and in believing without institutional belonging, even though the proponents of this approach, such as Grace Davie, recognize it has, to some extent, a transitional character, as argued by David Voas in *The Role of Religion in Modern Societies*.[6] Then there is rational choice theory, which

---

[3] Casanova, *Public Religions in the Modern World*.

[4] Habermas, *Between Naturalism and Religion*.

[5] Sorkin, *The Religious Enlightenment*.

[6] Berger, Davie and Fokas *Religious America Secular Europe*: Voas 'The Continuing Secular Transition', in Pollack and Olson, (eds), *The Role of Religion in Modern Societies*.

assumes a steady demand for religion variously manifest according to the supply, notably whether this is provided by 'lazy' monopolies or vigorous competition. It is in relation to ideas of a steady demand for religion that an examination of the very variable channels of secularization, as originally set out in my *A General Theory of Secularisation* (1969 and 1978) becomes crucial. That is precisely why the comparative analysis of these channels which now follows takes the former DDR as the focus for comparison and a test-bed case for the central role of culture and socialization rather than the some assumed steady demand, whether stimulated by the continuous pressure of existential need or postulated by biological theories seemingly reviving the 'religious instinct'. Biological theories have been put forward with remarkable confidence, and are constantly extended, even into a supposed instinct for art.[7] Yet biological theorists have taken very little interest in how a universal instinct, in this case for religion, can show itself with such vigour in Poland, where 96 per cent believe in God, and so weakly in the former East Germany, where 30 per cent believe.

The usual defence put forward by those few scholars of the socio-biological school who take the cultural and historical evidence into account, leans on the notion of functional equivalence, which in the case of East Germany has to mean communism. However, the 'religion' of communism collapsed 20 years ago, if not well before, and nothing has taken its place since 1989, in spite of opportunities for any amount of expansion in the 'supply' of religion from several competing sources. The Jehovah's Witnesses have been relatively successful, particularly in the area of Chemnitz, but that relative success dates back to pre-socialist times and is bolstered by a certain consonance between their rational style of argument, and the deposit of rationality, as well as the hope of heaven on earth, left by socialist education.[8]

The Remarkable Secularity of East Germany compared with West Germany

After the mid-twentieth century East and West Germany followed very different paths, politically and religiously. However, there is some evidence of a distinctive form of secularization emerging in East (then Central) Germany well before the First World War. The area had been the most Protestant region of Germany and had therefore experienced a greater degree of religious individualization and a weakening of the communal tie still retained in Catholicism. Moreover the

---

[7] Runciman, *The Theory of Cultural and Social Selection*; Runciman has provided a defence of the biological contribution to comparative sociology, though it seem to me that this form of biologism has something of the economistic character of transferred metaphor found in Rational Choice Theory, with which has some affinity.

[8] Wohlrab-Sahr, Monika, 'Religion *and* science or Religion *versus* Science: About the Social Construction of the Science-Religion Antagonism in the German Democratic Republic and its Lasting Consequences', in Pollak and Olson, (eds), *The Role of Religion in Modern Societies*, 223–48.

union of throne and altar also associated Protestantism with authority, power and submission to the state. Secularist and anti-clerical movements emerged early in the East of Germany and many 'free-thinking' associations were founded there in the late nineteenth and early twentieth centuries. In addition National Socialism was strong in some parts of the region and weakened the ties of denominational culture. As a result East Germany was already semi-secularized even prior to the communist assault. The newly imposed communist government offered an ideological exchange whereby East Germans would be treated as the innocent proletarian victims of Nazism provided they accepted their assigned role in the progress of communism and its comprehensive world-view. National identity, which provided a base for religious resistance in Poland, could not exercise that role in East Germany because it had been so thoroughly discredited between 1933 and 1945 by the Nazi regime.

This then was the situation in which a rapid state-sponsored secularization took place. It had less to do with modernization, given that modernization moved forward much more quickly in West Germany, and a great deal to do with changes in regime. The situation has been commented on by numerous analysts, such as and Michael Hainz,[9] and Monika Wohlrab-Sahr, Olaf Müller, Detlef Pollack and Gert Pickel in *The Role of Religion in Modern Societies*.[10] Whereas in the 1940s most people in East Germany and in the West had some affiliation with the Church, by the time of the second millennium the differences had become striking. 21 per cent in West Germany accounted themselves highly religious whereas in the East only eight per cent did so. In the West 57 per cent of those questioned accounted themselves religious and 22 per cent irreligious while the comparable figures in the East were 28 per cent and 64 per cent. In short, two out of three in West Germany were well-disposed to religion while two out of three in East Germany were indifferent or hostile. In East Germany it is even possible not to know what it is you do not believe in. Of course the differences might be somewhat less striking were one to compare the Protestant North-West of Germany with the Protestant North-East, taking Hamburg with its irreligious majority as the point of reference. Here we have a constant problem in this type of data: one requires figures taking into account region, migrant status and ethnicity. Presumably active Christians were over-represented among those millions who fled the DDR. Or again, Catholic Latvia is not as Lutheran Latvia or Post-Protestant Groningen in Holland as Nijmegen. But even making proper regional allowances the West-East contrasts in Germany are nevertheless dramatic. In 1998, 18 per cent of West Germans declared they had 'never believed in God' while among East Germans

---

    9   Hainz Michael, 'A Central European Perspective on both of Germany's Differentiated Landscapes: Description and Explanation', in Šimon Marinčàk, (ed.), *Religion: Problem or Promise? The Role of Religion in the Integration of Europe* (Košice: Dobra Knina, 2010: 207–32).
    10   Müller, Olaf, 'Religion in Central and Eastern Europe' in Pollack and Olson, *The Role of Religion in Modern Societies*, 63–92.

the figure was 58 per cent. In East Germany a high degree of active dissociation from either belief or affiliation meant that the various dimensions of irreligion and religion alike were closely related and internally consistent, whereas in West Germany the higher degree of acceptability enjoyed by religion meant that large numbers of people were institutionally detached or semi-detached without counting themselves irreligious.

West Germany is religiously pluralistic with a noticeable penumbra of 'spirituality' though not one so large that it makes up for losses in traditional religion. Withdrawals from the Church in West Germany peaked in the sixties and the nineties, and continue today. In their discussion of these withdrawals Pollack and Pickel in *The Role of Religion in Modern Societies* report that the highly educated are no longer over-represented, a trend which is observable over much of the continent.[11] They also note a pattern among the better educated both of greater identification with the Church and of greater dissociation. However, the crucial data of secularization in West Germany are that whereas at the mid-century half of all Catholics attended regularly, by the millennium this had dropped to a quarter and the gap between the generations had greatly increased. Among Lutherans those over 60 who regularly attended outnumbered those between 16 and 29 by four to one. In spite of the high proportion of those who consider themselves 'religious' the implications for commitment to institutional Christianity are obvious. The situation of the established Church in England is directly parallel.

Some Wider Comparisons in Northern and Central Europe

Here I extend my comparison between East and West Germany. I do this, first, within the northern secular heartlands, briefly contrasting Lutheran Denmark and post-Protestant Britain, Holland, and Switzerland. Then I take in other extensively secularized countries in the sometime communist bloc, notably Latvia, Estonia and the (post-Catholic) Czech Republic. These are the core countries of European secularity, with the exception of highly secular Franco-Belgian region centred on Paris, where the key element is not the Protestant version of the Westphalian Church-state system but the war of the Catholic Church in alliance with the forces of the *ancien régime* with the French version of the Enlightenment in alliance with Republican nationalism.

Denmark is the nearest Lutheran neighbour to the former DDR and its capital Copenhagen lies roughly at the mid-point of the secular belt running from Birmingham to Amsterdam, Hamburg, Stockholm, Berlin and Tallinn. The religious condition of Denmark suggests how East Germany might have evolved had it not been part of a much bigger entity at the epicentre of European

---

[11] Pollack, Detlef, and Pickel, Gert, 'Religious Individualization or Secularization' in Pollack and Olson, (eds), *The Role of Religion in Modern Societies*, 191–220.

geo-political tensions. Denmark exemplifies an astonishingly stable pattern of Scandinavian religion with high levels of identification with the Church and low levels of dogmatic assent and regular practice, as well as a fairly uniform Social Democratic ethos. Danish religion is an accommodating habit of the heart associated with a church in an iconic landscape. Its combination of a folk-Church and Social Democracy illustrates the extent to which political culture and religious culture mirror each other throughout Europe.

Danish religio-political homogeneity has geographical as well as historical roots. If one compares Denmark with Britain the country consists of a small, flat peninsula with adjacent islands occupied solely by Danes, whereas Britain comprises two main islands divided into major ecological niches occupied by five different ethnic groups, each with a distinctive version of Christianity. Denmark lies at the junction of the Baltic and the North Sea whereas Britain is a relatively secure territory looking towards the Atlantic, able to generate a partial pluralism outside the established churches which later became complete pluralism when exported to the even greater safety of North America. By European standards Britain is unusually diverse religiously, whereas Denmark is unusually homogeneous though both have a history of (mostly) settled evolutionary change rather than revolution. Problems have been solved one by one rather than arriving in battalions. Moreover regular attendance at the respective state churches is not so very different, say, two per cent per Sunday.

At the same time Britain has experienced a rapid secularization affecting Catholics as well as Protestants. Over a quarter of a century regular Catholic practice has dropped very seriously. As analysed by Anthony Heath, declining religious identity is associated with a decline in all traditional identities, such as political loyalty, a sense of close solidarity with others of the same class, and a specifically British consciousness. Moreover, increasing numbers have shifted from a working- to a middle-class identity. In the case of religion, in 1964 just over a quarter either did not claim a religion or said they never attended a religious service. In 2005 over two-thirds did so. In 1964 around three quarters of those who claimed a religion attended services whereas in 2005 only half did so.[12] On the other hand, where class and party have declined in their capacity to offer normative guidance, religion has retained its hold over the ethical norms of the religious minority. Overall one may conclude that the rather generalized notion of individualization received some support, which would be consistent with the idea that a dominant Protestant culture weakens the communal tie. When the Irish historian Roy Foster refers to the relative weakening of the Catholic Church in Ireland as 'Protestantization' one intuits what he means.

Further evidence might have been supplied by the rapid secularization of post-Protestant Holland that followed the break-up of segregated socio-religious 'pillars' in the sixties, or by the gentler secularization of Switzerland. In Holland

---

[12]   Heath, Martin and Elgenius, 'Who do We Think We Are? The Decline of Traditional Identities' in Park, Curtice, Phillips and Johnson, *British Social Attitudes*.

less than half the population are religiously affiliated and over three-quarters attend less than once a month. The decline in belief in God, now held by six persons in ten, is greater than the decline of belief in the supernatural. Unsurprisingly belief and affiliation are closely related, especially among Catholics and conservative Protestants. Religion declines as younger cohorts replace older ones, as it does in Britain. In Switzerland, a country socially segregated by geography, religion has become increasingly plural and exercises decreasing influence on education, media, welfare and leisure. Between 1900 and 2000 membership of the Reformed churches fell from 57.8 per cent to 35.3 per cent while the Catholic Church has experienced some decline, though a less severe one, since the 1970s. Belief in God stands at 84 per cent, far higher than in Holland.

My final comparison is between East Germany and other countries of the ex-Soviet bloc. Of the three Baltic countries, Estonia, which is very largely Lutheran, apart from the considerable Russian minority, is the least religious, with six per cent attending church in the course of a month, while the comparable figure for Latvia, which is of mixed confession, is 15 per cent, and for Lithuania, which is Catholic, 32 per cent. Estonia is closest to East Germany with 42 per cent believing in God, whereas Latvia and Lithuania are quite similar to each other with about seven persons in ten believing. Estonia is distinctive in one crucial feature: religion is associated with German dominance, and national feeling therefore retires to the level of folk culture, and even pre-Christian religions. Exactly the same is true of the other highly secularized country of the ex-Eastern bloc, the Czech Republic, in particular Bohemia, which lost its German population in the post-war ethnic cleansing. The re-catholicization of Czech Lands that took place in the seventeenth century after the defeat of the Protestant Czechs, was associated with Hapsburg (German-speaking) dominance. The negative impact of forcible conversion, especially when associated with cultural dominance, (for example, the very late semi-forcible conversion of North-Eastern Europe in the late Middle Ages), is long-lasting. Belief in God in the Czech Republic stands at 35 per cent, only slightly above East Germany. Interestingly trust in the Church was at its highest in several Eastern Bloc countries, Bulgaria, the Czech Republic, Slovenia and East Germany, just at the point of communist collapse. The transfer of political hope to the Church was later found unjustified.

This is not the place to reproduce the complex data that allow the late Yves Lambert, in a fairly recent article, to write of 'A Turning Point in Religious Evolution in Europe'.[13] I simply note religious stability in Italy with 40 per cent regular church attendance (in spite of the 'fragmentation' analysed by some Italian sociologists),[14] and there is also some stability in much of Southern and Eastern Europe. Belief in God in Portugal stands at 95 per cent and in Italy at 93 per cent,

---

[13]   Lambert, Yves, 'A Turning Point in Religious Evolution in Europe', *Journal of Contemporary Religion*, 19 (2004): 29–46.

[14]   Garelli, Franco, *Forza della Religione e Debolezza della Fede* (Bologna: Il Mulino, 1996).

while in Croatia, Slovakia, Romania and Greece it stands at 80 per cent, 76 per cent, 93 per cent and 91 per cent respectively. Even taking into account the rapid post-Franco secularization in Spain, especially among younger people, belief in God there stands at 85 per cent.

Lambert identifies the negative effects of radicalization in the sixties on the churches and on moral ethos generally. He considers there is a decline in exaggerated expectations of self-realization and permissiveness among the young, and he wonders whether a more pessimistic assessment of modernity might be associated with rising levels of belief in life after death. The great competitors of religion, above all Marxism and certain kinds of rationalism have gone into decline, and Lambert believes there is a new climate which he refers to as 'pluralistic secularization'. Religion has passed through the filter of individual subjectivity and is firmly non-authoritarian, but it can find a new credibility as a source of meaning, ethics, sociability and identity.

The Character of the DDR: Nature and Artefact

What kind of society was the DDR? Mary Fulbrook in *The People's State* believes it was in some sense normal, whereas Arvid Nelson, writing about its approach to nature in *Cold War Ecology* and Eli Rubin, writing about its approach to artefacts in *Synthetic Socialism*, disagree.[15] Arvid Nelson and Eli Rubin provide a lens for thinking about the former DDR in terms that are wider than what we conventionally label as religion, but nevertheless bound up with fundamental attitudes to the world, above all to Nature and the nature of the human artefact. Furthermore those who postulate a religious instinct, whether existentially or biologically based, or who regard religion as a functional requirement of society, are prone to regard communism as sharing key characteristics with religion. Indeed Arvid Nelson uses the word 'religion' both with reference to some purist forms of Marxism and to the German reverence for *Natur*. Marxism picks up the religious idea of human dominion over Nature through the exploitation for human purposes of the powers of production, while being less sympathetic towards the equally religious, or at any rate, religiously romantic reverence for Nature, in Caspar David Friedrich, for example. For Germans the landscape, whether of the Rhineland or the Brocken, is iconic, just as the English landscape is iconic for English people, above all in wartime. Music and literature are both accorded a quasi-religious respect in Germany, and Marxist ideology consistently attempted to harness the great names of the East of Germany, Goethe and Schiller, Bach and Handel, – and even Luther

---

15   Fulbrook, Mary, *The People's State East German Society from Hitler to Honecker* (London: 2005); Nelson, Arvid, *Cold War Ecology: Forests, Farms and People in the East German Landscape, 1945–1989* (London: Yale University Press, 2005); Rubin, Eli, *Synthetic Socialism: Plastics and Dictatorship in the German Democratic Republic* (Chapel Hill, NC: University of North Carolina Press, 2008).

and Schleiermacher – to its own genealogy of progress. Ironically the Leipzig Gewandhaus Orchestra played a major role in the fall of the regime in 1989, along with the Church, above all in the Nikolaikirche, one of the city churches where Bach was in charge of the music. By a further and less pleasing irony the statue of Frederick the Great, a monarch previously demoted to the status of Frederick the Second, was re-erected in the Unter den Linden in the eighties to provide further legitimation of the communist regime by way of a link with the Prussian imperial past.

What exactly is Mary Fulbrook's case for the normality of the DDR, or rather for the widespread existence of normal life? She admits, of course that a society based on surveillance and manipulative intervention, and that hems its citizens in behind a wall lest they flee conditions social scientifically designed to release their human potential, was far from normal. All the same she emphasizes the mundane ordinariness of life in the DDR, particularly as people grew up who knew nothing different. That is what socialization means and what it does under almost any regime not undergoing chronic collapse, whether it is Soviet Russia as recounted in Orlando Figes' *The Whisperers* or Danzig under the Nazis in Gunter Grass' *Peeling the Onion*.[16] After all, the young Gunter Grass thought Nazi Germany sufficiently 'ordinary' to join the Waffen SS. Mary Fulbrook refers to the DDR as a 'participatory dictatorship' or the 'honeycomb state' and describes how East Germans became 'used to a society in which they were assured of child-care places and cheap holidays; of education, training and guaranteed employment; of a degree of comradeship among workplace colleagues, and relaxation in work-based sporting and social activities, on outings and anniversaries'. She compares the DDR to the more individualistic and competitive society of the Federal Republic in order to claim a real basis for Ostalgie. Her conclusion is almost elegiac: 'In the end, in the context of a collapsing economy that precipitated the end of the Cold War, the individual search for material well-being and personal freedom won over the utopian dreams born in the violence of the Second World War'. Interestingly enough this view is shared by many today in the former DDR, where there is an amnesia about the real character of the communist state, and where the *Nomenklatura* have slipped back into positions of power under different nomenclature, including the business elite.

Of course, when you switch the criteria of power and privilege from economic entrepreneurship to political rectitude you are bound to rely on lies, on corruption and privilege on the basis of personal connections to the power elite. At the same time, though the power elite in the DDR was tiny, the wider state involved millions in mass organizations and the party, and some areas were open to negotiation provided limits were strictly observed. East Germans did not necessarily see themselves as dupes, or willing tools, of totalitarianism. In any case it was not possible to cut off the population of the DDR from wider currents of change

[16]   Figes, Orlando, *The Whisperers: Private Life in Stalin's Russia* (Harmondsworth: Penguin, 2008); and *Natasha's Dance: A Cultural History of Russia* (Harmondsworth: Penguin, 2003); Grass, Gunter, *Peeling the Onion* (London: Vintage, 2008).

in modernizing societies, including youth culture, especially pop music, and increasing individualization. What perhaps does not come across in Fulbrook's account is the degree to which people became passive, perhaps because they regarded initiative as dangerous. The health service, for example, was bedevilled by bureaucracy and the total inadequacy of supplies and investment, as well as the interference of political priorities and – something ubiquitous in the Eastern bloc – 'health rationing by power, privilege and (re)productivity'. Pro-natalist policies, in some ways shared with the previous regime, though not on a racist basis, had various results: an increased birth rate and much lower infant mortality. The dying fared less well.

What then of the results of planned secularization? Here Mary Fulbrook's comments bring out the special position of pastors and priests, defined as socially unnecessary and yet in some ways forming an irreducible island in DDR society. Catholics formed a minority of about one million and rapidly regrouped to develop a way of living with the regime which survived the 40 years with a certain élan, except where whole villages were destroyed, for example, by the introduction of brown-coal mining at which Gunter Grass himself worked for a couple of years. As for Protestant pastors, they were even less dependent on the state for professional education and employment than the academic elite and the cultural intelligentsia. Some of them may even have entered the Church because they were inadequately conformist at school and found theology the only area of study open to them. Data about Christian businessmen show a similar profile. Under communism they were independent minded people excluded from advanced education, while after 1989 they were people who tried to conduct business with integrity.

In spite of dwindling congregations the institutional structure of the Protestant churches remained intact. In the 1970s the role played by church hospitals, homes for the elderly and disabled, orphanages, and social outreach work with alcoholics and 'asocials' led to a policy of domestic co-option, and to the Church-state agreement of the 6 March 1978, as well as infiltration by the Stasi. The relatively de-centralized organization of the Protestant churches allowed space for dissident spirits at the grass-roots, and pastors offered opportunities for discussion and debate about pollution and the militarization of youth. These protected spaces provided the crucial preconditions for the growth of dissent in the 1980s and so for the extraordinary situation where 'anachronistic remnants of the bourgeoisie' brought about what some called the 'Protestant Revolution' of 1989.

This is where an autobiography by Theo Lehmann, as edited and translated in *Blues Music and Gospel Proclamation* is interesting, because it brings together in unlikely combination two sources of social change, the Church and youth culture, especially popular music.[17] Lehmann was born in 1934 into one dreadful 'normality', and lived out most of his adult life in the other dreadful 'normality' described by Mary Fulbrook. His father was a pastor who had been a missionary

---

[17]   Lehmann, Theo, *Blues Music and Gospel Proclamation* (Eugene, Oregon: WIPF and Stock, 2008).

in Tranquebar, South India for the Leipzig mission, a historic venture founded as early as 1706. He returned to Germany at the beginning of the war as pastor at Christchurch, Dresden-Stehlen, where he and his family experienced the appalling bombing of Dresden on 13 February 1945, and the brutality attendant on the Russian victory. An interesting detail is that his father's sister joined the Jehovah's Witnesses, who were and are quite strong in that part of Germany, and whose combination of a rational style with a utopian hope appealed to straightforward socialist non-believers more than to marginal Christians.

Important for Theo Lehmann's future development was his clear detestation of any kind of regimentation, whether at school or in the kind of mass society promoted by the Nazis and the communists alike. The Protestant *Junge Gemeinde* brought out his rebellious spirit to the point where he (briefly) joined the communist *Frei Deutsche Jugend* in protest. Even liturgical responses irked him and clearly the kind of autonomy offered by the pastorate was appealing. Church is for nonconformists as well as conformists, especially in societies as intent on conformity as those endured by Theo Lehmann. He describes himself as constantly at loggerheads with the Church to which in the end he gave his whole life. His father showed much the same independent spirit when he became Professor of Mission and Dean of the Theological Faculty at the University of Halle.

After some characteristic problems with his Abitur examination Theo Lehmann eventually moved from the Leipzig mission seminary to reading theology at the Leipzig Karl-Marx University where he was greatly influenced by Helmut Thielicke. His hopes of a position at Halle University were dashed by an unfavourable political report, but more important for his future was hearing dance music and the blues on the American Armed Forces Network radio. Jazz was not only exciting on its own account as the spirited music of slaves 'made free by God', but had a conspiratorial quality because labelled decadent. Indeed, popular music as such has been credited with a major role in the collapse of the Berlin Wall on account of its capacity to bind together young people on either side of it. At any rate, jazz provided the music that accompanied Lehmann's wedding in the chapel of the Moritzburg Castle, Halle, and it became the subject, not without problems, of his doctoral dissertation.

When Lehmann eventually became pastor in Chemnitz, a city designed to be model of socialist society, he linked blues music to a conservative Evangelical gospel to create a new kind of youth worship. This was his very own show and it became a model for the whole of the DDR, attracting hundreds, even thousands, of young people. The rest of the story includes the regular attendance of the Stasi and of unofficial informers, intent on causing dissension between members of his team and between him and the Church authorities. Just how far this went he only discovered, to his acute distress, on reading his Stasi files after the fall of the regime.

In his *Cold War Ecology* Arvid Nelson gives a detailed and scholarly account of the approach of the communist elite in the DDR to agriculture, and the forest in particular, which goes to the heart of what went wrong and bears directly on the religious question. The communist elite, imposed by the Soviets, saw itself as the vanguard of modernity and harbinger of the future by virtue of having the keys to the unfolding of the historical process. That meant it was not enough to be on the right side of history in principle, but also necessary to prove that the productive powers of Socialism exceeded those of western capitalism, notably as represented by West Germany. In addition there would be a certain satisfaction in showing the Soviet victors how to bring Socialism about in an efficient way, in particular by harnessing the cybernetic and computer revolutions.

Actually the Soviets were themselves intrigued by the same Promethean dream, though they recognized two drawbacks. One was the difficulty of reconciling the key role of the party cadres and/or the workers with a leading role for scientific technocrats. The other difficulty was the nature of extremely complex systems. Just one mistake in the calculations or fault in the cybernetic model can prove catastrophic, whereas a policy of pragmatically seeing how things work out enables you to pull back from disaster.[18] After all, as events in 2007 and after have shown, even capitalism can end up in big trouble if overtaken by hubris (or pride and greed), and you get your sums wrong.

The communist ideology saw itself as the political embodiment of modernity and science, which in turn was yet another version of human domination over Nature. 'Modernity's conflict with custom defined and shaped the European landscape as much as economics' says Nelson. One has to understand the religious resonance of Nature and the potent notion of close-to-nature permanent forest (or *Dauerwald*), which framed the struggle between the modern industrial forest and the primeval forest of German lore. That same struggle framed what happened in East Germany after the Second World War and provides one clue why the Nazis, with their sense of sacred soil as well as blood, took better care of the forest than the communists, in spite of the strains imposed by looming defeat.

Nelson shows that East Germany had suffered much less damage than West Germany during the war, but it was poor in most resources apart from wood, and it had lost vast areas of territory as well as suffering ethnic cleansings involving some twelve million Germans and crippling reparations to the Russians. In addition the control of the countryside and the mobilization of the productive forces of the rural economy had been one of the least successful as well as one of the most brutal aspects of the communist experiment in Russia since 1917. If the communist elite in the DDR could not deliver in a sector so mythically saturated and politically sensitive it would be exposed as a failure by its own most cherished criteria of judgement. Failure was unthinkable, and any signs of failure had to be suppressed, which was one of the reasons the DDR was (with Romania) among the most secretive countries in the whole Eastern bloc.

The regime officially embraced science, but scientific data were dangerous because they documented heresy. One could not concede defeat to the revanchist, neo-fascist warmongers, exploiters and polluters of the West. The paradoxical

---

[18]   Spufford, Francis, *Red Plenty* (London: Faber, 2010).

result was that in order to fend off the western threat the DDR became a militarized society, as well as one notorious for modes of exploitation that ruined the forest, particularly with clear-cutting, and resulted in massive industrial pollution. As Nelson points out, 'East Germans, at the epicentre of the Soviet bloc's environmental catastrophe, formed the earliest environmental movement in the Eastern bloc in the early 1970s, under the shelter of the Protestant Church'.[19] The threat to the environment, the evident increase in pollution, and the militarization of society, were causes that could be taken up, in particular by an educated pastorate, in the one free space left in East German society. The Church retained the resources to resist the materialism that guided DDR policy. Indeed, the Church, historically lampooned for not following its own prescriptions, was able to show that communism likewise failed by its own criteria, though without a doctrine of sin to account for the failure. At the same time the more gullible elements of the Western intelligentsia were still prone to accept the apologetics of the DDR, though the evidence of forest death, water pollution and decrepit factories stared them in the face.

One might frame the issues of the forest in terms of contrasts between spirit and matter, care or respect and domination, sustainability and exploitation for maximum short-term advantage. But the issue of the use of plastics in the DDR posed a rather different contrast between the disposable and the enduring. Plastic was 'a hissing and a byword' in the West because it represented the inauthentic and disposable, and therefore the waste and wastefulness of consumer society. That is exactly what the leaders of the DDR thought in the years immediately following the Second World War. They considered it far better to create products that were authentically rooted in the national culture of the people. Wood and working in wood was authentic whereas plastic and above all Bauhaus functional architecture was an international style originating in inter-war capitalist Germany. It was true that the Nazis did not approve of Bauhaus functionalism either, but that was not a sufficient reason for communists to embrace it.

However there were considerations of politics and practicality that brought about a change of mind. Stalin died in 1953, to be denounced in 1956 by Khrushchev. Stalinism favoured expensive monumentality, for example the Stalinallee running east from the Alexanderplatz in East Berlin and designed to challenge capitalist building projects on the other side of the Brandenburg Gate in West Berlin. Stalinism also favoured production over consumption, but the deep discontent that surfaced in the disturbances of 1953 led the East German communist Nomenklatura to consider whether it might be better to offer carrots to consumers as well as holding sticks over workers and making demands for ever higher production targets.

This is where practical considerations started to bite. In spite of the fact that the DDR was not well endowed with natural resources, it was the beneficiary of Germany's high standards of education, including a long tradition of technological

---

[19] Nelson, *Cold War Ecology*, 150.

innovation. Innovation had long been encouraged in Germany, and had been adopted in part to put Germany ahead of its political and military rivals, like the French and the British, who had pre-empted the profits and resources of empire. Now it was a matter of putting East Germany ahead of capitalist Germany as the potential flagship of the Eastern bloc. It could not rely on Russian support, not at least in the way the FBR could rely on the USA, so it made sense to turn to its one great resource: the chemistry industry. Chemicals now emerged at the heart of planning. Of course the chemistry industry, like plastics and Bauhaus functionalism, had tainted capitalist associations, and had been implicated in Nazi policies and plans for war.

All the same the wrong associations could be reversed if chemicals, plastics and Bauhaus architecture were mobilized for the benefit of the people and the people's Economy. In particular plastics could be deployed as cheap and above all durable goods for furnishing apartment blocks and Bauhaus principles could be deployed to produce apartments on a large scale. The ensemble of plastic furnishing and Bauhaus architecture, with its new and decisively modern aesthetic, could now be embraced and driven forward by all the propaganda resources at the government's disposal. Institutions in Halle and Berlin devoted themselves to the creation of a set of basic designs, standardized but with built in variations.

Numerous journals and magazines devoted themselves to advertising their usefulness and ideological acceptability, in particular to the New Woman who was now both a worker and in need of efficient and practical apartments and furnishings in her role as home maker. In the magazine *Kultur im Heim* illustrations showed the new products as 'beautiful in Form, Practical, and Joyfully Colored'. Plastics went on display at the Leipzig Trade Fairs and by the time of the GDR's twentieth anniversary in 1969 the promised flood of plastics was well on its way. However, the failures of the East German economy meant that when plastics did flood the *Volkswirtschaft* they did so as part of a massive recentralization of the industry.

Eli Rubin suggests that the legally enforced 'most purposeful' substitution of plastic created highly centralized meaning that inhered in plastics and was absorbed by the people. If the power of the Stasi was hard power this dissemination of an approved product as symbolizing and materializing the proclaimed ideals of the regime was soft power. The two forms did, of course, reinforce each other, so that one of Rubin's key interlocutors was identified as suspect because she failed to conform to socialist expectations by her exclusive use of wood and metal furniture. That was the novel way in which the East German state redefined original sin. Yet curiously the plastic revolution had permanently replaced the 'authentic' culture of the past with its time and labour saving artefacts, including ubiquitous and iconic egg cups as plastic chickens, and in due course it became part of the cult of Ostalgie and a reminder of an alternative modernity.

And this is where Eli Rubin disagrees with Mary Fulbrook in her *The People's State* and other authors he labels Fulbrookians as to whether this 'welfare dictatorship', keeping its population in by force behind a wall, was in its everyday life a normal society. A normal society is not so described simply because most of time people think more about mundane concerns than the power of political dictatorship, or its omnipresent machinery of surveillance or the privileged life style of its apparatchiks. Eli Rubin does not accept this understanding of normality any more than he accepts the straightforward dismissal of the GDR as a totalitarian society replicating the dictates of Soviet power. For him the plastics revolution stays on as part of the 'Wall in the head' Germans refer to when thinking about the continuing difficulties of German integration.

One essential plank in the planned secularization of the DDR was the careful ideological construction of the clash between science, including Marxist pseudo-science, and religion. In her discussion of this crucial aspect of the campaign to eliminate religion Monika Wohlrab-Sahr in *The Role of Religion in Modern Societies* shows that it even succeeded in infiltrating the otherwise highly resistant Catholic sub-culture.[20] She concludes that the anti-religious campaign based on the opposition of science and religion 'was not only embodied in political ideology and state institutions ... but actually resounded in the world-view of large parts of the population' as documented by the World Values Survey. By contrast, the same campaigns in the Ukraine, as described by Catherine Wanner in *Communities of the Converted*,[21] were much less effective and even counter-productive given the association of religion with Ukrainian nationalism. Monika Wohlrab-Sahr also documents how nonconformist attitudes could lead at least one or two lively spirits to embrace (for example) Catholicism without being strong believers.

As already suggested above German culture had historically nurtured the seeds of such a construction, and these seeds had already taken root in what was later to become the DDR. The East-West divide in church participation was already evident in 1910, particularly where, as Max Weber put it, plebeian intellectuals had adopted socialism itself as a this-worldly eschatology. Positivism was particularly influential in establishing a dichotomy between religion and science with its double strategy of disenchanting the world and setting up science itself as a form of salvation in competition with both politics and religion.

This dichotomy has also been influential in the story of how religion and science have interacted in the West, and in his writings John Brooke has shown how genuine problems associated with evolution were (mis)constructed in terms of a narrative based on a fundamental clash.[22] In the DDR, of course, political salvation and scientific salvation were regarded as intimate allies not as competing. In West Germany the principle of the functional differentiation of spheres as between religion and science prevailed, so that biology books tended to point out differences in mode of approach and kinds of understanding. In the DDR by contrast books initially treated religion as irrational and later in the 1970s ignored

---

[20] Wohlrab-Sahr, 'Religion *and* Science or Religion *versus* Science', in Pollack and Olson, (eds), *The Role of Religion in Modern Societies*.

[21] Wanner, *Communities of the Converted*.

[22] Brooke, John, *Science and Religion: Some Historical Perspectives* (Cambridge: Cambridge University Press, 1991).

it altogether. Fundamentally educators in the DDR stressed antagonism while the Federal Republic adopted a pluralistic relativism.

Monika Wohlrab-Sahr concludes that elements of internal secularization within Protestantism may make it less able to resist antagonism and disenchantment than Catholicism.[23] The comparative data already cited for Lithuania, Latvia, and Estonia, and for much of Northern Europe, give this contention some colour of plausibility, over and above the impact of state-sponsored secularization in the DDR. Just conceivably it is not an historical accident that Wittenberg and Prague are two of the epicentres of secularity, the other being Paris. How and why science and education have historically been negatively related with religion in much of Europe and positively related in the USA is another question, as is the contrast between the secularizing potential of Protestantism in Europe and its vigour in the USA.

---

[23]   Wohlrab-Sahr, 'Religion *and* Science or Religion *versus* Science', in Pollack and Olson, (eds), *The Role of Religion in Modern Societies*.

PART 3
Religion and Politics;
Democracy and Violence

Chapter 10
The Religious and the Political

My focus is on the extraordinarily complex issue of religion and democracy, and to some extent on the related and equally complex issue of religion and violence. Both issues are obscured by rival types of propaganda, and to insert a social scientific understanding of what is involved in the face of assertions by contentious gurus concentrating on surface evidence and selecting what suits their book is far from easy.

Sociological Principles

There are some broad sociological principles needing to be set out right at the beginning. The first is that if one views a given world religion (and in a sense there are only three) as a group of themes with a strong family likeness, then the cultural realization of those themes will vary enormously according to type of society, type of social context, and historical situation. Indeed, its realization in one context may be the reverse of what it is in another. For example, the authoritative structure of the Roman Catholic Church may well constrain it to collude with conservative authoritarian regimes, such as those of Salazar in Portugal or Franco in Spain, and to that extent work against freedom of conscience and democracy. Yet the same authoritative structure enabled the Catholic Church to stand up against authoritarian regimes in Nazi Germany and Communist Poland, as well as the national security states of Latin America and the Philippines. In those contexts the Catholic Church could help clear a space for democracy, even though liberation theology clearly assumes Catholic hegemony. The same modernizing capacity exists in contemporary Islam. About half of the one and a half billion Muslims today live in democratic societies, and those Muslim societies where democracy has made little progress are mostly in the Middle East. In Islam as in Catholicism hegemony is assumed.

The context is also important with regard to the meaning of a particular religious practice. For example, female headdress of various kinds may signify seclusion and subordination in some Islamic contexts, but in the West, particularly when adopted by professional women, it may serve to symbolize not only a resistant identity but an identification with a desexualized role for women in an over-sexualized western society.

The second principle is that Christianity will be translated according to the type of society which adopts it, and, at least initially, in a way consonant with the rationale governing its adoption. With regard to the latter, Christianity in

Northern, North-Eastern and Eastern Europe was often adopted because Christian potentates were extending their power by absorbing adjacent territories, or because the monarchs of those adjacent territories sought to gain the advantages of association with a major civilized centre, as in the case of Vladimir of Kiev after his visit to Constantinople. Kings like Vladimir of Kiev or Clovis are not likely to abandon an heroic style in a hurry simply because they have acquired the gospels as part of the cultural package.

It is more likely that Christ will be recast in heroic mould in the way illustrated in the Anglo-Saxon poem *The Dream of the Rood*. From 995 AD onwards Olaf Haraldson almost literally rammed Christianity down the throat of his people, but by dying at the battle of Stiklestadt in 1030 he was assimilated to the Christian pattern of victory through suffering as St. Olaf. When William I of Normandy overwhelmed Harold at Hastings in 1066 he built an Abbey to Our Lady of Victories by way of thanksgiving, on the Old Testament principle that the Lord is a man of war. The sociological inference is obvious. In heroic or courtly or commercial or capitalist or nationalist societies the Christian (and antecedent Jewish) repertoire of themes will be raided selectively according to criteria of contemporary relevance. Poland and Serbia will see themselves as martyr nations; Protestant businessmen will adopt the Parable of the Talents as legitimation for canny investment.

That is not to say that Christianity is so retuned that it simply reflects its socio-historical location. It is to say that when, for example, Christian gentleness and loving-kindness become fused with a society based on knighthood you have the ideal figure of the 'verray parfit gentil knight', while in Victorian society you have the ideal of the 'Christian gentleman'. What is in essence a pan-human virtue, pertaining to the *gens*, but espoused in the New Testament, acquires a link to status location in a given type of society, and in this case a link to a particular gender. The ideal of gentleness or loving-kindness is not lost but takes on a socio-historical colouring.

The point is best illustrated by quoting Simon Schama on commercial and Calvinist Amsterdam. In *The Embarrassment of Riches* he writes:

> As in so many other departments of Dutch culture, opposite impulses were harmoniously reconciled in practice. The incorrigible habits of material self-indulgence, and the spur of risky venture that were ingrained into the Dutch commercial economy themselves prompted all those warning clucks and solemn judgements from the appointed guardians of the old orthodoxy. It was their task to protect the Dutch from the consequences of their own economic success, just as it was the job of the people to make sure there was enough of a success in the first place to be protected from. This moral pulling and pushing may have made for inconsistency, but it did not much confuse the artisan, the merchant or the banker in their daily affairs. The peculiar coexistence of apparently opposite value systems was what they expected of their culture. It gave them room to manoeuvre between the sacred and profane as wants or culture commanded, without risking

a brutal choice between poverty or perdition. And they certainly did not need Calvinism to tell them that riches had better embarrass, but need not lose them salvation. That lesson had been drunk with Dutch capitalism's mother's milk, in the earliest accounting between northern trade and the Christian gospel.[1]

The third principle is that every important religious or ideological position, judged by us as positive or constituting an advance, trails an inevitable cost. Monotheism is judged to be an advance because it seeks the inclusion of a unified humanity under one God. That, however, gives it an aggressive edge, both in relation to other monotheisms with a similar inclusive mission, and in its encounter with resistant particularities. The affirmation of the One actually creates the Other, especially since the monotheistic thrust often comes to specify an *axis mundi*, or key location, such as Mecca, Jerusalem or Rome, and thus to fuse universal claims with particular empires. That in turn is linked to the way the interim solidarities achieved by 'inclusive' particular empires war against wider pan-human solidarities.

Again, justice and peace are often embraced as twin virtues, but an emphasis on justice may lead to revolution or to just war at the expense of peace, while the embrace of peace at any price leaves the field to the powers of injustice. Love of neighbours in one context means not using violence towards them, and in another means using violence to defend them. A parallel kind of cost is entailed in the making of qualitative judgements, for example, that slavery and the subordination of women are wrong, since one cannot then 'respect' the Other when the Other rejects that judgement. Indiscriminate respect and tolerance are by definition incompatible with moral discrimination, or, indeed, a vigorous insistence on truth. Costs are unavoidable: one cannot fully implement all the 'goods' all the time. Even the ideology of progress entails relegating 'others' to a by-gone time zone while respecting other people's authentic culture may well entail leaving them there.

The Cost of Human Solidarity

At this point one encounters a particular type of cost associated with world religions but equally present in nationalism, whether or not ethno-religious as in Poland, or secular as in France or in Baathism and Kemalism. Religious and/or nationalist solidarity entails a cost relevant to both democracy and violence since (ideally) democracy seeks as far as possible to abjure violence in the settlement of internal conflicts and in the assertion of overall solidarity. In practice all the major forms of solidarity, religious, political and nationalist, are ambiguous and double-edged. All have fortified the One against the Other.

---

[1]   Schama, Simon, *The Embarrassment of Riches: An Interpretation of Dutch Culture in the Golden Age* (London: Fontana/Harper Collins, 1991: 371).

The way in which this cost of solidarity works out is of such major importance for democracy and violence that it has to be treated in some detail. World religions are premised on a concept of pan-human solidarity located in a particular faith, that is, in its drive to universal inclusiveness, and in its embrace of what is normally judged a pan-human virtue: truth. One has to say immediately that this is not the revisable truth of science, negotiated in terms of theories and supporting evidence, but a mode of framing permanent truths of existence. Religious truth operates at a discursive level distinct from the level of scientific truth. To see humankind as flawed and in need of redemption, or to respond to the creation as declaring the glory of God is to make a religious affirmation not to put forward a scientific proposition. In the matter of scientific discourse we have more or less agreed criteria for negotiating disagreements, but these are far less clear in the matter of religious discourse. How does one negotiate the poetic assertion: 'The world is full of the glory of God'?

This is true even within religions, let alone between them, for example as between broad hermeneutic principles selecting key texts as governing the rest, and literal readings for which a text is authoritative and God-given throughout, or as between text, tradition, experience and reason, or as between individual conscience and ecclesiastical authority. This problem of over-arching criteria as a basis for negotiated settlements about truth within or between religions is regularly latched on to by those who claim religion is divisive, as well as potentially violent and undemocratic.

However, the issue is much more complicated. One has perhaps to begin with the role of religion in establishing solidarity, that is, the *consensus fidelium*, realized on the basis of what is shared. That is, in itself, a fundamental achievement, and finds a particular expression in organic societies where authority is vested in religious and political authorities, both allied and conflicting, as in Western Europe, or vested in religio-political authorities, as in Byzantium and the Caliphate. The moment that is undermined by an appeal to the individual conscience in the interpretation of scripture, and its eventual secular translation in terms of individual judgement *as such*, unity is in principle beyond recovery. The 'wars of religion' over the century or so between Luther and the Treaty of Westphalia in 1648 were in fact fought for a number of politico-religious reasons, and the settlement of 1648 proposed only an interim solution, based on the unity of religion in a given jurisdiction, whether Catholic, Lutheran, Calvinist or Anglican.

Notwithstanding this interim solution, the principle of individual judgement still remained at large, either working within state churches, for example in the Lutheran Collegia Pietatis or the Inner Mission, or to some extent outside, as in England and North America. During this period of interim stabilization religion functioned as one marker of local identity, with a relatively minor role in struggles between local identities, for example, the struggle between Catholic France and Protestant England (and Holland) in the eighteenth century. That role as a marker has persisted, especially in areas of mixed religion, such as the Balkans and the

Caucasus, but conflicts even in these areas have characteristically been about political and ethnic supremacy and control of economic resources.

The achievement of consensus in organic society based on a principle of sameness had become a problem in societies increasingly based on a combination of identity and difference and experiencing a secular extension of the religious principle of individual conscience. Alternatively the consensual principle mutated into a secular nationalism endowed with a quasi-religious principle of unity, as in the case of republican France, or else into an ethno-religious nationalism where religion defined who was and who was not included, as in Poland. Nationalism of whatever kind 'secularizes' the *consensus fidelium*, as well as the idea of chosenness, and characteristically expels groups who are perceived as not belonging: ethnic or ethno-religious cleansing is the historical rule.

The essential problem for democracy was to separate the religious sacred, centred on the unity of the faithful, from the social sacred, centred on the unity of the nation. That problem was solved most easily in societies like Holland, Britain and in colonial and post-colonial North America, and least easily in societies where the religious marker functioned to ensure unity against oppression, as in much of Eastern Europe. In between were societies like France, Spain and Italy where two principles of unity were in conflict: organic secular nationalism and organic Catholicism, *Cattolici* and *laïci*. In Russia the principles alternated: from 1917 on there was an aggressively secular ideology, and from 1989 on there has been an increasing identification with a nationalist Orthodoxy.

Four Stages in the Christian West

Each of these trajectories has to be pursued in turn with regard to religion and democracy, but before that is attempted four stages have to be looked at specific to Christianity in the West. The first two of these relate to the space (or the distinction) between God and Caesar, between the kingdoms of 'this world' and the kingdom of God. In the first three centuries of its existence Christianity was a quasi-universal, non-violent, voluntary society, cherishing the space between God and Caesar. Once established in power, that space narrowed to comprise two mutually supporting and intermittently rivalrous jurisdictions, with the ideal voluntary society implicitly shunted off into monastic sidings. The second two stages involved first an interim stabilization, (Anglican, Presbyterian, Calvinist and so on) in which the national sacred and its consensus remained in close alliance with the religious sacred and its consensus. In the Presbyterian/Calvinist case the themes selected from the Christian (and Jewish) repertoire were city, saint/citizen, heart/sincerity, exodus, wayfarer, assembly, covenant and commonwealth. These all contained democratic potential, once an interim religio-political unity (for example in Massachusetts) broke down. At that point their potential was, so to speak, on the loose, and in the North American context the way was open to the kind of universal voluntarism embedded in the First Amendment.

The mutation of saint into citizen, of the ecumenism of the heart (and of faith understood as trust) into sincerity, all played a part in breaking down the principle of hierarchy with its emphasis on face and honour as bound up in inherent status.[2] So too did the mutation of the principle of an Elect chosen by God irrespective of status into the principle of converts electing (that is, choosing) to adopt a faith. The principle of free religious choice, together with its secularized equivalents, tended mutually to support each other, so that successive mobilizations further and further down the social scale could take on religious as well as secular form. The Pentecostalism now expanding throughout the developing world is the most recent example of the religious mobilization (without revolution) among lower status groups. In Europe, insofar as the organic principle survived, religious and secular mobilizations were more likely to be rivalrous, and negotiated democratic outcomes less likely.

The foregoing sketch of a sequence can be put in another way. Platforms are established in religious consciousness, often through ritual disputes, such as those over offering the cup to the laity in Hussite Prague, or the division between a lay nave and a priestly chancel, or conflict over vestments, and these disputes fought in a constricted ritual corridor can become generalized to society at large. The 'perspicuity' of Scripture can become the universal right of private judgement. When Luther defied the authority of Pope and Emperor at the Diet of Worms by insisting on the ultimate authority of Scripture he effectively inaugurated modernity, because the next and obvious step involved private judgement.

Concepts like commonwealth and assembly in Christian liberty can be translated more widely in terms of political organization. For example it is sometimes asserted that Methodist modes of organization transmogrified into English trade union organization; and it seems the Korean constitution was initially based on the Presbyterian notion of covenant. There is a long revolution to be traced here, with its earliest stages rooted in tussles over texts, words and symbols. However, we now need to revert to those early stages, before exploring the nexus of religion and democracy, religion and violence, in contexts other than the North Atlantic, that is, in Latin Europe and in ethno-religious Eastern Europe.

The Christian Repertoire and its Bifurcation

The first stage of Christian formation prior to the Constantinian establishment is fundamental, because it sets in motion a radical mutation of Jewish themes, in particular, the universalism already present, for example, in Genesis, Isaiah and Jonah, and the interiority fostered in Jeremiah. It makes a huge difference that Christianity spiritualized the concept of nation, as well as the idea of the sacred capital, Jerusalem, (and its temple), as the universal body of Christ and as the New Jerusalem above, the 'mother of us all'. It also makes a huge difference that Christ

---

[2]   Seligman, Weller, Puett, and Simon, *Ritual and its Consequences*.

was not a leader of fighting men, or a 'family man', as Mohammed was. That is consonant with the emergence of a universal voluntary association defined as a kingdom of God set over against the kingdom of Caesar, rather than a territorial tribe and a genealogy of blood based on a new sacred capital in Mecca, and proposing world conquest. In facing the imperial representative, Pontius Pilate, Christ (once again) rejected violence and declared his kingdom was not of this world. Thus non-violence was built into a new universal (ecumenical) spiritual union, separate from the state and from its monopoly of violence. The communion of Christians was to be such that they 'called no man "father"', and rendered 'no man evil for evil', cherished affective bonds based on spiritual fraternity not the family, shared goods through the diaconate, and refused to take each other to law to settle disputes. In relation to religious law they were further defined by 'faith' and inwardness, rather than by external conformity. In relation to each other they were united across the old boundaries of 'bond or free, Jew or Gentile', in particular by a common language (or tongue) symbolized at Pentecost as reversing the divisions of Babel. Such a community has aspirations towards perfection which go beyond anything likely to be instituted on the plane of ordinary politics.

However, with political establishment, the perfectionist strain associated with a voluntary group, and relativizing both family and property, is likely to be pursued in the voluntary context of monasticism, or to live on as a radical iconographic motif juxtaposed to the motifs more appropriate to established power. This bifurcation of motifs and of types of organization, means that Christian civilization will be marked by creative tensions between humility and honour, between inwardness or conscience and lawful obedience, between peaceability and justice, between self-giving in love and self-giving in defending one's neighbour against assault or injustice, between 'the world' embraced and 'the world' rejected.

Given the perfectionist thrust of New Testament Christianity and its emphasis on *kairos*, established Christianity has to limit the built-in tensions by reversions to the Hebrew Scriptures (the Old Testament) or by the partial adoption of classical concepts like Stoicism. The Old Testament offers a concept of Solomonic kingship, based on temporal continuity, territory and temple, consonant with established imperial power, and it restores the centrality of the family running 'from generation to generation', and appealing to natural birth rather than second birth in the spirit. Gospel perspectives, emphasizing the temporal proximity of the other kingdom, partly give way to an equable Wisdom appropriate to the everyday and to long-term expectations. Thus at the cathedral of Monreale in Sicily the Norman kings were represented iconographically as Solomonic figures whose destiny might be to re-conquer the physical territory of Jerusalem. In that way the Christian revolution is forced by social realities into partial reverse.

We have now covered the revolutionary first two, and the second two, phases of a 'Western' development: the initial repertoire and its partial reversal. We need now to look at particular trajectories, such as those of Latin (or Southern) Europe, Protestant North-West Europe, and Eastern Europe.

The Latin pattern is one of strife between religion and radical liberalism in the enlightened tradition, above all in France in the period of the Third Republic when severe tensions led to disestablishment in 1905. The French model of the Enlightenment, initially Deist, in the long-run generated a tradition of conflict between the secular and the religious, which was exported to Turkey, to Latin America and to some extent the French colonial empire, and taken up by revolutionary elements in the western intelligentsia. The French Enlightenment differed from all other Enlightenments, German, English, Dutch, Scottish and American, in regarding religion as a form of organic and authoritarian unity opposed to democracy, and needing to be subdued or even replaced by an organic unity founded on the secular nationalism of a lay Republic. The strife over a secular rather than a religious definition of nationalism in Spain and Italy had rather different outcomes. Two rival and undemocratic traditions, secular and religious, clashed in the Spanish Civil War, as well as in the Mexican and Russian Civil Wars, pushing the Catholic Church into a collusion with conservative authoritarian regimes. But the outcome of the Second World War enabled the Catholic Church to embrace Christian Democracy as its centre-right route to democracy and as the only viable alternative to totalitarian communism established in Eastern Europe and its proxies in the communist parties of the West. In the wake of Vatican II the Catholic Church partially repudiated the kind of Catholic *intégrisme* adopted in the mid-nineteenth century in reaction to secular liberalism, and saw itself more as a major player in the democratic politics of Western Europe. As the communist threat was seen off, so Catholic voting declined and, deprived of a revolutionary threat, *Democrazia Cristiana* in Italy went into crisis.

Two other patterns of relationship between religion, violence and democracy (and, one should add, secularization) are worth canvassing: that of the outer Protestant rim of Scandinavia, Holland and Britain, marked by steady democratization without religion as such being at the heart of contention; and that of Central and Eastern Europe where the Enlightenment was itself absolutist, and religion associated with nation-building, though with some exceptions, notably in what is now the liberal Czech Republic.

In Britain, (including Canada, Australia and New Zealand), in Scandinavia and Holland, the Protestant religion has generally helped make the path to democracy easy. Indeed, a faith which emphasizes personal conscience rather than ecclesiastical authority has some affinities with democracy, and the proportion of Protestant countries with a record of stable and early democracy is uniquely high. Insofar as there are Catholic minorities (and this includes the USA), they have traditionally been outside the elite sectors and unlikely to espouse an organicist conservatism, though something like that was tried in the post-independence Irish Republic from 1922 until the collapse in the 1980s with the emergence of the 'Celtic Tiger' economy. Insofar as most Protestant countries developed steadily over a long period, without major pile-ups of difficult problems and did not suffer the trauma of military defeat, the path to democracy was relatively smooth, though Norway had a brush with the extreme left in the twenties, and Sweden with the right in the thirties. Insofar as there was a religious pluralism among Protestant groups (examples here might be the relationship between the pietism of the Bergen hinterland and the old left, or between English nonconformity and the Liberal and Labour parties), their political allegiances were spread across the parties without the emergence of a specific politico-religious bloc.

Moreover, the conservatism of the state churches was moderate in tone, and there were many Anglicans and Lutherans with concerns for welfare provision. The clergy of the Protestant state churches were in any case not a separate echelon but integrated into the universities and middle classes. The specifically religious parties of Scandinavia have been small and mainly represent the values of people on the periphery anxious about the moral styles espoused at the centre. In this respect Holland was distinctive, since, like Germany, it had a large regional, and to some extent Catholic, population, with specific political representation in pursuit of equality in a country where the key elites were mostly Protestant. The disaster which overtook German democracy 1933–45 is too complex, and in my view too specific, for discussion here, but it does not undermine the overall relationship between Protestantism and democracy. What the German case does raise is the issue of the relation between Protestantism and nationalism, which has been generally positive, partly because Protestant reading of the Old Testament produced identifications with the history of Israel, above all in the USA but also in Ulster and England. On the one hand a moderate Enlightenment encouraged identifications with Rome and Athens at the elite level, while readings of the Bible among the people at large encouraged identifications with Israel, and even a somewhat ambivalent philo-semitism. The Jewish populations of the Anglo-Saxon world simply amplified religious pluralism, and often inclined to the centre-left, at least till recently. One might add that Protestant minorities in Czech Lands and in Hungary were differentially associated with democratic liberal nationalism.

The situation in Eastern Europe was in many ways the reverse of the situation in the Protestant North Atlantic countries. Many of the countries concerned were part of the Austro-Hungarian Empire, the Prussian Empire or the Russian Empire, all of them with histories of enlightened absolutism. That reminds us that historically enlightenment and absolutism have often gone together, and illustrates the sociological principle put forward earlier to the effect that the destination of a given idea (religious or secular), depends as much on context and type of society as on its intrinsic character. Those countries not under the rule of the 'Christian' empires were under the rule of the Ottoman Empire, which had only a muted or 'shy' Enlightenment.

Throughout much of Eastern (and Central) Europe the emergence of movements for national self-determination brought into being an ethno-religiosity, with a strong xenophobic as well as – except in Bulgaria – an anti-semitic component, and ideological attachment to ideas of suffering, as in Poland, or suffering martyrdom, as in Serbia. For that matter imperial Russia also nourished messianic tendencies in association with nationalism, and these have resurfaced strongly since the demise of communism, so much so that the Church and the army now emerge together as the two 'most trusted' institutions in contemporary Russia.

The attempted revolutions of 1848 were liberal, nationalist and democratic, but the record of newly independent countries, particularly between the two world wars, includes marked tendencies to a conservative authoritarianism, even Fascism, with some association between religion and agrarian or peasant parties. Whether political regimes were conservative authoritarian, or indeed, communist authoritarian, the Orthodox Church retained its Byzantine inheritance of '*symphonia*' between Church and state. In Romania, for example, collaboration was strikingly close, both under monarchical and communist authoritarian governments. Monarchs and communists alike dealt harshly with dissidents.

Yet the association of religion with nationalism in the circumstances of communist decline, economic failure and moral bankruptcy meant that nationalist, religious and democratic forces emerged in liaison in the final years of the twentieth century and the opening ones of the twenty-first, not only in Eastern Europe but in the Western Ukraine and Georgia. Indeed, the revolutions beginning in 1989 and continuing up to the Orange revolution in the Ukraine in 2004, probably had stronger religious aspects than was the case with the liberal nationalist revolutions of the nineteenth century. Religion provided much of the symbolism of revolution, above all in Poland, though it could not provide a coherent policy, and attempts to reinstate religious moral positions in terms of state law mostly failed, though in Poland at least the Church had some degree of success. The clearest identification of a Church with democracy as such was in East Germany (the former DDR). Though the communist government had been uniquely successful in reducing identification with Lutheranism to a minority, it was the Lutheran Church that provided the main havens and venues for dissidence. There was, however, little increase in the everyday influence of the Church or in the levels of belief and attendance post-1989. As in the rest of Eastern Europe there was a moment when the Church provided the one continuing institutional presence able to carry the search for a new autonomous identity. One might add that in Eastern Europe as a whole, including Russia, the sense of religious community in association with the affirmation of national identity is not necessarily pro-western or pro-capitalist. Indeed, there is considerable suspicion about western materialism, consumerism and rampant individualism, as well as a dislike of religious pluralism as likely to undermine ethno-religious unity. Greece, for example, nourishes a religiously toned nationalism suspicious of the EU agenda, and of migrants and multiculturalism, in part because of a perceived threat from its traditional enemy, Turkey. According to Richard Pipes, Russia under Putin has reverted to a classic combination of autocracy, Orthodoxy and messianism (assisted by gas and oil) after the kleptocratic free for all under Yeltsin. In Russia the distinction between state and society remains weak. The rule of law is less important than stability.[3]

---

[3]   Pipes, Richard, *Russian Conservatism and its Critics: A Study in Political Culture* (New Haven: Yale University Press, 2006).

An Overview

An overview of this variegated scene suggests that Protestantism has provided uniquely easy passage for democracy, in spite of a partial association of state churches with elite strata and a conservatism of throne and altar, for instance in Scandinavia and Germany. By contrast, in the Orthodox world the traditional Byzantine *symphonia* of Church and state has produced an identification of Church with nation, not with democracy, and certainly not with pluralism. Yet the circumstances of communist dominance and then of its collapse made possible some links between religion, national independence, and democratization.

The Catholic Church, being a body extended through many cultures, entertains various tendencies depending on its location and interests. The fortress mentality of nineteenth-century Catholicism, with its authoritarian, *intégriste* and anti-liberal stances, was breached by Vatican II, but there is still a sense, represented by the present Pope, that the Church is the natural educator of nations, as well as sole long-term guardian of Europe's historical and cultural identity.[4] Moreover, the Church faces an increasingly aggressive secularist agenda, insisting that dialogue be conducted solely on its own terms. In other words, we have an illiberal version of liberalism which seems to have adopted the old Catholic view that error has no rights, and disavows those cultural continuities of the European identity in which Christianity is profoundly implicated.

The dominant liberalism has also been forced to question its own commitment to pluralism and multiculturalism in view of the increasing Islamic presence, demographically and politically. That is an anxiety it shares with the Vatican, though some of the attitudes of the Catholic Church, for instance in relation to sexual morality and the public display of religious symbols, give it a community of interest with Islam. There is another sense in which Christianity and Islam are allied, and that is with respect to their shared emphasis on the communal rather than the individual. Both originated in communal societies and in any case their understanding of 'the religious' is inherently solidary and communal. That stress on the solidary and communal, especially in Catholicism and Islam rather than in Protestantism, is in tension within the negotiated compromises inherent in multicultural societies defined by a combination of accepted difference with an overarching shared civility. Islamic minorities press for inclusion under the rubric of a multiculturalism and civil society, while at the same time linked to societies more inclined to the unity of religious and national identity and the close alliance of religious and secular law. If the Catholic Church has largely abandoned that integral vision Islam has not, thus creating a dilemma as to how far liberal tolerance can extend to minorities, increasingly segregated in cultural ghettoes at a

---

[4] On the major change achieved by Vatican II, at the instance of Bishops in the Anglo-sphere and Northern Europe in alliance with Latin American Bishops, at the expense of the Southern Latin Europeans, cf. Wilde, Melissa J., *Vatican II: A Sociological Analysis of Religious Change* (Princeton: Princeton University Press, 2007).

considerable distance from the values of civil society. How Islamic minorities, and indeed Islamic majorities, select from their own repertoire, without an intervening enlightenment or a reformation other than movements like Wahhabism, remains an undecided question. As in the Catholic case, it seems to depend on where Muslims are, so that in the United States they mostly assimilate to the pluralistic ideal, whereas in Europe they are divided, and in Pakistan (say) they are menacingly hostile to minorities. But, as was observed earlier, if half of Islamia is now under democratic governance, the crucial factor inhibiting democracy is presumably not Islam.

Chapter 11
Christianity, Violence and Democracy

The Argument

My argument is simple. Normatively understood, Christianity is that particular kind of transcendent vision that looks for 'peace on earth, goodwill toward men'. However, it encounters the social sacred, as articulated by Durkheim, which partly absorbs it, and the resistant secularity of politics, power and violence, as articulated by Machiavelli, which largely deflects it. Mediating between these mighty opposites stands Wisdom, or practical reason, operating as peaceably as may be for the time being. Secularization takes various forms: the *partial* absorption of Christianity as the sacred legitimation of empire, countered by voluntaristic protest movements operating outside the social space of political necessity, and successive exposures of raw secularity, from Machiavelli to Hobbes, Social Darwinism and the Freudian deconstruction even of love. However, the Enlightenment is yet another partial secularization, converting the visionary hopes of Christianity into rational potentialities in history, thereby generating the category of secular religion, cherishing unappeasable hopes of political utopia on earth, and/or a liberation of the self. In both versions it encounters the necessities of politics and of the social sacred embodied in ritual and hierarchy. Liberal Enlightenment is, therefore, a project based on *a mistake about the world*, the *saeculum*. However, the attempt to embrace mere secularity on the Humean empiricist model, as a way out of the impasse is itself not viable.

If this rather terse paragraph seems less than immediately self-explanatory, the rest of the chapter is devoted to unpacking it.

Setting out the Frame

I want to achieve a fresh angle of vision on the religious and the political by moving the goalposts. I am going to shift the boundaries of what we conventionally mean by secularization and the transcendent, and I am going to assume the steady persistence of a secular regimen of politics, power and violence associated with our involuntary membership in society as such. Through all the changes and chances of history and culture over millennia this mundane reality can be taken for granted.

However, the regimen of power and violence is only exposed *theoretically* quite late in the history of Christendom by Machiavelli and his various successors, from Hobbes to Sorel and Pareto, though one might suggest that Machiavelli's analysis of power was earlier anticipated by Ibn Khaldun within a context of a religion much readier to accept secular realities than Christianity. In Europe it is only in the Renaissance that the primordial and implicit secular practice is converted into an explicit secularization. Other explicit secularizations follow, such as the Darwinian exposure of the realities of power and violence in Nature, and its transfer to social relations through Social Darwinism and versions of Nietzsche, and the Freudian exposure of the dynamics of the psyche. Counter-posed to these raw outcrops of the explicitly secular, I trace various incursions of what I call the Christian transcendent, which I see as having a significant association with movements based on the voluntary principle, and therefore operating in social space partly removed from the imperatives of power and violence. These movements, for example Primitive Christianity, monasticism, the Waldensians, the friars, the Anabaptists, some of the Puritans, the Evangelicals and the Pentecostals, have the potential to embody the Christian vision of peace. Whether that vision is realized depends on their social location, for example the Cluniac role in the Crusades, the Dominican involvement in the Inquisition and the Jesuit role in the courts of Counter-Reformation Europe.

In between the various outcrops of the explicitly secular and the incursions of the Christian transcendent, I place the 'social sacred' – or the protecting veil thrown over the lineaments of society, as well as the mediating notion of wisdom or practical reason, holding back both the pressure of the Christian transcendent and the raw reality of the explicitly secular. Wisdom works in the constantly extended interim between the raw present and the forward looking hopes and apocalyptic anxieties of the peaceable kingdom.

The latter part of the argument deals with expressions of the transcendent within the immanent frame characteristic of modernity. These expressions take the form of rival Enlightenment visions, partly derived from the Christian transcendent, and embodied in the nation or the party, or the party in the form of the nation. They also take the form of subjective utopias sought in the self, and inimical to the social realities of institutions, whether political or religious, and to all such institutions entail with respect to authority, hierarchy and ritual. The individualistic vision collides with the imperatives of the collective, and in some of its expressions it even seems to dispense with any framework of meaning and purpose. For example, one in 20 Danes is an explicit atheist, but one in five is a functional atheist, that is, one for whom God has no relevance whatever.

The Specifically Christian Transcendent

The Christian transcendent is in tension with the sacred understood in Durkheimian terms as a manifestation of the majesty of society rather than the judgement and mercy of God. I am referring to the explicitly Christian transcendent because the Islamic transcendent seems more closely related to the Durkheimian sacred. Though in Islam God himself is totally transcendent, his presence is realized

.

in holy lands, holy places and holy temples, rather than in a kingdom 'not of this world'. The Islamic kingdom is of this world and thus inherently political, whereas the Christian kingdom resists incorporation in the political sphere. The difference is crucial, so that Islamic law can form the basis of ordinary society while Christian grace cannot. While it is clear that all over the Christian world the Passion and the Resurrection are acted *out* in public, especially in Catholic and Orthodox countries, they cannot be acted *upon* as a basis for ordinary political practice. The action of the Passion cannot be realized politically but belongs to the arena of the Church understood as a divine society set over against the City of Man. That is because it is against the grain, not as Stanley Hauerwas maintains, with the grain.[1] You can only think self-offering a collective political tactic, and the power of the Resurrection a political potentiality, if you believe, against the facts, that Christianity is with the grain. The City of Man is at best governed in terms of reciprocity and justice, and for the most part it is in practice governed by norms of domination, honour, face, prestige, revenge, and a struggle for survival. One cannot forgive one's political opponents sitting on the bench opposite, or admit one's own trespasses, without breaking the rules of collective solidarity. Nations do not offer themselves up in love to redeem the international order.

I now need to give some account of the Christian transcendent as it goes against the grain and has some association with voluntary groups operating in social space outside the strict imperatives of politics. I have in mind here the monastic ideal of seeking the peace of God in the solitary place, and the principles of members of the Society of Friends as they tried to establish peaceable relations in Pennsylvania. For the sources of such ideals and principles I go back to Karl Jaspers on the Axial Age beginning about 1,000 BC,[2] and to Max Weber on religious rejections, or transformations, of the world.

The Axial Age, paradigmatically represented by Christianity and Buddhism, replaces the heroic ethic of self-assertion, honour and shame associated with loyalty to the family and the tribe, with an ethic of disinterested self-offering ignoring all particular boundaries. In its Christian version it simultaneously 'puts the body under subjection', questioning the imperatives of sexual reproduction central to Genesis, and affirms the body as the vehicle of God's self-emptying in Christ. The Word became flesh, and divine love became vulnerable in 'the form of a servant'. Whereas in tribal society time is characteristically experienced as constant recurrence and as seasonal rotation, according to the order of nature, and whereas in Buddhism Nirvana is timeless, Christianity anticipates an advent or epiphany in due time. The Christian transcendent eclipses all the particular

---

[1]　Hauerwas, Stanley, *With the Grain of the Universe* (London: SCM Press, 2001); a defence of Hauerwas is provided by Sam Wells in 'The Nature and Destiny of Serious Theology' in Richard Harries and Stephen Platten, (eds), *Reinhold Niebuhr and Contemporary Politics God and Power* (Oxford: Oxford University Press, 2010: 71–86).

[2]　Jaspers, Karl, *The Origin and Goal of History* (New Haven: Yale University Press, 1955).

locations of holy land, holy place and holy temple, and seeks to replace the regimen of violence, always potentially present in the earthly city, with the spiritual temple of the body of Christ made real, realized, in the common language of Pentecost, through the gift of tongues reversing the mutual incomprehensibility of Babel, and in the shared sacrifice of the common meal, known as the Eucharist or Holy Communion.

As time is tilted towards a second advent, suffused by hope and apocalyptic anxiety, so the Christian 'way' is understood as a journey or pilgrimage towards a more 'abiding city', a New Jerusalem 'above', which is 'mother of us all'. Membership in this city is voluntary, because it requires a new birth according to the spirit not the flesh, and a ceremony of admission. This ceremony is a baptismal passage through water to a new life of grace. Some scholars argue it is precisely this idea of a journey, realized in personal biography and in collective history that is made problematic by modernity. At the same time the idea is reaffirmed in contemporary life by the increasing popularity of pilgrimage.

What then of the aspiration to peace? Peace is envisaged in the animal kingdom, as well as in society between man and man, and beyond that between man and God, and inwardly in the heart. The key texts are in Isaiah 11:1–9, in Micah 4:1–5 where the prophet anticipates a peaceable kingdom on the mountain of the Lord, in the Sermon on the Mount, and also in the Epistle to the Hebrews 12:22–4 and in the Epistle to the Ephesians 2:14–18 where Christ breaks down 'the middle wall of separation' distinguishing Jew from Gentile to inaugurate a 'general assembly' on Mount Zion. The three mountains together symbolize the breaking in of the transcendent, while on the hill of Golgotha the self-offering or sacrificial gift of God secures peace, vertically and horizontally. This is then echoed liturgically. The Eucharist is punctuated by 'Peace be with you: and with thy spirit', by the kiss of peace, and in the closing phases by the prayer 'Grant us thy peace'.

The boundaries between Jew and Gentile are erased, the taboos and ritual acts protecting these boundaries, such as circumcision and food prohibitions, abolished, and ritual itself subordinated to inward sincerity. Peace displaces war, sincerity ritual, the poor the wealthy, the universal the particular, and choice automatic membership. Clearly, so comprehensive a revolution not only encounters resistance or reaction, but socio-logically engenders it, because (for example) even inwardness requires outward and material expression if it is to reproduce itself. In the same way, universality creates the resistant 'Other'. The cost of universalism is counted in the resistance of the particular and rival forms of universalism. Faith (or trust) cannot displace law, without either embracing an impossible perfection fulfilling the law, or an antinomian collapse into moral anarchy, 'sinning the more that grace may abound the more'. Human helplessness and recourse to irresistible grace can be interpreted as licence 'to love God and do as you like'. Once again, this is not simply theology, but the alternative moves or options built into the symbolic socio-logic of Christianity, and frequently realized in Christian history, especially in times of revolutionary crisis (or *kairos*), whether by George Fox or by John of Leyden as he presided over a mixture of moral anarchy and dictatorship.

So far I have repeated my own earlier arguments, though with an emphasis on the key motif of peace in the symbolic socio-logic of Christianity, given my current focus on the coiled up resistance of our social nature as that is built in to power, politics and the regimen of violence.[3] I now need to bring out the theme of choice as realized in voluntary movements with the potential to escape or transcend the necessities of power. I have already suggested some of the incursions of the transcendent in Christian history found in voluntary movements from Primitive Christianity to Pentecostalism. Of course, even a voluntary group needs forms of authority, and has to negotiate disagreements through rules agreed or imposed. The New Testament is hardly a manual of principles of negotiation, and there is much that cannot be settled by waiting on the spirit to bring about consensus. Alternatively, a voluntary group can split up, which is in practice what happens throughout Christian history. Voluntary groups seek to fuse people together in a shared, chosen solidarity, but fusion soon ends in fission.

Once the voluntary group becomes established in power and takes over/is taken over by the state, a fresh power dynamic comes into play. For one thing Christian leaders are now drawn from state-bearing elites, reared on the assumptions of the powerful, and senator and bishop sit adjacent to one another. If social unity is sought through religious unity, sectarian fission must give way to fusion, unity must be imposed and dissidents excommunicated. If Christianity covers the whole of life, comprehensively, rather than being just a ritual practice, the urge to social or imperial unity will create a universal institution, with a universal head, a *Pontifex Maximus*, sitting adjacent to the Emperor, just as bishop sits adjacent to senator. Whereas the distinction between the kingdom of peace and grace and 'the principalities and the powers', created a boundary between Church and world, the boundary now runs through, that is, *inside*, the Church-state system. The result is that the space between Christianity and 'the world' is converted into a space between Church hierarchies and secular hierarchies, while another space emerges inside the Church between 'secular' clergy and 'religious virtuosi' who pursue Christian ideals in bounded communities, which are in their turn stabilized by a 'rule' administered by authoritative 'fathers-in-God'.

The kingdom of peace will be progressively postponed, while in the interim the secular dynamic of power begins to invade the Church. Although power is intrinsic to government, whether for good or ill, it also corrupts, and the corruption of the vehicle of hope creates protest movements seeking to restore the pristine gospel: the *virtuosi* emerge, segregating themselves from the wider context of society to create islands of peace. However, these peaceful groups, whether inside or outside the Church, require strong authority since consensus cannot automatically be assumed. The pre-conditions of society as such are *in part* replicated in groups designed to subvert them, otherwise protest itself cannot survive.

---

[3]   Martin, David, *Pacifism: An Historical and Sociological Study* (London: Routledge, 1965).

The Social Sacred

My basic contrast can be dramatized by comparing the voluntary, mobile, peaceful character of Pentecostalism with Catholicism as a traditional identity still rooted in place, even today. By place I mean the tutelary saints of city and hearth, the crosses erected by highways or in high places, and the territorial organization of the parish or diocese. I am also referring to the symmetry between ecclesiastical and social hierarchies (notwithstanding the spectacular instances of social mobility via ecclesiastical preferment), and the continuity of tradition from generation to generation secured by automatic paedo-baptism. Paedo-baptism, meaning the baptism of infants, converts a voluntary sacrament into an involuntary rite of passage of reception into a 'natural' community, analogous to circumcision. Catholicism has been the religion of emplacement, mimicking the secular practice of power, which is an inevitable development, given the mingling of personnel in the nurseries of political and ecclesiastical leadership.

However, Catholicism devises normative constraints on the secular practice of power, notably the just war and the just price. In time it develops a critique of capitalism and the inhumane domination of utility, and of the associated Protestant understanding of work.[4] Catholicism also retains a space between the Christian transcendent and the social sacred, through aspirations to a sanctity which is *not* biologically transmitted, through the doctrine of the two swords, ecclesiastical and temporal, and through the assertion of the universal over the local. At the same time the disruptive potency of the transcendent is redirected to support the regime it symbolically undermines, setting up an internal dynamic of legitimation and de-legitimation, above all in iconography. Iconography, as Emile Mâle shows in the Introduction to *The Gothic Image*, links the higher order with the lower at the same time as it overturns the higher in the name of the lowly, or of 'the cringing ones', to render the New Testament more precisely.[5] For example, monks became part of a wealthy 'estate' praying for the rest of society, and receiving gifts from the higher orders to secure a place in Paradise, just as the higher orders demanded service from lower orders in return for the 'service' of protection. The Church earths the lightning of the transcendent, standing between God and man in more senses than one.

For this Durkheimian type of society it is a very serious matter whose insignia dominates the high and holy place, whose emblem flies over the citadel, whose flag is burnt in the public square, whose profane activity pollutes it, whose statue is toppled by whom, whose language is treated as normative, especially for the naming of places, whose icons and holy pictures are defaced or whitewashed out, and whose holy book used as lavatory paper.

---

   [4]   Hughes, *The End of Work: Theological Critiques of Capitalism* (Oxford: Blackwell, 2007); I am thinking in the British context of Eric Gill and David Jones and their diffuse relation to Chesterton, Ruskin and Morris.

   [5]   Mâle, Emile, *The Gothic Image* (London: Fontana, 1961: 1–26).

So-called 'secular' societies can display sensitivities very like those of conventionally 'religious' societies. When Estonians proposed moving a memorial to Soviet war dead their action was described as 'blasphemous' and a 'desecration'. In Russia at the present time secular and religious expressions co-exist: the cult of Lenin continues in his mausoleum, and Yeltsin's body rested in the recently restored Cathedral of Christ the Saviour in the first state funeral under Orthodox auspices since 1894. So strong is the position of the Orthodox Church today (now reunited at home and abroad), that no party in Russia finds it politic to promote an anti-religious agenda. It was President Putin, the ex-KGB Head, who said Christianity was the bedrock of European civilization, a sentiment one would not expect to hear even from Gordon Brown or Angela Merkel, both of them children of Christian pastors.

Wisdom, Set between Raw Survival and the Visionary Gleam

So far we have been dealing with a polar contrast between the voluntary and the involuntary, the unbounded and the located, the potentially peaceful group and an established Church not only involved in political power as a functional necessity for good or ill, but embroiled in its raw and expansive dynamic. Beyond that, a Durkheimian understanding of the potency of the social sacred has been contrasted with the tension introduced by the Christian transcendent. I now have to insert the Spirit of Wisdom, Sophia (or practical reason understood as its secular incarnation), as another middle term between the raw use and abuse of secular power and the tension introduced by the Christian transcendent. Whereas the Spirit can break out in flames in the voluntary sector, or erupt in folk Catholicism when ignited by the supernatural and miraculous, it can also operate as a 'pure and peaceable' mode of governance. Stephen Sykes has analysed wisdom at work in the person of Gregory the Great and in the maxims that guided him as a monk separated from power and a politician responsible for justice and the survival and the good of the state.[6] The biblical model here is Solomon, the wise and just ruler of a prosperous nation. In the various writings attributed to him, Solomon concentrated on everyday maxims and proverbs for the proximate future, rather than canvassing an eschatological hope of the 'other kingdom' and the associated anxiety of the apocalypse. For the Solomonic tradition the flow of time is relatively stable, and the office of faith is stoically to withstand its depredations rather than to cherish any ultimate hope of transformation. Were this an essay in political theology rather than sociology I would treat the Solomonic tradition as an instance of government understood as an institution of a good created order. Perhaps I would also say that what are in my view the restrictions placed by the political order on the dynamic of redemption, for example forgiving your political opponents for their mistakes, do not entail

---

[6] Sykes, Stephen, *Power and Christian Theology* (London: Continuum, 2006).

some restriction of that dynamic to the Church. After all, my argument implies that ecclesiastical politics exhibit the same features as politics in general.

The Rationality of Religion in the Public Sphere

The role of wisdom, conceived in the form of Sophia, and allied to practical reason, raises an issue which may appear philosophical, but has important sociological implications. It concerns the rational, or at least the reasonable, articulation of religion in the public sphere. Keith Ward, in his *Is Religion Dangerous?*, argues for a reasonable account of faith, and Roger Trigg, in *Religion in Public Life*, argues for a rational account.[7] If religion, or rather Christianity (since this is the focus both for Trigg and myself), is a mode of rational thinking, then it appears in the political forum as of right.

But what are the aspects of religion capable of a rational articulation? Presumably they concern the idea of God the Creator (or the transcendent) as argued for in Natural Law, and the status of the human, with all that is taken to imply with regard to abortion, euthanasia, contraception, issues in bio-ethics like stem-cell research, and normative concepts of gender. Yet it is precisely in these areas that religious interventions strike many observers as problematic. I have already suggested that the drama of redemption and resurrection can be acted *out* in public (for example in Greece) but not acted *upon* in public, but even with regard to God the Creator, the European Union was the site of a debate, with the allies of the Pope on the one side, and much of *laïque* Western Europe on the other. Issues of gender notoriously divide parts of Eastern Europe, for example, from secularist voices in Western Europe. These two arenas of contention have both been decided in favour of the secularist view, and the victors are increasingly inclined to press home their advantage, dismissing religion as an essentially private affair. From a secularist viewpoint Europe does not have a soul, and Jacques Delors' quest for 'a soul for Europe' is simply a recipe for conflict. Who is in a position to declare which of the traditions that historically have contributed to the formation of modern Europe is normative today: Christianity, monotheism, Enlightened deism or paganism, ancient, romantic or modern?

Christians hold various views about the appropriate contribution of religion in the political forum. The Protestant view varies within a spectrum running from a ceremonially 'established' Church expressing a view as a Church (or ecumenically) but on the model of a voluntary pressure group, to a populist notion of a moral majority and a very different idea of individuals reflecting conscientiously as Christians on such issues as may arise and maybe coming to quite variable conclusions. However, in Germany the Protestant and Catholic churches have tended to express joint views on questions in the area of eugenics, in part because

---

[7]   Ward, Keith, *Is Religion Dangerous?* (Oxford: Lion Hudson, 2006); Trigg, *Religion in Public Life*.

the Nazi past renders such questions very sensitive. In Britain by contrast, eugenics is a less sensitive area, though still subject to contestation.

The Orthodox view stands at the far end of a spectrum of positions, holding to the traditional Byzantine notion of the *symphonia* between Church and state, but also reluctant to question the state, provided its institutional rights are safeguarded, especially when it comes to religious competition. Thus in Russia the open attitude to religious competition in the early 1990s has become more restrictive, and in Greece the Church, especially under its recent vigorous leadership, has been concerned with restricting religious competition and maintaining religious teaching in the schools, as well as with pan-Orthodox political action (for instance with respect to Serbia) and the essentially Orthodox character of Greek identity over, for example, the issue of religion being specified on state identity cards. In Romania and in Moldova there have been major tensions over which brand of Orthodoxy represents the national identity, and these have roots in historic disputes over appropriate ethnic borders.[8] The Catholic Church varies in its approach between guarding its specific rights where it is a minority, and promoting legislation in accordance with natural law and its role as guardian of civilization where it is a majority.

What then are the areas of tension with regard to religion in the public sphere? As Charles Taylor has shown, the mainstream Christian churches of the West, especially their leaders, share most of the values of secular politicians precisely because what Taylor calls 'the modern moral structure' is the product of an interaction between Christianity and the Enlightenment, notably the human rights agenda, including 'happiness' (or 'felicity' argued for by Thomas Aquinas long before Thomas Jefferson).[9] The areas of contention are likely, therefore, to concern the status, governing conditions, and freedom of activity of religious bodies, above all the socialization of the next generation through education. Where Church and state have fought over the body and soul of the nation, as in France, education becomes the focus of the struggle, whereas where the struggle has been muted, as in Scandinavia, an agreed minimum of Christian knowledge mutates into generalized understandings of religious traditions. Then there is the issue of proselytism, so important to the New Religious Movements of particular concern to James Beckford. Finally, there are issues clustering around sex, gender and bio-ethics where sectors of the churches have views on the essential constitution of 'the human' strongly opposed to the more or less dominant secular consensus.

---

[8]   Hann, Christopher, (ed.), *The Post-Socialist Religious Question: Faith and Power in Central Asia and East-Central Europe* (Berlin: Lit-Verlag, 2006).

[9]   Taylor, *Sources of the Self.*

Outcrops of Raw Secularity

In one sense the Constantinian establishment of Christianity can be regarded as a secularization, and if that were followed through, all the sacral elements embodied in the legitimation of monarchs like Justinian, Alfred and Charlemagne would be accounted secular. However, that particular shift in criteria is not what interests me here. My present concern is with explicit outcrops of a continuing raw secular practice, running counter to the explicit incursions of the Christian transcendent. The first and great secularization comes with the Renaissance view of power as articulated by Machiavelli and his successors up to the German military theorists and other European geo-politicians in the nineteenth and twentieth centuries. There is on the one hand a combined Christian and classical tradition of statecraft, combining the classical hero with the saintly administrator, and on the other the dynamic of political survival. What Machiavelli and the Machiavellian tradition exposes is the dynamic of political survival. This exposure scandalized Christian Europe in a way it would not have scandalized more 'secular' civilizations, such as China, unaffected by Christianity, and the sentiments travelling in its wake.

The second great secularization is associated with Darwin. In one way that was not about raw social power at all, but about raw power and the struggle for survival in the natural world. Nevertheless there was a Christian version of a redeemed cosmos, and a harmonious conception of Nature such as one finds luminously expressed in Haydn's *The Creation* and his setting of James Thompson in *The Seasons* as well as in Handel's setting of Dryden's *Ode to Saint Cecilia*. Nature 'red and raw' did not chime with this view. Moreover, the survival of the fittest soon found expression in Social Darwinism, in debased versions of Schopenhauer's 'life force' and Nietzsche's supra-moral superman, in pagan faiths of blood and soil, and scientific racism. Colin Kidd, in his recent book on the Bible and the forging of race in the Protestant Atlantic world (but not only there), has indicated how Enlightenment racism and scientific racism strained against the Biblical vision of monogenesis in Adam, even though there were plenty of Christian writers capable of subverting that vision, in particular by latching on to the idea in Genesis of the cursed lineage of Ham, and identifying the children of Ham with 'inferior races'.[10]

This is a very complex story, and Darwin himself held firmly to the unity of humankind, but a racism based on the authority of science was very widespread. It was not finally ejected from all respectable science until the years after the Second World War. Just what amalgams were possible can be judged by the combination of Christianity and science represented by a character in Chekhov's short story 'The Duel'.[11] The theme could be continued with the deconstruction of love in the myths of Freudian psychoanalysis, and other 'masters of suspicion'. The Christian

---

[10]   Kidd, Colin, *The Forging of Races*: *Race and Scripture in the Protestant Atlantic World, 1600–2000* (Cambridge: Cambridge University Press, 2006).

[11]   Chekov, Anton, 'The Duel', in Anton Chekov, *The Russian Master and Other Stories* (Oxford: Oxford University Press, 1992: 90–92).

narrative of the soul on its journey, so central to Puritan introspection and the genesis of the intimate diary, becomes what Philip Rieff called *The Triumph of the Therapeutic*, above all in the United States.[12]

The Dubious Secularity of the Enlightenment

But how far was the Enlightenment itself an expression of the secular? Once again, much depends on how you move the goalposts in marking out the boundaries of the religious (or the mythic) and the secular. John Gray, in his *Black Mass*, argues that the political perversion of religion, in particular the redeployment of the Christian myth of the Apocalypse to promote utopian visions of a world made new, is *the* key to modern history.[13] One of the great themes of the theory of secularization has envisaged *the* transition from the religious to the political, but in reality there has only been a partial transition for 'the time being', meaning by that our current modernity. In the course of that transition, the power of God held back in the transcendent realm, is translated into human empowerment, unleashing thereby a torrent of exemplary violence. In terms very like those used by the historian Michael Burleigh and the sociologist, S. N. Eisenstadt, John Gray, as a political philosopher, instances the terrible history from the Jacobins to the Bolsheviks, as well as the Russian anarchists like Bakunin, and contemporary radical Islamists, American neo-conservatives and neo-liberal Evangelicals.[14]

It is not only the idea of the transition from the religious to the political that needs to be questioned, but also the idea of the transition from the mythic to the scientific. Enlightenment thinking purports to be scientific but it is infiltrated by precisely the myths it pretends to undermine and disprove, in part because such myths are more securely embedded in generic human experience, or rather, I would say, the specific Christian rendering of that experience.

Where it most obviously differs from mainstream Christianity is in altering, indeed excising, the Christian coding of the resistance to 'heavens below' through the concept of original sin. The neo-conservative vision of universal democracy imposed by the exercise of American power (for example in Iraq), depends on an optimistic Enlightened translation of Christianity, such as you find in Thomas Jefferson, and with even fewer Christian infusions in Thomas Paine. The horrors of the past, in this account, can be attributed not to a generic human violence, whether biologically or culturally based, or an inherent political dynamic (or, as I suspect, both together), but to specific social formations, above all those that united religious power to political power, Church to state. Strike off the chains

---

12 Rieff, Philip, *The Triumph of the Therapeutic* (London: Chatto and Windus, 1966).

13 Gray, *Black Mass*.

14 Burleigh, Michael, *Sacred Causes: Religion and Politics from the European Dictators to Al Qaeda* (London: Harper Collins, 2006); Eisenstadt, *Fundamentalism, Sectarianism and Revolution*.

imposed on the human by such social formations, insert a 'wall of separation' between Church and state, and there would emerge a new humanity in the image and likeness of American democracy. So much for culture, so much for tradition.

This theme of 'secular religion' has been long-established in the sociology of religion, though John Gray has lent it a new lease of life by the verve with which he presents it, and by a pessimistic and atheist perspective darker and more unrelieved than any found in mainstream Christianity since the bleak and sardonic imaginings of James Hogg in his *Private Memoirs and Confessions of a Justified Sinner*.[15]

At one point in *Black Mass* John Gray interprets the Cold War as a conflict between rival versions of the Enlightenment, based respectively in Washington and Moscow. That is clearly correct, and there is no inherent connection between Enlightenment and democracy, any more than there is an inherent connection between Christianity and democracy. It is worth adding that there is an equally plausible connection between Enlightenment and autocracy, particularly the kind of autocracy that pulls down even the flimsy partitions between state and established Church, for example in the St. Petersburg of Peter the Great, and in imperial Berlin and Vienna. This is reform from above, not democracy from below, and it characterized massive swathes of the history of Enlightenment.

The ambiguity that characterizes the relation between Christianity, peace and violence is reproduced, and arguably exacerbated in the Enlightenment, precisely because divine power and judgement has been translated into human power and judgement. Both liberalism and anarchism as movements based on human liberation and autonomy spawn pacific and violent wings. The pacific anarchist tradition of Kropotkin is joined at the hip to the anarchist tradition of violence promoted by Bakunin, just as liberal imperialism in the nineteenth century (and very recently) is joined to liberal pacifism. Both are integrally related to the way the pacifist tradition in Christianity is joined at the hip to the apocalyptic tradition.

The histories of liberal nationalism are replete with mass mobilizations of 'the people' which require ethnic cleansing as a pre-condition of democracy, and not just in Kemalist Turkey in 1922. The origins of nations as 'imagined communities', whether under autocratic aegis (as in Spain in 1492), or created by mass mobilizations, characteristically require the expulsion of the alien. Contemporary politics are infiltrated by the hopes and anxiety of apocalypse, and not just in the various velvet and orange revolutions in the wake of the communist collapse. There is a persistent pressure for a charismatic leader, who is 'whiter than white', who will purge the corruptions of the old order, and who in turn becomes corrupted. The persistent mythic structure of politics turns on the mystery of innocence corrupted, and on the new order of the world (the *novus ordo seclorum* printed on every American one-dollar bill) subverted by the evil ways of an older, sadder, more resigned world. The 2005 revolution in the Ukraine began in what looked like the passion narrative of an upright leader literally poisoned by the representatives of the old (Soviet) order, and the revolutionary mobilization in

---

[15]   Hogg, James, *Private Memoirs and Confessions of a Justified Sinner* (Harmondsworth: Penguin, 2004).

the Madan (or central square) in Kiev was marked by quasi-eucharistic and baptismal celebrations. Within months, the pure new leader was being accused of corruption by his almost equally charismatic second-in-command, until she in turn faced charges of financial irregularities.

The Subjectivization of the *Eschaton*

One uses a phrase like 'the subjectivization of the *eschaton*' in heavy quotation marks, and mainly to indicate a connection between what Charles Taylor calls 'The Turn to the Self' and the immanentization of the *eschaton* in political religion.[16] Once again, one is dealing with a political translation of Christianity, in particular by way of Luther and pietism, freed from the constraints of the collective and the sacramental. Certainly these constraints have a history of oppression weighing heavily on the minds of subject populations, but the constraints built into collective solidarities are not necessarily oppressive. Sociologically one has a choice of 'oppressions' not a choice between subjective liberation and the oppressions of group solidarity. As will be indicated below, authority, ritual and collective constraints are all pre-conditions of the social, rather than antithetical to authentic sociality. The genuine claims of the individual to autonomy, along with claims to respect through the human rights agenda (once again a fusion of Christian and Enlightened motifs, based on a shared image of our human status) are in tension not only with other claims similarly based, but with the claims of constitutive social identities. The demand by a Dutch political pressure group for the age of consent to be reduced to the age of four represents a claim based on notions of autonomy and liberation at odds with other claims similarly based, and with any number of constitutive identities, such as a Catholic identity, a Muslim identity or a Jewish identity. Somehow claims are advanced as if all possible items on the agenda of human rights were of the same weight and kind, whereas in practice they are often claims to special treatment by organized interest groups. The political and cultural wars currently opening up in the extended European Union do not arise *solely* because the more recent members of the community are not up to speed with respect to the liberal revolution in the politics of gender.

'The Turn to the Self' assumes two *semi-secular* forms. First it locates the pursuit of fullness, redemption and paradise in the depths of the inner self at the expense of collective redemption; and second, it converts self-offering into self-expression. This gives rise to a tension between an understanding of the self in terms of sincerity, spontaneity and authenticity, and the inherent requirements of social order (cosmic or otherwise), in terms of authority, internalized discipline, ritual and courtesy. Social institutions, including the Church, become identified with oppressive structures and unacceptable demands, including long-term commitments. The spirit wanders at will under the impulse of unappeasable desire. This epiphany

---

[16] Taylor, *Sources of the Self*.

of the self is incapable of recognizing the structural realities of politics exposed by Machiavelli, and recognized by Christianity under the code name of sin. From this comes the contemporary apathy and scepticism about politics.

The semi-secularization of Christianity through the rejection of self-offering in favour of self-expression draws its nourishment from resources embedded deep in Christianity, and even in Judaism. The priority of the inner spiritual condition over 'mere' external conformity, taught in the parable of the Pharisee and the Publican, has been taken literally 'to heart', as has the prophetic emphasis on the law written 'on the inward parts' and the reduction of the religious requirement to doing justly, loving mercy and (less inviting), 'walking humbly with thy God'. The opposite of the subjective and individual translation of inward grace is *Halakah*, the objective performance of ritual obligation, without emotion or desire, because that belongs to one's collective social identity. In Adam Seligman's formulation in *Ritual and its Consequences: an Essay on the Limits of Sincerity*, the *halakhic* obligation may be as divorced from meaning as it is from desire, though in Christian rituals the meaning is profoundly embedded in the act, even when the act is so habitual as to be automatic.[17] It can be argued that precisely the attempted reduction of religion to inward states reduces the stakes when it comes to conflicts over doctrine. If the criterion is sincerity rather than truth, one example of sincerity is as good as another, and arguments about truth become surplus to requirements. The eclipse of truth by sincerity is very much a marker of the advanced semi-secular condition, and it leads to pan-relativistic conclusions as inimical to institutional academic disciplines as to institutional religions. If there are no hierarchies of truth, judgement and moral or aesthetic value, no agreed canon of excellence, what becomes of the role of the teacher, let alone of the priest or the imam? No wonder the Roman Catholic Church holds to verities which the contemporary intelligentsia in deconstructivist, relativistic, anti-canonical mode, puts at risk. And the Catholic Church is hardly alone in that: contemporary uses of language are saturated in agreed values about what is 'acceptable', as well as infiltrated with intimations of the sacred and what constitutes a violation.

The issue of the canon lies close to the heart of those putative contemporary secularizations which go beyond the semi-secular to embrace something on the verge of mere secularity. The philosopher Stewart Sutherland quotes Alasdair MacIntyre on the question of canonicity as saying that 'an encyclopedia [can] no longer be a set of canonical books for an educated public, since increasingly such publics [have] disintegrated'.[18] I disagree with both MacIntyre and Sutherland, but if that were indeed so, then the university, at one time seen as a replacement for the universal Church, would be going the way of what it purportedly replaced, or (alternatively) the university and the universal Church, the humanist and the Christian, would stand and fall together.

---

[17]   Seligman, Weller, Puett, and Simon, *Ritual and its Consequences*.

[18]   Sutherland, Stewart, 'Nomad's Progress', *Proceedings of the British Academy*, 131 (2005): 443–63.

Sutherland argues that the associated privatization of moral and aesthetic truth, as well as theological truth, undermines a metaphor as fundamental to (say) Plato as to Christianity: the pilgrimage to the 'abiding city' which is to come. Sutherland cites his fellow Scot, David Hume, here as the Enlightened thinker who most undermined the philosophical pre-conditions for such a metaphor to work existentially, in spite of Kant's attempted restoration. 'Man', to use the phraseology of the Shorter Scottish Catechism, does not have a 'chief end'. He only comes to an end. In Sutherland's formulation pilgrims have been replaced by tourists who are lovers of sights and sounds, dealers in experience for its own sake, *going* nowhere. In short order the empiricist project leads to a dead end, and the meaningless succession of one damned thing after another on Matthew Arnold's 'darkling plain', and the tensions of transcendence introduced in the Axial Age have run their course.

Sutherland's preferred nomad is Shostakovich, who managed to survive the three dangers of exile, execution and deformity of talent and integrity. One is bound to ask: whence come these evaluations of a canonical composer?

There are various possible responses to this. One, expressed by another philosopher, Anthony Kenney, holds that the contemporary world has become all too replete with passionate pilgrims, meaning by that fundamentalists in the USA, Africa and the Middle East, including hitherto secular Turkey. It is a view compatible with the argument of John Gray, even though Gray extends the range of what is meant by fundamentalism.[19]

For a concluding response I turn again to Charles Taylor, who would, I suspect, ask about the philosophical basis and subterranean religious sources that underlie criteria of judgement like 'integrity' and 'deformity of talent'. He would renovate meaning and purpose under the rubric of 'fullness', and perhaps point to a Heideggerian and phenomenological upending of the whole empirical project. In his most recent summa, *A Secular Age*, Taylor has traced the transitions from Christianity to Enlightenment to the modern 'secular age', and has made clear that each stage is a further secularization of the moral priorities of the previous one.[20] He does not explicitly attempt to do what I have attempted to do here, which is to trace the religious models underlying much of what appears to be secular politics. Instead he has argued that the West has undergone a transition from a condition in which the transcendent is presupposed, to a fragile, precarious condition of contradictions and cross-pressures, where the taken-for-granted, against which it would be necessary to define a critique, assumes the primacy of the immanent.

---

[19]   Spoken contribution by Anthony Kenney to the debate on Charles Taylor's *A Secular Age*, at the British Academy, 2 May 2007 on the occasion of Charles Taylor receiving the 2007 Templeton Prize.

[20]   Taylor, Charles, *A Secular Age* (Cambridge, MA and London: Harvard University Press, 2007); my comments focus in particular on Chapter 15. The whole of the chapter above is an extended version of my contribution to the British Academy debate on Charles Taylor's work on the occasion of his receiving the 2007 Templeton Prize, 2 May 2007.

The critique as proposed by Taylor argues for openness to the transcendent rather than dogmatic closure. An analysis such as that offered here is compatible with that view, except that I have traced the shadow of the transcendent animating the political tradition, with the bare structure of the dynamic of power showing through the disguises of political rhetoric. Back stairs advisers may propose Machiavellian stratagems, but politicians with mass electorates to mobilize continue to rely on the appeal of the secularized transcendent. The bare political truth is unacceptable, but the sacrificial language of the secular transcendent with its vision of the better future is capable of mobilizing even a modern electorate.

Chapter 12
Protestantism and Democracy

I have repeatedly argued that from a sociological viewpoint a religion can be construed as a repertoire that extends over a distinctive spectrum, with some central tendencies and many marginal possibilities. A central tendency of the Protestant sector of the Christian repertoire is to stress the authority of the Word of the Bible and to suspect sacred hierarchies of authority, while a marginal tendency of the repertoire is to insist on local congregational autonomy and even to reject leadership altogether. These particular central tendencies and marginal possibilities have clear implications for democracy and they will be emphasized or played down depending on the historical situation and the kind of society in which they are disseminated. To give an example, the ideal of congregational autonomy constitutes one widespread version of Protestant organization but it is not likely to make much impact in a feudal society based on a hierarchy of superimposed social strata each with specified obligations to the other.

The Protestant model of congregational autonomy and the feudal system represent differing ways of structuring power and they are incompatible. In a feudal society, as in any other kind of society, the dominant social mode of the society will restrict the likely impact of incompatible models of organization and restrict congregational models to the sectarian underground. The dominant social mode will also influence how those religious forms that are compatible conceive of power, while at the same time the ideal religious vision carried by underground forms will infiltrate and modify how the society understands and legitimates its distribution of power. Christian visions of how things ought to be ordered socially will interact with the everyday secular practices of social life. That interaction will create a situation where Christianity both stabilizes and challenges the dominant structure of social power.

Religion, understood as an ensemble of beliefs and practices, stabilizes societies and changes them. It moulds societies and is moulded by them. Much depends on the relation of a given religion to power. Christianity was seriously changed when it was adopted by the Roman Empire as the imperial religion and it was again altered when it was adopted by monarchs as the state religion in the early modern period. In particular the ensemble of beliefs and practices we call religion will be inflected and deflected by whether it is a minority without power or a majority in power. Of course a religion can also be a minority in power, as were Sunni Muslims in Iraq until quite recently or Dutch Protestants in apartheid South Africa, in which case it is more than likely to be oppressive. Likewise it can be a majority out of power, as in Poland and Ireland, in which case it is more than likely to coalesce with the cause of national liberation. In Mexico, where Protestants were a small minority, they became associated with the forces of change, particularly in the period prior to the Civil War beginning in 1910. The same was true in other parts of Central and South America, where the small minority of Protestants, along with the whole North Atlantic cultural world, became associated with liberalism and progress, and in particular with the separation of Church and state.

Power offers opportunities, but also imposes systematic constraints, based on its inherently variable distribution and on the political dynamic inherent both in legitimate force and in violence. Thus a religion which is established and in political power has an opportunity to implement its ideals, but it is at the same time held back by its close integration with established structures of authority, status and interest, as well as by what it needs to do to stay in power in its own territory and to deal with external threats. By contrast, a minority experiences rather different opportunities and constraints. In the Christian tradition, and particularly in the Protestant tradition, groups such as the Methodists, Quakers and Unitarians, emerge outside the structures of established power. They lack a territorial base, and depend on free personal choice rather than automatic birthright belonging. These groups have a potential to pick up radical elements in the foundation documents of Christianity, above all in the Gospels, though whether that potential is realized depends on the context. In the American South, for example, the Southern Baptists retain their suspicion of the state and their democratic modes of self-government, but they are also a form of local established power. In general minority groups outside the arcana of power *may* develop relatively egalitarian forms of internal organization, giving their members experience of personal responsibility, and also encouraging them to embrace reform or to cultivate a pacific ethos. Such groups may even imagine and seek a radically altered human and social order.

The Socio-Logic of Unintended Consequences

However, things rarely turn out as intended. That is a universal rule applying to religious and political visions alike. So the consequences of Protestant religious groups seeking to realize an imagined future cannot be foreseen. To take a well-known example from the history of North America and Northern Europe, certain Protestant groups curb their personal consumption, reject luxury and regard hard and disciplined work as a divine vocation. However, in the course of a generation or so, they create an abundance which tempts them to relax their dedication to disciplined work. These groups now learn to cope with the embarrassment of riches and may over time succumb to the pleasures of luxury. Unintended consequences of this kind may not be the only consequences. Once people relax and are perhaps minded to pursue profit for its own sake rather than as a by-product of religious virtue, they become assimilated to an amoral economic dynamic. (This assimilation is analogous to the process whereby religious groups originally inspired by egalitarian and peaceable ideals acquire political power and become assimilated to the amoral dynamic of domination.) According to this amoral economic dynamic everything and everybody has an impersonal price and that may mean that disputes over religious differences cease to matter much. The incidental consequence of such a dynamic may be mutual tolerance in religious matters simply because all energies have been rededicated to profit and to free competition with anybody and everybody. Assimilation to the dynamic of economic gain may result in the moral anarchy of a ruthless competition equally indifferent to rival religious traditions and to the moral demands of care for the poor, the needy and the bereft. At the same time this indifference can help foster a laisser-faire democracy. The point here is simply that religious ideals can become part of an extended sequence of consequences not originally foreseen. One can never know by what route the pursuit of a religious virtue like hard work and personal discipline ends up by fostering consequences quite other than those initially pursued.

The Variety of Possible Routes

The examples just given suggest there are numerous different concatenations of religious principles and social visions, some of them reinforcing each other while others are in conflict with each other. It also suggests that characteristics central to the Protestant repertoire, or marginally present within it, may end up by fostering first tolerance and then democracy. The shift from moral discipline to amoral profit is only one of those routes. It may be that moral responsibility continues to motivate some of those who have come to enjoy wealth and power, so that they engage in projects for the amelioration of the condition of the less fortunate. Whether or not one counts Jimmy Carter and Woodrow Wilson successful presidents they certainly retained their ideals even when standing in the courts of power. That too is part of the history of North America and Northern Europe.

Another feature of the Protestant repertoire that may help foster tolerance and democracy is the emphasis on individual interpretation of Scripture. Once people are free to devise their own interpretations of the authoritative text they are liable to disagree. One result is that Protestant groups constantly break up into rival denominations. The religious field becomes fragmented, which in turn may pave the way for a plural society where no faith is strong enough realistically to seek political dominance. At that point all may agree it is in their mutual interest to separate religion from the state and ensure that no particular religious group acquires privileged access to political power.

Yet another Protestant feature liable under certain circumstances to foster tolerance and democracy is the emphasis on inward sincerity rather than outward conformity to religious dogmas. Protestants who pursue sincerity at the expense of doctrinal rectitude may create a climate in which doctrinal rectitude becomes a matter of little moment. An emphasis on sincerity may help reduce religious teaching to its ethical implications and, by a further shift, reduce it to modes of conduct which contribute to a tolerant, free and democratic social order. That is now the situation in many Protestant societies, and it is not surprising that governments with an interest in civil peace are more than happy to support such a shift. The test the American legal system applies to the claims of religious bodies is the Protestant one of sincerity.

All the examples just given are simple thought experiments to illustrate the way ideas and images can work out in practice. Clearly it is not enough to think in terms of one particular principle. One needs to think in terms of the interaction of principles, for example between hard work understood as a divine vocation and a principled confidence in the ability of believers to discern the plain meaning of a text for themselves. Of course, the principle of the personal interpretation of a text needs facilitating circumstances, in particular the widespread practical availability of texts, which is why the invention of printing was so crucial for the success of Protestantism. The relation of the invention of printing to the spread of Protestantism may lead in turn to an association between Protestantism, education, literacy and the emergence of a national vernacular literature. In this way it may promote debate and eventually facilitate a furious competition of ideas. That is precisely what occurred in England in the revolutionary period of the 1640s when the Puritan Republic was inaugurated. Debates over religious questions may evolve into the town meetings characteristic of early American democracy. Passionate preaching in the open air to large numbers may provide models for political rhetoric directed at moving and persuading large crowds. The rhetoric of President Obama lies directly in this line of succession.

Conditions which Facilitate or Deflect Protestant Principles

The realization of a given principle depends on certain conditions being fulfilled. Not merely that, but there needs to be a certain consonance between the principle and conditions. For example the expansion of the principle of personal interpretation may depend on the increasing freedom of a given stratum, say the merchants, from immediate dependence on a rigidly defined aristocratic hierarchy based on blood and genealogy. Clearly the idea of personal interpretation assumes direct and autonomous access to the transcendent and is incompatible with fixed hierarchies and intermediaries, particularly where aristocratic and ecclesiastical hierarchies and intermediaries are allied together. There is a complicated interaction here: the rise of personal interpretation depends for its success on a weakening of hierarchical mediation and it also serves further to weaken hierarchical mediation. That is one reason why Protestantism took off in the burgeoning towns of the late Middle Ages and early modern period.

Once the idea of a free citizenry is established, as in North America, religious principles may be translated into political ones. Thus the idea that Christ died for all and that we are invited to decide in his favour as our personal saviour may, given the existence of a free citizenry, translate quite easily into the idea that we are all of equal dignity and are all invited to exercise free personal decisions in every sphere, including the political. If we can participate and announce our arrival in the religious sphere, why should we not participate and announce our arrival in the political sphere? The free churches of Victorian England were mainly composed of people outside the power elites and they announced their arrival on the social scene both by building up their religious communities and by supporting political parties that promoted their social advancement. They turned the Liberal and the Labour parties inter alia into organizations to achieve equal rights.

Of course, some conditions assist the realization of a principle, while others may deflect it, in which case another principle from the basic initial repertoire may be called upon to compensate. Several circumstances and principles may need to come into play at once. Personal interpretation may not be powerful enough on its own. In the sixteenth century it needed to coincide with the desire on the part of princes to assert unqualified and (maybe) centralized sovereignty in their dominions, and in addition to expropriate the wealth of the Catholic Church for their own purposes. If that particular precondition of change and Reformation turns out to be critical, the principle of personal interpretation may be deflected, for the time being at least, and the Protestant movement channelled in support of the formation of the nation state.

When a deflection of this kind occurs it may result in other deflections. Thus in the early phase of nation building the personal discipline inculcated by Protestantism may be deployed by the ruler, as it was in Germany, to shore up the organization of the kingdom. German Pietism inculcated disciplines that helped ensure the smooth running of the state. Moreover, the principle of personal interpretation may mean as much weight is accorded to the Old Testament as to the New Testament. That may easily lead on to identification with the God of Judaism as portrayed in the Old Testament and therefore with the nation understood as a modern realization of God's Chosen People. Personal choice may then be partly subsumed in national solidarity, and the consequence may then be that religious difference is interpreted as treason, given that political treason is the (early) modern version of religious heresy. Instead of the international Church being seen as the universal New Israel, the new early modern nation under 'the godly Prince' may be regarded as particularly blessed by God and equipped with a divine mission to conquer and subdue others. That was precisely what happened to the Boers in South Africa, and the Protestants of Northern Ireland. Such paradoxical consequences attend the realization of all ideas, not just religious ones. For example, the supposedly universal secular Enlightenment can be converted into racial attitudes toward the unenlightened, as Colin Kidd has persuasively documented.[1]

---

[1] Kidd, *The Forging of Races: Race and Scripture in the Protestant Atlantic World 1600–2000.*

The Working Out of the Protestant Trajectory in History

Phase 1: Protestantism and the Nation

In the circumstances of the sixteenth and seventeenth centuries religion became a factor in the rivalries of princes and (later) of nations, and the resulting wars were only brought to an end by invoking the principle of each nation following the faith espoused by its ruler. This principle variously coexisted with Catholic, Protestant, and Enlightened autocracies, which meant that the democratic potentialities of certain Protestant principles were temporarily deflected and frustrated. At the same time a critical path existed for their realization through an incipiently democratic combination of Christianity and Enlightenment, particularly in the Protestant nations of Holland, Switzerland, England, Scotland, and the United States. Though the thrust to personal choice was partly reversed, at least for a while, it nevertheless found this pathway for its eventual realization.

Not only was there an incipiently democratic possibility open through a combination of Christianity and Enlightenment but it was also possible to combine the idea of automatic membership in a territorial Church with the emergence of self-selected groups of devout persons cultivating the inner life, sustained by a highly personal and emotional piety. The way was open for the emergence of an empathetic sentiment capable of powering reform, notably the abolition of slavery and the amelioration of working conditions with the onset of the Industrial Revolution.

The national Church coexists with the growth of these self-selected groups but in time it also coexists with the idea that Christianity is an entirely personal matter quite apart from any active participation in the religious group. The result is two rather different forms of secularization. One is the conformity of the Church to the national idea. The other is the evanescence of personal piety in the cultivation of the autonomous and religiously dormant person. Finland has combined both forms of secularization. There is a vigorous nationalism associated with the Finnish Lutheran Church and assiduously fostered by the clergy, especially in times of threat from Russia. There is also a highly inward form of personal religion, either attached to the Church in a rather nominal way or else active in revivalist groups.

However, a national Church is not the only possibility. Attention to the teachings of the New Testament, particularly the Gospels, may foster the idea of a community devoted specifically to the realization of those teachings. Such a community can conceive itself as 'a City set on a hill', and ordered as though everyone were an active member in the Church and subject to its disciplines. Communities of this kind tend to stress duties rather than rights, and also to run into a dilemma inherent in Christianity, given that its initial scriptural charters stressed inward sincerity rather than obedience to detailed regulation. The alternative to a city set on a hill is the self-selected group sometimes set up in a segregated territorial area. In this segregated plot of land spiritual high-flyers strive to realize the injunctions of the New Testament with regard to non-violence, mutual love, and even shared property. These injunctions have a way of seeding themselves outside the boundaries of specifically religious communities and feeding into a semi-secularized pacific ethos, active also in social amelioration and charitable endeavour, with particular influence in incipiently democratic Protestant societies.

I use the term 'incipiently democratic' because the record of Protestant societies with respect to democratization, though arguably better than most other religious forms, is variable. Individualization and regard for individuality, particularly in association with pluralism, as in the USA, has considerable democratic potential, but a great deal depends on facilitating circumstances. These circumstances are maximal where the societies concerned are powerful enough not to be constantly overrun; where national unification is early achieved; where Protestantism is not faced with a large non-Protestant minority; where societies live in a protected niche, such as an island in the case of Britain, or on a continent without seriously threatening enemies, as in the USA; and where institutions can be slowly built up and problems solved one by one without destructive revolutions.

Even where all these conditions are fulfilled and the nations in question are world-powers, indeed world empires, the advance to democracy can take centuries, and is bound to proceed by degrees, beginning with the enfranchisement of males, usually based on a property qualification. In the developed West democracy does not come to full fruition until the twentieth century with the enfranchisement of women and the full incorporation of minorities. After all, the USA is often celebrated as a model democracy but the black minority had to wait till the second half of the twentieth century to achieve something like equality in the sphere of citizenship.

Where such conditions are not fulfilled other developments are possible. Germany provides an example of an economically and culturally advanced nation where several crucial conditions for the achievement of democracy were not fulfilled. It was unified later that most other countries; it was religiously divided; the 1848 Revolution failed; the country was geopolitically at the centre of an unstable continental balance of power; it was run autocratically and it fostered a culture of obedience and order, including military order. Protestantism was fully incorporated in that order through a union of throne and altar.

Protestantism has, of course, been conventionally associated with the revolutions that made the modern world, or rather with the revolutions we use to define modernity, above all the industrial revolution. In most of Europe that association has been accompanied by secularization, whereas in the United States the reverse has been the case, with the essential proviso that the separation of Church and state was achieved earlier than any where else. That was partly because successive migrations to North America involved several different ethnic groups, for example English, Ulster Irish, Dutch and German, and several varieties of Protestantism. These ethnic and religious groups differed from each other in numerous ways but they were not so culturally distant or antagonistic that mutual accommodation was out of the question. As time went on it became clear that Protestant pluralism and the constant proliferation of fresh varieties of Protestant religion made a single dominant Church impossible. The presence of these competing Protestant varieties provided an opportunity for powerful elites attracted to a semi-Christian or Deist Enlightenment to put forward and eventually to realize the idea of a wall of separation between Church and state.

However, this is an area where we encounter the sheer complexity of the relation between repertoires and the social conditions that either assist or inhibit their realization. Christianity early proposed a separation between the things that belong to Caesar and the things that belong to God. That came in time to include the positive evaluation of the man or woman of conscience who put loyalty to God and principle above social conformity, even though all churches, once established, persecuted or harassed those who refused to conform. The circumstances of the death of its founder at the hands of 'Church' and state, the three centuries in which Christians were themselves divided among themselves as well as being an intermittently persecuted minority, built in a nonconformist and potentially voluntarist deposit, as well as a reverence for the righteous victim and the non-violent martyr for a cause. Such models and images can be drawn on in appropriate circumstances, and they can become influential in the culture at large far beyond the boundaries of ecclesiastical communities.

Here time and space require me to truncate a complicated story. Let us assume that the Reformation needed to be promoted from the top as well as from below, that it was associated with new modes of communication, especially print, and that it had an elective affinity with the culture of commerce and trade in Northern Europe as Protestant nations became the lead societies of their time. All these cooperating factors made the association of Protestantism with national and economic power a virtual inevitability. The same is true of its association with the idea of a learned ministry and therefore with a stratum bound in with national elites and their changing ethos. At the same time it had a personal and lay potential with popular, even populist overtones, present in the radical wing of the Reformation and capable of powering successive mobilizations further and further down the social scale, especially in America and the Anglo-sphere generally.

Phase 2: Successive Popular Mobilizations – Evangelical and Pentecostal

These mobilizations, which included the revivalist mobilization of whites on the American frontier and of the black slave population of America, can be credited with helping to save the Anglo-sphere from violent revolution. There was therefore an alternative model of the road to modernity available apart from the route involving a war between the Enlightenment and the Catholic Church whereby the Catholic Church for a century backed itself into a corner in its alliance with elites opposed to modernity, including capitalism. This alternative route, as followed by Protestantism, allowed an intermittent alliance between religion and politics rather than the replacement of religion by politics mandated by the rival model. It also meant the replacement of the learned ministry by a charismatic pastorate, which in the circumstances of the post-Civil War American South increased the chances of a clash between a Biblically based religion and some forms of modern science, as distinct from modern technology. A learned ministry may accept modern science, and even contribute to it, as is indicated by the contribution of Mendel, as a monk, to the foundations of genetics. Fundamentalist movements, whether Christian or Muslim, particularly when led by poorly educated populist preachers, sometimes reject aspects of modern science they believe incompatible with the Bible or the Koran. By contrast such movements have little trouble with modern technology, since it is a means to an end and enables them to propagate their message more effectively.

At the same time the role played by relatively uneducated religious leaders made possible the emergence of an Evangelical faith, in particular Pentecostalism, capable of fusing together black and white revivalism. This revivalism not only coalesced with white conservatism in the American South but also fuelled the Black Civil Rights Movement, one consequence of which is the election of President Obama. Another consequence has been the emergence of a faith pre-adapted to cross any number of cultural species barriers in the developing world. Pentecostals now number some quarter of a billion followers in the developing world. The Pentecostal faith is particularly potent, given the widespread failure of politics in that world, because it offers a capsule of hope and mobility. This capsule is sustained by moral reform, hard work, opportunity for participation and mutual support, in alliance with a belief in a providence that will bring salvation here and now as well as hereafter. Whether and to what extent this faith eventually conforms to the pattern of corruption and exploitation exercised by political leaders (for example, Mugabe) in the developing world, or to some extent transforms the pattern, remains to be seen. How far the democratic potential of Protestantism can be realized in very varying circumstances from Nigeria to Korea, and how far the Catholic Church has separated itself from its ancient alliances with political power and its territorial character, to operate progressively in a multicultural, mobile and transnational world is too extensive an issue to be pursued here. Clearly the Catholic Church has preserved a communal potential capable of blossoming into a critique of unbridled capitalism.[2]

The contrast underlying my argument is essentially between a faith based on mediation, for example in relation to the central issue of confession and priestly absolution or morally and financially buying time in purgatory, and one based on direct access, inwardness, personal choice and response. Insofar as Protestantism can be said to embody the latter set of characteristics they have a clear affinity with democracy. However, Catholicism also has elements in its repertoire that can be deployed in a democratic cause, including the very elements that work in the opposite direction when the Church is too closely allied with the forces of social hierarchy, such as its centralized, hierarchical structure and public visibility. In Germany the Catholic Church was socially located in a way which allowed it to be in the main associated with democratic potential and the same alignment has been possible in the USA and parts of Asia and Africa. In the right social and historical circumstances Catholicism can deploy those parts of its repertoire that

---

[2]   Hughes, *The End of Work: Theological Critiques of Capitalism.*

speak of human dignity and rationality, of social justice and the role of subsidiary organizations mediating between the state and the individual. Protestantism and Catholicism have both deployed the repertoire of original sin, corruption and concupiscence bequeathed them by Augustine to varied purpose depending on context, either stressing man's incapacity to do anything pleasing or good, or else tolerating the vices and moral vicissitudes attendant on the human condition and not attempting the dangerous ascent to 'the high that proved too high, the heaven for earth too hard'.[3]

Liturgical Postscript

One arena in which the arguments just outlined about the role of a repertoire in relation to the opportunities blocked or made available by context is liturgy, especially in the early modern period where opportunities arose for Protestantism to implement some central but intermittently dormant elements in the original Christian repertoire. These elements are inwardness, which includes the emphasis on mature and conscious personal choice, and the equality of all before God, particularly through a universal participation both in sin and in the image of God. Once these elements were released into the cultural mainstream their initial impact was expressed in the arena of liturgy by way of a sustained attack on mediation, on priestly hierarchy, on automatic adherence by virtue of birth, on formal recitation and on the kind of virtue that rested on habit and was nurtured by habitual devotion.

   The attack was incipiently democratic and amounted to a profound revolution capable of ushering in the modern world through the creation of the modern subject. However, the Protestant revolution was inherently unstable and capable of undermining itself through more and more extreme, and sometimes contradictory, manifestations. Thus a reformed liturgy might begin by attempting to include everybody through common prayer, but this itself was still an outward form of worship inhibiting the pure spontaneity of individual believers. This generated demands for a genuine spontaneity, and these demands appealed to the authority of the Bible. However, the Bible, like common prayer, constituted a stabilized text warring against the freedom of the spirit. The result, from early modern England to the American frontier and contemporary Africa, has been resort to prophesying, and the recurrence of a dilemma faced by Saint Paul in the earliest Church when it came to the problem of 'discerning the spirits, whether they be of God'. After all, Paul himself had recommended praying and singing 'in the spirit'.

   Ramie Targoff, in her remarkable discussion of this complicated controversy, shows how dilemmas of this kind released a new potential for a devotional poetry, itself capable of providing a carrier for the collective sentiments of seventeenth-century believers, controlling and disciplining otherwise unmanageable expressions

---

[3]   Browning, Robert, *Abt Vogler*.

of faith. However, we today remain firmly in the Puritan tradition as expressed, for example, in the romantic poetics of Wordsworth where poetry is defined as the spontaneous overflow of powerful feelings. This is because we privilege the private spontaneous voice over what we take to be the artificiality of collective sentiments expressed in formal liturgy. Nevertheless, the power and eloquence we today find in the devotional poetry of the seventeenth century was based on 'the two central principles that governed the Book of Common Prayer – the intertwining of the singular I and the collective we, and an absolute preference for formalized over spontaneous voice'.[4]

Ramie Targoff notes one other paradox of some historic and contemporary moment. Whereas the (American) Bay Psalm book claimed to put scriptural fidelity above poetic eloquence, it also claimed that God had so effectively hidden from us the nature and poetry of Hebrew verse as to assist not only the production of our own poetic forms, but to do so in a manner consonant with our own country. Thus, the political and cultural independence was already built implicitly into the liturgical forms embraced by New England. One never knows just where the Protestant pressure for liturgical reform will end up. Ramie Targoff does not say so, but the Protestant pressure against formal liturgy was also in part responsible, both in England and North America, for the universal popularity of Handel's *Messiah* in the nineteenth century and up to today as the supreme collective expression of a biblical piety, free of all priestly institutional religion and liturgical form, beyond shadowing the sequence of texts in the Prayer Book lectionary. Millions attend performances of *Messiah* who have no interest in liturgy, or for that matter, in any other kind of classical concert. Protestantism in this mode achieves a mass expression outside the ecclesiastical framework, but also finds itself remarkably vulnerable to cultural change. What was intended as a return to the heart of the Gospel finds itself outflanked by heart-work and sincerity regarded as inherently valuable, whatever the content.

---

[4] Targoff, Ramie, *Common Prayer: The Language of Public Devotion in Early Modern England* (Chicago: University of Chicago Press, 2001: 87).

Chapter 13

Multiple Ironies and Necessary Paradoxes: A Review of Religion, Fanaticism, and Violence

This chapter began life as a review for the *TLS* of three books on religion and violence, *The Myth of Religious Violence: Secular Ideology and the Roots of Modern Conflict* by William Cavanaugh,[1] *Fanaticism: On the Uses of an Idea*, by Alberto Toscano,[2] and *In the Name of God: The Evolutionary Origins of Religious Ethics and Violence*, by John Teehan.[3] It gradually extended itself beyond the normal contours of a review. I include it here since it summarizes the fundamental arguments that underlie my approach to the issues raised in most of the earlier chapters of this book.

Religion, violence and fanaticism are all hot topics and are often treated by lay sermons in academic guise even and especially when the approach is self consciously 'scientific' as in John Teehan's exercise in cognitive science, *In the Name of God*. The more 'scientific' the claim the greater is the missionary zeal to preach to the unconverted and to offer moral advice to the world, supposedly based on the supposed new knowledge. Zeal is only increased if the new knowledge shows we are so programmed we can do next to nothing about it but wait till our cave man brains trigger a cave man response. Boys will be boys and cave men will be cave men, and you might think there was no more to be said once that dire reality had been revealed. Not a bit of it: lay sermons wax ever more urgent in documenting the built-in resistance to their liberating scientific truth.

Among the most impressive of recent contributors to the serious side of the debate about religion, politics and violence over the past decade have been Hans Kippenberg,[4] Hans Joas[5] and Mark Juergensmeyer.[6] Joas is a Catholic and Juergensmeyer a Protestant, and both have been morally motivated by experience as activists in peace movements, as well as a proper academic curiosity. That

---

[1] Cavanaugh, *The Myth of Religious Violence*.

[2] Toscano, *Fanaticism*.

[3] Teehan, *In the Name of God*.

[4] Juergensmeyer, Mark, *Terror in the Mind of God: The Global Rise of Religious Violence* (Berkeley, CA: University of California Press, 2000).

[5] Joas, Hans, *War and Modernity: Studies in the History of Violence in the 20th Century* (Cambridge: Polity, 2002).

[6] Kippenberg, Hans, *Gewalt als Gottesdienst*.

is what you might expect, because if my own experience is anything to go by, participation in the highly charged, fractious and sometimes intolerant atmosphere of peace movements immediately raises theoretical and existential problems. Canon John Collins and Bertrand Russell did not have peaceful relations in the course of their CND campaign to ban the bomb. I recognized my son Magnus as a kindred spirit to my earlier self when he was hauled into a police car in Whitehall during some peace demonstration, still hotly addressing a fellow protester 'but it is more complicated than *that*'.

It definitely is more complicated than *that* and it is hardly surprising academic treatments reflect prior commitments, because this awkward set of issues alters its shape as you take up position to find the best angle and then revolve the lens. If you look at the different views of historians of the so-called wars of religion to garner some overview of the actual role of the religious factor, as William Cavanaugh does in *The Myth of Religious Violence*, you need to canvass how they take position as well as the objective pressure of evidence. If you think religion an expression of in-group/out-group dynamics, either socio-biologically or sociologically, the question of specific blame attached to religion goes down the tubes. If like Alberto Toscano in his *Fanaticism*, and indeed in the whole Marxist and Marxisant tradition, you believe religion is the beautiful or threatening spume blown up from the surface of real forces, blame is equally otiose.

The question 'where are you coming from?' is strictly impertinent and ought not to matter, but where you stand is very prone to shape what you see and the direction of your response. There is no way the serious scientific observer can stand above it all, pointing the finger at this or that horror, and exclaiming with all the moral superiority of Disgusted of Oxford 'Just look at that!' Yah-boo science is as tiresome as yah-boo politics, and when it comes to the sources of war the former easily degenerates into the latter. Maybe secular fanatics killed their thousands, but for sure the religious fanatics killed their tens of thousands. The Evil Ones of recent history, Hitler, Stalin and Saddam Hussein, are batted around as knock down rhetorical counters. Yah, Stalin was typically 'religious' in his paranoid intolerance of opposition, and don't you know that Hitler never renounced his Catholicism? Boo, how is it you so easily forget it was biologists, many of them supporting the sometime progressive cause of eugenics, whom Hitler recruited? Yah, President Bush, the Evangelical Christian, bombed Muslims for the material benefits of oil. He is so unchristian it makes one want to join the noble army of atheists. Boo, anti-God warrior Hitchens wanted to bomb Muslims into liberal rationality, forgetting Hussein was a secular Baathist. So perhaps God is great after all.

All three treatments discussed here belong to profoundly disparate research communities, with extensive bibliographies that barely overlap each other, though all are to this or that extent on the left. All are serious contributions, and extremely well and clearly written, though in very different prose genres. John Teehan uses a brisk no-nonsense style of rational assessment and calculation, backed by an aggressively mechanistic vocabulary of mental tools and triggers. He is the typical academic cub bristling with 'Have I got news for you'. William Cavanaugh uses the more extended sentence structure of someone saturated in humanistic traditions of interpreting the depth and historically located resonance of signs. Alberto Toscana also creates a rich and layered text, but makes virtuoso use of the ironic magisterial and materialist Marxist mode of cultural criticism. He turns positions on their heads and executes more and more dizzying dialectic cartwheels before telling us plainly about the debilitating effects of cynical intellectual attitudes on serious commitment.

William Cavanaugh is a radical Catholic theologian who has written passionately on Pinochet and Chile, John Teehan is a cognitive scientist and science fiction writer who sounds like an American culture warrior in his obsession with what you might call the 'Bad News' Bible, and Alberto Toscano is a Marxist and journalist with varied teaching assignments, for example at Goldsmith's College and the Workers' and Punks' University of Llublijana.

I begin with Cavanaugh because if religious violence is a myth, in Georges Sorel's sense of a story serving to motivate and mobilize a particular brand of politics, (in this case associated with the rise of the nation-state and its own appalling violence), then Teehan's explanation of a *specifically* religious violence stemming from a generic potential biologically written into 'our evolved human psychology', is otiose. After all 'ought' implies 'can'. What interests Cavanaugh is the relatively recent and politically embedded construction of the notion of the religious and its dubious binary partner, *the* secular.

This is not quite the same as the notorious difficulty of framing either substantive or functionalist definitions of religion in order to make any generalized statements about it, which cognitive scientists usually dismiss as pettifogging obscurantism. Nor is it a variant on the point recently reinforced by Talal Asad about the changing grammar of the secular over historical time, understood as a binary in some ways generated by Christianity itself and related to the early Christian distinction within between faith and the world. Equally Cavanaugh is not here exercised by the major difference between the sacred and profane distinction and the related distinctions between the religious and the secular and faith and the world. These are just some of the problems and issues feeding into a broader philosophical contention that the very concept of religion, so easily flung around for polemical purposes, is 'essentially contested' as well as constructed. Yet these standard counters in the debate are not at the heart of Cavanaugh's concern.

Cavanaugh's problem is with the religious/secular distinction specifically as it emerges in the discourse of the early modern period, and its use in the rhetorical armoury of the 'secular' nation state against all other forms of solidarity and loyalty, whether aristocratic, civic, religious or imperial. He argues that when it comes to our own contemporary debate, fuelled and fanned no doubt by 9/11, the essential violence of the religious, understood as something given rather than constructed, is falsely contrasted with the innocence of the secular, and in particular our western secular democratic and liberal innocence. This is where Cavanaugh might have drawn on Reinhold Niebuhr's analysis of the irony and innocence of American history, because America provides the pre-eminent instance of power defending its dominance as for the benefit of others, though the British and French are also adept at bearing other peoples' burdens for the greater good of all.

Cavanaugh discerns a contumacious rhetoric of liberal innocence, which persists however much our innocence is intermittently marred pro tem by what needs, alas, to be done, to keep rogues and rogue states in order. Our liberal rationality is contrasted with the irrationality of religious 'Others', since what *they* do goes way beyond what might be thought appropriate as an understandable response to the plundering of their patrimony by western colonialism.

I would enter some caveats about this line of argument, since 'we' do have to make interim and morally ambiguous decisions about whether to intervene forcefully in (say) Sierra Leone or to abstain (say in Darfur), but there can be little doubt that the self-serving and self-deluding nature of American real-politik is on all fours with the self-serving delusions of real-politik in general. Though any attempt to characterize religion universally and ahistorically is dubious, it is pretty clear the discipline of international relations can characterize the universal dynamic of real-politik in pretty well any time and place. For example, one can say with some confidence that alliances for defence and attack, when made between two plus one or more state actors in a situation of disequilibrium, will be forged on the basis of real-politik, to the virtual exclusion of religious or ideological considerations. Given the polemical role assigned to the notion of 'wars of religion' that generalization is of major importance.

Nowadays, self-defined secularists know who plays the role of the cosmic bad guys in the drama of those who are with us in the fight for scientific truth and liberal freedoms and those who are against us. The bad guys are mainly Muslims. But Christians cannot be let off the hook, partly on historical grounds but also because that would let down the anti-religious cause as such. To be honest, says our honest atheist, most Christians are crypto-fundamentalists really, and liberal Christians are an absurd anomaly, not only confusing the issue but afraid to face the ghastly truth of what they are supposed to believe. Only allow Christians at large into politics and out of the sphere of the private closet where they belong, and they too would shed the pacific mask hiding their fanatical face.

After all, that is the nature of religion and the evil result of ignorant superstition throughout the ages. This gives rise to the curious empirical claim that being wrong empirically has some association with being malevolent morally, though the symmetrical claim that being right empirically is associated with being good is less clearly spelled out, and for very good reason too. I recollect quite well how Hitler's rocket scientists were empirically right on the ball when they targeted my London suburb in 1944, but I awarded them no marks for benevolence.

The overall conclusion seems to be that pedants may pussyfoot as they will about the definition and historical sources, origins and uses of the concept 'religion', but we plain men, among them our cognitive scientist John Teehan, know what we are talking about when we characterize 'religion'. Unfortunately the plan truths of plain men are not always as plain as they claim. William Cavanaugh is a subtle man and he argues that if we do not understand the *history* of the *political uses* of these our basic coinages, in particular 'the secular', we literally do not know what we are talking about.

What is that history, and how has it distorted our understandings in a way that enables us to cite the divisive intolerance and chronic violence of 'religion' as the plain man's view of the matter? Why is the same prejudice not quite so immediately available to characterize other forms of human solidarity, such as kin, tribe, nation and the political party? That is the question Cavanaugh addresses. He seeks to enquire just how and why the specific violence of religion became a standard trope of western discourse, apart from its 'obvious' truth? After all 'the obvious' is usually a suspect category in the academic world, as any biologist might tell you when you cite the obviously divine design features of the Lesser Celandine.

It may be that every now and again we naively note something that does not quite fit that obvious truth, but the lack of fit is not allowed to upset the Kuhnian paradigm, unless we happen to be unusually well motivated by a hermeneutic of suspicion. Mere open-mindedness will not be a sufficient condition of suspicion, though arguably a necessary one. Why would the great champion of Catholicism, Charles the Fifth, sack Rome in 1527, and why was Christian Byzantium sacked almost beyond recovery in 1204 by Venetian Crusaders rather than by Muslims?

We may also attempt, as any historian must, to weigh the different factors, economic, political and religious, in wars conventionally labelled religious. We have to document, as Cavanaugh does, how it comes about that in so-called religious wars co-religionists often fight on opposing sides and vice versa. Maybe the key dividing lines are located elsewhere than the 'sectarian divide'. At least that hypothesis needs to be entertained, even though some recent historiography has been concerned to bring the religious factor back into the 'wars of religion'.

Cavanaugh denies that religion is essentially violent to a greater degree than other types of factor and modes of solidarity, such as kinship, nationalism and the political party. Here he differs somewhat from Kippenberg in *Gewalt als Gottesdienst*.[7] Kippenberg argues that the post-axial world religions are not all that different from each other when it comes to violence, because they are rooted in archaic practices of divinely sanctioned sacrificial killing which are reactivated much later by threats to the solidarity of the group. At the same time Kippenberg traces this reactivation to mainly 'secular' factors, like territorial incursions and displacement. Hans Joas, however, is perfectly clear that war is an inherent component of modernity rather than any kind of primitive throw-back.[8]

The question for Cavanaugh is when, where, under what conditions, and in what *types* of society, religion turns violent. We have to ask when precisely were the modalities of violence likely to include a religious factor or to achieve a religious expression. We have to ask, for example, about societies where the Eucharist lies at the heart of the social bond, because where it does, issues like the division of nave and chancel, giving the cup to the laity and clerical dress, code the defence

---

[7]   Kippenberg, *Gewalt als Gottesdienst*.

[8]   Joas, *War and Modernity*.

of hierarchy against the assaults of equality. Here, of course, Cavanaugh's analysis might well be compatible with Toscano's Marxist analysis of fanaticism whereby the form of 'society' in Roman imperial times was political, and in medieval times 'Roman' Catholic and religious.

Consider the following observation guided initially by the norms of educated and enlightened opinion, rather than a 'hermeneutic of suspicion'. While in Heidelberg recently I was told the town was torched in the seventeenth century and I 'naturally' assumed this happened in the hugely destructive wars of religion which a certain brand of history tells us were happily brought to an end by the secular nation state through the Treaty of Westphalia in 1648. The point is important because these wars provide exhibit A in the chamber of horrors attributed to religion.

Not at all: Heidelberg was torched in 1689 as part of the hugely destructive wars of the Palatinate. These wars had a religious element in the expulsion of Protestants from France in 1685 and of the Catholic James the Second from England in the Glorious Revolution, but the key elements were the defensive/aggressive power politics of the Catholic French alarmed by the successes of the equally Catholic Hapsburgs against the Muslim Turks. The resulting alliances and coalitions followed the usual patterns of power politics, promoting aggressive French aggrandizement inter alia as the first line of defence. The key question concerns the dynamics and modalities of power not the special malignancy of religion.

Another example might be provided by the intolerance and violence that ensued in Spain with the completion of the Christian *Reconquista* in 1492. There are various ways of accounting for the persecutions and expulsions that followed what had been the relative if intermittent religious tolerance of multicultural Spain in the late Middle Ages, but two of them are particularly problematic. Clearly the change cannot be accounted for by religion as such, given the earlier history of tolerance over centuries. Equally the overall tenor of history does not entirely support the alternative hypothesis that Muslims and Jews are nice whereas Christians are nasty. We are driven back to the essentially historical question of where, when and under what circumstances religious faith or secular ideology is prone to turn violent and intolerant. For example, one might try out Cavanaugh's analysis based on the homogenizing sociologic of sacred monarchies as they centralize their domains, and, later, on the same homogenizing logic pursued by secular nationalism, in particular ethnic cleansing.

It is precisely this type of analysis we need to apply to the wars of religion as a key exhibit in contemporary polemics. In the course of a wide ranging discussion Cavanaugh suggests that far from the nation state being the happy consequence and solution to the 'wars of religion', effectively bringing them to an end for the public good, the rise of the nation state was the unhappy cause of them in the first place. He cites Tilly, 'War made the state and the state made war', and he quotes Gabriel Ardant to the effect that in the process of state building the most serious precipitant to violence, and the greatest spur to the growth of the state, was the attempt to collect taxes from an unwilling populace.

Another source of the violence, according to Michael Howard, was the resistance of local elites to the centralizing efforts of monarchs and emperors. As Quentin Skinner pointed out, the failure of the Reformation in France and Spain had something to do with the fact that monarchs had already absorbed churches into their patronage systems. That is precisely what the *Patronato* entails. Elsewhere the energies of the Reformation could assist in spoliation of the Church both by monarchs and the nobility, and in England the 'bare ruined choirs' and well appointed aristocratic homes created out of converted abbeys are with us to this day.

So far I have stressed the dynamics of power politics creating the conditions leading to warfare, and that is entirely consonant with discussions of violence as produced by the dynamics of varying coalitions of 'them' and 'us', the in-group and the out-group. If one reads John Teehan's cognitive scientific analysis, *In the Name of God*, with care, it is as susceptible to an understanding of violence as selected for in terms of 'us' and 'them' as in terms of the particular 'religious' expressions of social solidarity.

It seems you can construct a theory of religion and violence either on a socio-biological basis or on a sociological basis but the understandings you arrive at will contain very similar elements, which is encouraging. Both types of theory can come up with the idea that the boundaries erected by Jewish tribal particularity, as defended by command of a jealous God, can be reinforced by the borders erected by a universal monotheism based on the difference between the redeemed and the unredeemed. Indeed, the Jewish theologian Franz Rosenzweig made that observation a long time ago. One has to recognize how moral advances often ratchet up collateral costs. Given the overlap between the understandings of sociology and cognitive science illustrated in this example, it is hardly surprising Teehan's account of our evolved psychology of morals, notably his exploration of successive extensions of the scope of moral sensitivity, can also be found in Hobhouse's *Morals in Evolution*, published in 1906. Cognitive science rediscovers familiar truths, and renders them rich and strange with its new linguistic and conceptual equipment.

Teehan's book is partly addressed to colleagues in religious studies, and once again one has to note the kind of problem he typically runs into, in spite of his evident erudition and desire to be fair. He has taken advice about the harsh logic of 'the ban' in early Judaism, as well as utilizing the work of Susan Nidich on the ethics of war in the Hebrew Scriptures, yet in his critical scrutiny of biblical texts he selects just those which fit his theses about signalling loyalty to other members, survival value and boundary maintenance. The text 'He that is not for me is against me', attributed to Jesus Christ and George Bush, needs to be set against the text 'He that is not against me is for me'. The gospel texts about the bad news in store at the final assize for those out-groups rejecting the universal good news, have to be related to a host of other texts. These texts make the last judgement turn on the indiscriminate exercise of 'the most excellent gift of charity', for example in the Matthean text 'Inasmuch as ye did it unto one of these the least of these my brethren ye did it unto me' or the Common Prayer Book text, with a nice Anglican sense of the via media 'Do good unto all men but especially to them that are of the household of faith'.

The trouble with all this is that Teehan has slight interest in how texts are selected according to context and circumstance, or how in religious practice they are read, discounted or emphasized, and subject to systems of hermeneutic interpretation. When scholars in religious studies or the sociology of religion study and elucidate texts their focus is not only on an understanding of them as originally produced, especially when the production retrospectively recounts and interprets events centuries earlier, but in their variable use in contexts remote in time and place, for example Tolstoy's pacifist reading of Christ's teaching of the kingdom of God. The parable of the Talents can be deployed to bolster capital accumulation, provided you gloss being rich unto God as just being rich. Clearly one needs to go well beyond the Bible, yet Teehan takes no account of the fundamental gestures of the Eucharist as they bear on incarnation, incorporation, exchange of gifts, offers of peace, confession, reconciliation, sanctification and forgiveness.

Teehan is no conventional Christianophobe. Yet one has to ask why the careful criteria for a just war are not central to his discussion of evolutionary changes in what he rather oddly constructs as the category of specifically 'religious ethics'. Among the many varied motives for war, men fight for justice, and for peace. An analysis of violence, whether religious or secular, supposing one can work at all in an ahistorical manner with such a binary distinction, has to enquire into its *proper* occasions. Teehan focuses instead on the difference between murder and killing in the various Mosaic codes and treats the difference as though it were reducible to the dynamic of in-group and out-group. What is murder among us is merely killing against them.

But in 1940 at Dunkirk the members of the rearguard of the British army were not 'murdering' the advancing Germans. They were killing them, and their actions were neither motivated nor justified solely or even largely by the logic of the in-group against the out-group. They killed Germans in a war that in principle fulfilled all the religious and non-religious criteria of the just and proportionate exercize of force, even though bishop Bell and others were later to criticize what they saw as disproportionate responses in attacks on German cities, such as Dresden.

Space prevents me exploring further the difference between the evolution of ethics and an evolutionary ethic, such as was proposed by the sociologist/ philosopher Herbert Spencer. In some ways Spencer anticipated Darwin, and was responsible for the phrase 'the survival of the fittest'. I need hardly remind Teehan of the potential consequences for the justification and pursuit of violence when we take our values from the facts of evolution. Of course, one can and should repudiate Social Darwinism as an illegitimate inference from the theories of Darwin, but it is nevertheless a simple fact of history, and one illustrating the way empirically good scientific ideas, like morally good religious ideas, can be used to justify all kinds of horrors, in this instance to justify the struggle of all against all for domination.

Some contemporary biological scientists may point out it is illegitimate to infer Social Darwinism from biological Darwinism, as they ostentatiously wash their hands in public and affirm their own moral purity compared with the rest of us. But they cannot purify history from what has been done in the name of science, and moreover done by scientists, any more than the followers of Jesus Christ can expunge the record of the Inquisition. As John Teehan points out, though without quite following his logic through, one does not exculpate religion from its actual record in history by simply claiming the worst aspects of its practice are a distortion of the best aspects of its message. Allowing properly for the differences between scientific and Christian discourse, the same applies to science. Science is a practice as well as an intellectual pursuit, most of it an empirically mistaken practice looked at historically, and much of it very far from 'pure' in its application. Scientists cannot parade in their white coats at the expense of the men in black.

Teehan's enquiry into religious violence is bound to be seriously lop-sided unless complemented by an enquiry into religious pacifism. He must know that the classical critique of Christianity has *not* been on account of its violence but because of its rejection of the necessary use of violence in the defence of a fragile civic order. There are two critiques of Christianity and they come from opposite directions. If an enquiry were undertaken into pacifism as well as war and violence it would be clear that religious pacifism arises no earlier than the first millennium BC, and is part of a great *cultural* leap viewing the world in the eschatological perspective of a coming kingdom of peace and righteousness.

Both religious *and secular* revolutionary violence is located in that same relatively recent eschatological anticipation, and so is the rejection of violence. The Christian revolutions divide into pacifist and activist/violent wings and the secular anarchist movements do the same, and one needs to understand why that is so in terms of the long durance of eschatological hope. For good and for ill, the Christian hope of a righteous kingdom 'come on earth as it is in heaven' feeds into and is part of the hope of a secular transformation, and one has to understand that the good and the ill, what Ruskin would have called the 'wealth and the illth', are mutually entangled. That is why it is entirely natural for a Marxist like Alberto Toscano to defend serious hope and commitment against the derogatory uses of the idea of fanaticism in contemporary polemic.

I learnt nothing essentially new from Teehan's pages about violence, as distinct from being better informed about the operating style of cognitive science. The 'cognitions' he proposes are mostly valid and interesting but they are also insights already canvassed in sociology, even though there is a minimal engagement with the subject. Perhaps this is an accident of mere ignorance, but it could also be a principled ignorance, because sociology works with cultural understandings whereas cognitive science works with biological explanations. Whatever the reason, it is a pity the most relevant complementary discipline is bypassed. You hamper yourself quite seriously if you discuss religious evolution without engaging at length with Robert Bellah, or if you analyse notions of purity without discussing Mary Douglas. It is not that sociologists doubt that there is a place for biological explanations, or fail to recognize there are limits to what Alfred Schütz called the 'world openness' of the psyche, but they are cautious about the kind of insouciant disciplinary imperialism they see in cognitive science, especially when it tells what we already know in yet another new jargon. Previously it was cybernetics, now it is cognitive science, and our everyday vocabulary, for example 'situation' and 'process', is littered with the linguistic detritus left by scientific fashion.

One major problem with cognitive science is the generality of what it has independently to offer the pursuit of scientific understanding. Its explanations amount to saying that we are programmed for incorporation in groups in which we compete and cooperate, but also programmed to fight for our own group against other groups competing for scarce resources, except when we are in coalition with them. X and not X. Edmund Burke said as much in 1757 in his *Philosophical Enquiry into the Sublime and the Beautiful*.

Teehan works through an analysis of Judaism and Christianity by way of commitment theory, kin selection, face saving, and what he calls 'costly signalling' that one is a trustworthy member of the group. This is amplified by comments on the cost effectiveness of (say) sacrifice, including self sacrifice, so it is no surprise Teehan quotes a colleague evaluating Jesus as a really smart evolutionary psychologist before his time. Christian ethics is based, therefore, on the direct or indirect payoffs of altruism, and the benefits have to be ratcheted up, for example in the book of Revelation, to offset the costs of belonging to a threatened group, including the unpleasantness of martyrdom. If anyone suspects having your breasts cut off or being fried on a grid-iron of being painful, they had better consult their felicific calculus and compare it with being dunked for ever in a lake of fire. Christianity is a bonus culture based on survival mechanisms that have been selected for, and it delivers eternal long-term benefits in return for short-term risk taking. The mordant Anglican poet Charles Sisson put this rather sharply as 'One short crucifixion, then reign for ever' and in Eliot's *Murder in the Cathedral* Archbishop Becket quite properly wondered whether his desire for the glory of martyrdom might deprive him of the martyr's crown. What goes unnoticed in all these translations of Christianity into utilitarian and other discourses is the way the social sciences can throw up a shadow theology, as for example the recent pronouncements of a distinguished economist putting the recent crash down to a towering concupiscence which transfers the chronic debt to others, unto the third and fourth generation. The redemption of that kind of debt is going to be very costly. Clearly we know sin under many synonyms.

All this reinforces the suspicion that cognitive science is a contemporary translation of the assumptions of philosophical utilitarianism and economics, as well as a companion piece to contemporary rational choice theory. Indeed, Gary Runciman argues something along these lines in his recent book, *The Theory of Cultural and Social Selection.*[9] Runciman is one of the very few sociologists to endorse cognitive science and he even adopts the language of memes rather

---

[9]   Runciman, *The Theory of Cultural and Social Selection.*

that of traits and themes. But I cannot see that his analyses, for example of the modification of the thematic repertoire of Christianity as it was incorporated in the feudal system, are anything other than what one would produce on general sociological grounds. Insightful they may be, but new in principle, or even put forward as a creative reorganization of what is already known, as proposed in the disciplinary propaganda of cognitive science, they certainly are not.

My doubts about the cognitive scientific approach to what may be the non-problem of a specifically religious, as distinct from a general potential for violence, are reinforced by my doubts about the related theories of cognitive scientists seeking to explain religion itself. These theories are as over-generalized in their grandiose claims, for example as put forward in Pascal Boyer's *Explaining Religion*,[10] as the theories of religious violence. It really is impossible to account for the variable presence and absence of religion, even supposing we know what that means, with an evolutionary constant. Christians used to take comfort from universal traces of what they thought were natural apprehensions of the divine, however distorted, but religion is not a natural given of that sort. It is culturally derived. In particular it is passed by socialization from parent to child, as has been pointed out in attacks on religious education in the home as 'child abuse', and if one cannot recognize that this implies the cultural nature of religion, one is either blinded by a priori assumptions, or egregiously incapable of scientific inference.

It needs saying, once again, that religion varies in its form and intensity, and in its absence and presence, under specifiable historical and social conditions. Arguments for a constant beneath seeming infinite variety, whether such arguments are based on religious, evolutionary, sociological or existential grounds, hold in reserve a catch-all argument locating the presence of functional equivalents where religion *appears* to be absent, or they appeal to the very long-term to throw up the evidence so conspicuously lacking at the moment. This explains what Teehan says about the flimsy nature of the secularization thesis, unaware it seems that the critique of secularization theory can be, and indeed is, quite differently based. Secularization theory can be criticized on grounds other than the 'natural' resilience of religion, or on grounds of an 'instinct' for religion.

The evidence is that no serious functional equivalents are to be located in those parts of Eastern Europe where religion had been previously weakened by association with perceived internal or external oppression, and was therefore vulnerable to hostile socialization. The conclusion has to be that 'religion' is a cultural product, given that the alternative explanation needs to posit an atrophy of the biological programme west of the Oder-Neisse line, where many people do not even know about the posited existence of the God they do not believe in, whereas east of the same line the biological programme is so hyper-active they find it difficult to imagine what disbelief in God might be. So, while supporters of a strong secularization theory are waiting for the predicted disappearance of religion in the USA and Poland, cognitive scientists, supposing they know anything at all

---

[10]   Boyer, *Explaining Religion*.

about the empirical evidence, are waiting for its predicted reappearance in the former DDR, Estonia and the Czech Republic, and indeed, in Uruguay. Thus far one has to report that the secularization theorists have the empirical advantage.

Cognitive scientific theories of religion begin with an evolutionary take on the much older theory of animism as a bed-rock of the religious attitude. They understand religious attributions of spiritual animation to mere objects as an evolutionary adaptation rooted in the need to assume the object is a crocodile rather then a log, on pain of being swallowed and therefore losing the opportunity to perpetuate your gene pool pleasuring your mate back at the ranch. In our modern world religion is therefore a chronic and increasingly dysfunctional propensity to react too quickly on the basis of seriously under-determined evidence.

But in his Marxist account of the uses of the idea of fanaticism Alberto Toscano argues precisely the opposite. He celebrates the human importance and indeed necessity of acting on under-determined evidence. Where Teehan suspects faith (aka 'blind faith') as socially dangerous, Toscano celebrates a dangerous faith as at the same time our human glory, for if we have fully determined knowledge we deny any human hope of a better world to come. There is no *vitam venturi*. Pentecostals in a Latin American *favela* have a better hope than others who accept the likely limits of their situation. Toscano links his embrace of dangerous hope to the recent interest of contemporary Marxists in St. Paul and his theology of hope. He considers the current criticism of religion by 'the new atheists' as little more than peevish outbursts by '*rentiers* of the Enlightenment', and contrasts it with Marx's sympathetic understanding of religion as 'the heart of the heartless world' and even with Hobsbawm's treatment of what Hobsbawm regards as proto-political religion in his *Primitive Rebels*.

Perhaps there is a theory of human action lurking here, which goes beyond the 'real forces' identified by Marx or the pre-potent underlying structures identified by cognitive science or cybernetics or ethology. It is based on the future not the past and takes seriously the attractive pull of a future hope on the present, and the role of what is perceived as truth, religious or scientific, in disrupting the kingdom of the lie. It would analyse the collateral damage inherent in faith, hope and love, alongside the collateral damage and opportunity costs of monotheism and universalism. 'Hope springs eternal' could be what makes the world go round, which might explain why the hope embedded specifically in language and in the future and subjunctive tenses, was culturally 'selected for' in the first place. Tristram Hunt, the Labour historian, wrote in his *Building Jerusalem* of the spiritual inspiration and inspiration brought to the new creation of Britain through all the horrors of the industrial revolution.[11] The hope of a heavenly city for all tribes and tongues being brought down to earth and 'secularized', which was generated in the past as part of the vision of Christians scattered to the four corners of the Roman world, acted as the fascinating catalyst of the future. Hope really does

---

[11]   Hunt, Tristram, *Building Jerusalem: The Rise and Fall of the Victorian City* (London: Weidenfeld, 2004).

help us survive our quotidian travails better than what Bertrand Russell miscalled 'the firm foundations of despair'. Our human 'good causes' shape and inform our horizons, our inspirations and aspirations, and are therefore 'causal' in exactly the same way as fighting for justice is causal. The 'causes of things' lie ahead of us and are within us, as well as pushing us from behind and acting on us from without. That is what 'agency' means.

Toscano's main target is the attempt to undermine radical commitment in Cold War analyses of totalitarianism. In particular he criticizes the crude fusion of religious and secular eschatology by Norman Cohn, and the polemical uses of the concept of political religion in Talmon and Monnerot. On the contemporary scene he attacks John Gray for an analogous fusion of religious and political in his critique of enlightened anticipations of historical progress as a mutation of Christian delusions. If the necessary enthusiasms of the past were in danger of deteriorating into fanaticism, then the necessary scepticisms of the present are in danger of deteriorating into cynicism. Rather nicely Toscano describes the assimilation of politics to religion as a 'blasphemous' reduction of the transcendent to the political.

In his own concluding lay sermon John Teehan has his own reservations about the impassioned negativity of some contemporary comment on religion. He believes we need to understand our programmed religious violence in order the better to release religion's undeniable potential for good, and assist such ability as culture may possess to 'strain at the leash of biology'. He notes the historic potential for violence in those seized with a visceral hatred of religion and is distressed by what he dismisses as the primitive mistakes in logic perpetrated by polemicists like Hitchens[12] and Harris.[13] In their misbegotten zealotry and superficiality he feels they have thrown away the chance rationally to persuade.

But then, as he points out, their black and white, either-or approach, based on under-determined evidence, is only to be expected given the way responses are triggered by our biological programmes. From his perspective it seems our cave man brains will have their way with us, whether we will or not. Why blame Hitchens and Harris, any more than one blames religious people, for acting as mere carriers for drives that ensure cave men do what cave men have to do? To blame them one would need a different vocabulary and one shared with Christianity. What Teehan's perspective fails to grasp is the absence of conceptions like agency and liberation, let alone rational suasion, justice and truth, from the premises and discourse of science.

---

[12]   Hitchens, Christopher, *God is not Great: How Religion Poisons Everything* (New York and Boston: Twelve [Hachette], 2007).

[13]   Harris, Sam, *The End of Faith: Religion, Terror, and the Future of Reason* (New York: W.W. Norton, 2004).

Name Index

Subject Index